SECURWARE 2020

The Fourteenth International Conference on Emerging Security Information, Systems and Technologies

November 21 - 25, 2020

SECURWARE 2020 Editors

Hans-Joachim Hof, INSicherheit - Ingolstadt Research Group Applied IT Security, CARISSMA – Center of Automotive Research on Integrated Safety Systems, Germany
Manuela Popescu, IARIA, USA/EU
George Yee, Carleton University, Canada

Printed from e-media with permission by:

Curran Associates, Inc.
57 Morehouse Lane
Red Hook, NY 12571

Some format issues inherent in the e-media version may also appear in this print version.

International Academy, Research, and Industry Association (IARIA)
412 Derby Way
Wilmington, DE 19810

Phone: (408) 893-6407
Fax: (408) 527-6351

petre@iaria.org

Additional copies of this publication are available from:

Curran Associates, Inc.
57 Morehouse Lane
Red Hook, NY 12571 USA
Phone: 845-758-0400
Fax: 845-758-2633
Email: curran@proceedings.com
Web: www.proceedings.com

Table of Contents

SECURWARE 2020

Forward

The Fourteenth International Conference on Emerging Security Information, Systems and Technologies (SECURWARE 2020), held on November 21-25, 2020, continued a series of events covering related topics on theory and practice on security, cryptography, secure protocols, trust, privacy, confidentiality, vulnerability, intrusion detection and other areas related to low enforcement, security data mining, malware models, etc.

Security, defined for ensuring protected communication among terminals and user applications across public and private networks, is the core for guaranteeing confidentiality, privacy, and data protection. Security affects business and individuals, raises the business risk, and requires a corporate and individual culture. In the open business space offered by Internet, it is a need to improve defenses against hackers, disgruntled employees, and commercial rivals. There is a required balance between the effort and resources spent on security versus security achievements. Some vulnerability can be addressed using the rule of 80:20, meaning 80% of the vulnerabilities can be addressed for 20% of the costs. Other technical aspects are related to the communication speed versus complex and time consuming cryptography/security mechanisms and protocols.

Digital Ecosystem is defined as an open decentralized information infrastructure where different networked agents, such as enterprises (especially SMEs), intermediate actors, public bodies and end users, cooperate and compete enabling the creation of new complex structures. In digital ecosystems, the actors, their products and services can be seen as different organisms and species that are able to evolve and adapt dynamically to changing market conditions.

Digital Ecosystems lie at the intersection between different disciplines and fields: industry, business, social sciences, biology, and cutting edge ICT and its application driven research. They are supported by several underlying technologies such as semantic web and ontology-based knowledge sharing, self-organizing intelligent agents, peer-to-peer overlay networks, web services-based information platforms, and recommender systems.

To enable safe digital ecosystem functioning, security and trust mechanisms become essential components across all the technological layers. The aim is to bring together multidisciplinary research that ranges from technical aspects to socio-economic models.

We take here the opportunity to warmly thank all the members of the SECURWARE 2020 technical program committee, as well as all the reviewers. The creation of such a high quality conference program would not have been possible without their involvement. We also kindly thank all the authors who dedicated much of their time and effort to contribute to SECURWARE 2020. We truly believe that, thanks to all these efforts, the final conference program consisted of top quality contributions.

We also thank the members of the SECURWARE 2020 organizing committee for their help in handling the logistics and for their work that made this professional meeting a success.

We hope that SECURWARE 2020 was a successful international forum for the exchange of ideas and results between academia and industry and to promote further progress in the area of security information, systems and technologies.

SECURWARE 2020 Chairs

SECURWARE 2020 Steering Committee

Steffen Fries, Siemens, Germany

SECURWARE 2020 Publicity Chair

Jose Miguel Jimenez, Universitat Politecnica de Valencia, Spain // University of Haute Alsace, France

Jose Luis García, Universitat Politecnica de Valencia, Spain

SECURWARE 2020

Committee

SECURWARE 2020 Steering Committee

Steffen Fries, Siemens, Germany

SECURWARE 2020 Publicity Chair

Jose Miguel Jimenez, Universitat Politecnica de Valencia, Spain // University of Haute Alsace, France
Jose Luis García, Universitat Politecnica de Valencia, Spain

SECURWARE 2020 Technical Program Committee

Aysajan Abidin, imec-COSIC KU Leuven, Belgium
Abbas Acar, Florida International University, Miami, USA
Afrand Agah, West Chester University of Pennsylvania, USA
Ashwag Albakri, University of Missouri-Kansas City, USA / Jazan University, Saudi Arabia
Asif Ali laghari, SMIU, Karachi, Pakistan
Luca Allodi, Eindhoven University of Technology, Netherlands
Ghada Almashaqbeh, NuCypher, USA
Mohammed Alshehri, University of Arkansas, USA
Eric Amankwa, Presbyterian University College, Ghana
Antonio Barili, Università degli Studi di Pavia, Italy
Ilija Basicevic, University of Novi Sad, Serbia
Malek Ben Salem, Accenture, USA
Cătălin Bîrjoveanu, "Al. I. Cuza" University of Iasi, Romania
Robert Brotzman, Pennsylvania State University, USA
Francesco Buccafurri, University Mediterranea of Reggio Calabria, Italy
Paolo Campegiani, Bit4id, Italy
Juan-Vicente Capella-Hernández, Universitat Politècnica de València, Spain
Roberto Carbone, Fondazione Bruno Kessler, Trento, Italy
Christophe Charrier, Nomandie Univ. | UNICAEN | ENSICAEN | CNRS GREYC UMR 6072, France
Bo Chen, Michigan Technological University, Houghton, USA
Tan Saw Chin, Multimedia University, Malaysia
Jin-Hee Cho, Virginia Tech, USA
Stelvio Cimato, University of Milan, Italy
Marijke Coetzee, Academy of Computer Science and Software Engineering | University of Johannesburg, South Africa
Jun Dai, California State University at Sacramento, USA
Mila Dalla Preda, University of Verona, Italy
Navid Emamdoost, University of Minnesota, USA
Rainer Falk, Siemens AG, Corporate Technology, Germany
Yebo Feng, University of Oregon, USA
Eduardo B. Fernandez, Florida Atlantic University, USA

Carlos Enrique Palau Salvador, Universitat Politècnica de València, Spain
Lanlan Pan, Guangdong OPPO Mobile Telecommunications Corp. Ltd., China
Brajendra Panda, University of Arkansas, USA
Travis Peters, Montana State University, USA
Nikolaos Pitropakis, Edinburgh Napier University, UK
Tassilo Pellegrini, St. Pölten University of Applied Sciences, Austria
Thomas Plantard, University of Wollongong, Australia
Maxime Puys, Univ. Grenoble Alpes | CEA | LETI | DSYS, Grenoble, France
Alvise Rabitti, Università Ca'Foscari - Venezia, Italy
Khandaker "Abir" Rahman, Saginaw Valley State University, USA
Danda B. Rawat, Howard University, USA
Leon Reznik, Rochester Institute of Technology, USA
Ruben Ricart-Sanchez, University of the West of Scotland, UK
Martin Ring, Bosch Engineering GmbH, Germany
Heiko Roßnagel, Fraunhofer IAO, Germany
Simona Samardjiska, Radboud University, The Netherlands
Rodrigo Sanches Miani, Universidade Federal de Uberlândia, Brazil
Stefan Schauer, AIT Austrian Institute of Technology | Center for Digital Safety and Security, Vienna, Austria
Stefan Schiffner, SECAN-Lab, Uni Luxembourg
Savio Sciancalepore, Hamad Bin KhalifaUniversity (HBKU), Doha, Qatar
Cecilia Labrini, University of Reggio Calabria, Italy
Altaf Shaik, Technische Universität Berlin, Germany
Christoph Stach, University of Stuttgart, Germany
Yifan Tian, Agari Data Inc. , USA
Scott Trent, IBM Research - Tokyo, Japan
Mathy Vanhoef, New York University Abu Dhabi, UAE
Andrea Visconti, Università degli Studi di Milano, Italy
Ian Welch, Victoria University of Wellington, New Zealand
Geng Yang, Nanjing University of Posts & Telecommunications (NUPT), China
Wun-She Yap, Universiti Tunku Abdul Rahman, Malaysia
Qussai M. Yaseen, Jordan University of Science and Technology, Irbid, Jordan
George O. M. Yee, Aptusinnova Inc. / Carleton University, Ottawa, Canada
Kailiang Ying, Google, USA
Thomas Zefferer, Secure Information Technology Center Austria (A-SIT), Austria
Dongrui Zeng, Pennsylvania State University, University Park, USA
Tianwei Zhang, Nanyang Technological University, Singapore

Copyright Information

An Information Flow Modelling Approach for Critical Infrastructure Simulation

Denise Gall, Christian Luidold, Gregor Langner, Thomas Schaberreiter, Gerald Quirchmayr
Faculty of Computer Science,
University of Vienna
Vienna, Austria
email: denise.gall@univie.ac.at, christian.luidold@univie.ac.at, gregor.langner@univie.ac.at,
thomas.schaberreiter@univie.ac.at, gerald.quirchmayr@univie.ac.at

***Abstract*—Building a realistic environment for simulating cascading effects in critical infrastructures depends heavily on information received from experts, as well as on an accurate representation of processes and assets related to critical infrastructures. The approach introduced in this paper provides the conceptualization and implementation of an information flow model as a foundation for the subsequent development of a multi-layered risk model. The designed models represent both a process view, with the focus on procedures carried out by critical infrastructures, and a more technical object view, by defining objects and parameters representing assets and interactions. Starting with an analysis of relevant threats and affected infrastructures, use case scenarios are prepared in textual form and subsequently evaluated together with critical infrastructure representatives in end-user workshops. Based on the respective use case, a process view is established in form of an activity diagram including information flows, displaying processes of critical infrastructures during a threat. The activity diagram supports the evaluation and collection of information during subsequent end-user workshops with the aim to review and substantiate the model. The object diagram provides technical aspects of the use cases, for supporting the realization of a simulation and a corresponding risk model. The approach was developed in the context of a national research project for analyzing cascading effects in and between critical supply networks. The resulting diagrams demonstrate how cascading effects can be modelled in a structured form to support discussions with and between experts of critical infrastructures and emergency services, and how such models can serve as a foundation for subsequent simulation.**

Index Terms*—*Information Flow Modelling; Critical Infrastructure; Infrastructure Simulation; Cascading Effects.

I. Introduction

In times of advanced automation in critical supply networks, critical infrastructures (CIs) need to be resilient against a multitude of threats in order to maintain public interests. Regarding the protection against threats against their own infrastructure, providers are in many cases well prepared. However, when facing cascading effects due to failures in other CIs due to intentional or unintentional causes, protection measures are harder to establish as possible cascading effects are often unknown. Therefore, it is an essential step to assist CI providers in identifying cascading failures in scenarios that are not part of the daily processes within the CI's own ecosystem, but pose relevant and potentially devastating threat scenarios. Historic examples underlining the gravity of cascading effects provide exceptional insights regarding the importance of resilience against external events, e.g., as shown in Oslo, Norway in 2007. This incident affected public transportation and underlying systems for around 20 hours. In addition, network systems were also affected by disruptions for around 10 hours and the central train station had to be evacuated due to a fire, triggered by a short circuit caused by a destroyed high-voltage cable [1].

In order to facilitate the mitigation of risks, an additional focus on the aspect of communication and collaboration among dependent CIs should be considered. Collaboration among CIs supports identifying dependencies between the infrastructures and thus enables them to prepare themselves specifically for impacts of cascading failures. Furthermore, sharing this information with external stakeholders like emergency services can lead to more efficient strategies for emergency services in case of large-scale incidents that require close coordination between first responders. An effective approach lies in the implementation of an adapted information flow model, which provides a framework that helps to organize how specific types of information are to be communicated.

In this paper, we present an approach for supporting CI providers and emergency services by creating an instantiated information flow model, composed of an activity diagram and an object diagram, based on a textual description of a threat scenario. The information flow model offers a new way to represent cascading effects of incidents in interdependent CIs in a structured form. The aim of this model is to facilitate discussions on the feasibility of cascading threat scenarios, and to encourage CI stakeholders to contribute to the shared knowledge represented by the information flow model. Simulations based on this shared understanding of threat scenarios will be able to optimize response to incidents based on those threat scenarios and help to coordinate first response with external actors like emergency services. In the context of CI networks, information flow does not only represent the digital information that is exchanged between CIs, but follows the broader definition of goods and services that are exchanged between infrastructures.

Our approach for information flow modelling is based on activity and object diagrams established from a textual description of a threat scenario. The information flow model includes an activity diagram for providing a process view and a technical view implemented by an object diagram, which provides a definition of objects and their parameters. The information sources utilized to derive the diagrams included multiple workshops with experts from CIs and emergency services. We evaluate the results in a case study derived from results carried out in the ongoing ODYSSEUS project [2].

Section II provides an overview of related work and the applied methodologies. The subsequent Section III describes the modelling approach including the modelling prerequisites, the activity and object diagram definitions, and iterative refinements of the models. In Section IV, we present a case study within the scope of the ODYSSEUS project [2] and evaluate the findings in Section V. Section VI provides a conclusion and an outlook on future work.

II. Related Work

The methodology used for the presented modelling approach was greatly influenced by the design-science methodology described by Hevner et al. [3], as well as initially by the Soft Systems Methodology (SSM) described by Checkland [4]. The design-science research methodology consists of seven guidelines, from which an in-depth understanding of a given design problem and potential solutions can be gained. We utilize the design-science principles to create a design artifact in the form of a conceptual information flow model. The refinement and evaluation of the resulting artifact is conducted by multiple workshops with experts applying the world cafe methodology [5] described below, as well as technical evaluations conducted by project partners for further refinement. The principles of design-science were applied in the iterative refinement of the modelling results in all phases of the process.

Regarding the execution and the results of the workshops, the adopted world cafe process consists of seven design principles, which offers the participants to share their expertise in small groups [5]:

1) Set the Context
2) Create Hospitable Space
3) Explore Questions that Matter
4) Encourage Everyone's Contribution
5) Connect Diverse Perspectives
6) Listen Together for Patterns and Insights
7) Share Collective Discoveries

In terms of information flow modelling, Kupfersberger et al. [6] propose an approach for defining a conceptual security-driven information flow model for international software integration projects that was evaluated in a case study regarding an EU cybersecurity project CS-AWARE [7]. The authors focus on the representation of internal processes, what relevant data is used and how the communication with other components is realized in order to derive the framework conditions of their model [6]. Considering the comparable environments between Kupfersberger et al. [6] and this work, a similar approach was chosen with a set of adaptions regarding a broader field of stakeholders, and the goal of creating a multi-layered risk model, as well as to satisfy the requirements mentioned above.

For establishing a model representing activities as well as information flows, a lot of available approaches exist, including UML (Unified Modeling Language) activity diagrams, Business Process Model and Notation (BPMN) or Data Flow Diagrams (DFD). In our context, activity diagrams based on BPMN [8] were identified as most suitable, since BPMN is an established standard for representing business processes and workflows, and is not restricted to a certain domain or organization. Additionally, BPMN is a suitable instrument for presenting processes to different user groups, and provides a notation for message flows between layers [9].

Regarding modelling a more technical view, UML class diagrams [10] were selected as this technique allows to develop a representation of objects and parameters. However, the model had to be slightly expanded to support information flows and to suit our domain by adding modelling entities for representing information flows including shared information.

III. Modelling Approach

Identifying dependencies and potential risks caused by cascading effects between CIs is a complex issue. CIs are in many cases highly dependent on the services provided by other CIs, and failures in both the physical and cyber systems of one CI may cause service disruptions or failures in other CIs. Another major concern for interdependency risks is caused by geographical proximity of CIs, since a catastrophic event in an area can cause major disruptions in CI services, with potentially high impacts on the population [11]. The model presented in this paper is specifically designed for dealing with such sophisticated multi-stakeholder domains by applying the design-science method [3] as well as the SSM [4]. These methodologies offer procedures and guidelines on how to retrieve information and model highly complex environments such as CIs and how to reveal unknown problematic issues.

Following the design-science method introduced by Hevner et al. [3], we pursue an iterative approach, including:

- Analyzing the modelling prerequisites, which includes defining threat scenarios in textual form, based on an analysis of possible threats affecting CI networks.
- Based on the previously defined use cases, activity diagrams are established including the most important information flows between CIs and emergency services.
- For obtaining a more technical view of the use cases, relevant objects and parameters necessary for simulation are identified and modelled in an object diagram.
- Both the activity diagram and the object diagram are further refined in multiple workshop settings, as described in Section III-D.

The goal of the modelling approach is to create a structured activity diagram from the textual threat scenarios, to be able to model cascading effects and message flows between CIs and emergency services. The model forms the foundation for later simulations of the critical networks and serve as a basis for CIs and emergency services to get more insights into cascading effects and their impacts.

A. Modelling Prerequisite

The basis for the modelling efforts described in this work are textually composed threat scenarios that describe procedures and cascading effects in CIs during threats. In order to create realistic scenarios, the first step is to gather more information on threats affecting CIs and their dependencies. Therefore, possible dangers in urban areas were analyzed by creating a catalog of various threats, based on static and dynamic sources dealing with disasters and emergencies. These data sources include the Swiss catalog of threats, disasters and emergencies [12], newspaper articles and reports from authorities and other relevant organizations, dealing with incidents and threats. The identified threats were evaluated in terms of likelihood and impact in combination with national and international historical data and current developments, which resulted in a first set of use case scenarios. The main categories of threats identified were social threats, natural disasters and technological threats, according to the Swiss catalog of threats, disasters and emergencies [12].

The first drafts of threat scenarios were validated and refined in a workshop with security and business continuity experts from multiple CIs. The workshop's goal was to receive as much information from end-users for establishing realistic use cases and for the subsequent modelling activity.

In line with the principles of the SSM [4], the end-user workshops were composed of a large variety of stakeholder groups, in order to be able to obtain their views and expertise, and to gain a holistic understanding of the dynamics caused by an incident as modelled by the threat scenarios.

In the context of the project, the main stakeholders are an interdependent network of CI providers and emergency services, who are an integral part of the threat scenarios in the incident response. They were deeply involved in establishing realistic threat scenarios, as the goal of the project is to support the stakeholders by providing simulations on cascading effects. Furthermore, security experts are part of the stakeholder group, as the introduced method allows to identify information flows and dependencies between CIs, in order to gain an additional perspective on the potential ramifications of cascading incidents. Similarly, simulation experts are part of the stakeholder group in order to ensure that the translation of real-world incidents into simulation is viable and realistic. Furthermore, the perspective of first responders is crucial in understanding the dynamics of large-scale cascading incidents. Therefore, the input of emergency services and other first responders as part of the stakeholder group is important

In order to facilitate information collection in end-user workshops, the SSM [4] offers an approach that supports gathering information from experts by enforcing participants to model a big picture of the domain. However, due to limited possibilities in the context of the project, the world cafe process [5] was chosen for data gathering from the stakeholder groups. In the context of the project, the setting of a world cafe offered every end-user the possibility to reveal their expertise and estimation of relevance for each defined event and the associated impacts.

The information gathered during the workshop was used as basis for the resulting updated textual description of the use cases, comprising threats, impacts and the threat response by individual CIs. An especially interesting area of discussion in those stakeholder groups are the cascading failures that affect more than one CI. While failures contained within their own infrastructures are usually well understood and managed, there is great potential in better understanding the dynamics of cascading failures affecting multiple CIs. CI operators rarely have the opportunity to discuss cascading effects in a broad multi-stakeholder set-up, leading to valuable information to be uncovered and incorporated into the threat scenarios and subsequent models.

B. Modelling Scenario Behavior in Activity Diagrams

The activity diagram presented in this section represents a process view of events, including cause and impact on dependent infrastructures, extracted from the textual description of the threat scenarios. This is an important basis for the subsequent scenario simulation, as it transforms all the events defined in textual form in the threat scenario description into structured sequences, including information flows between infrastructures.
Additionally, visual models facilitate the evaluation and adaptation of end-user provided content, since the visual representation and grouping of information facilitates comprehension of sequences of events and cause and impact relationships [13].

The transformation of textual information to the representation in the activity diagram starts by identifying all involved CIs and other relevant stakeholder assets, followed by the identification of tasks and activities that are performed by those assets during the threat scenario. Those tasks and activities that change the state of an asset during a threat scenario need to be considered for modelling. The identified activities are to be sorted logically and chronologically, as that may not be necessarily preset in textual form.

After identifying CIs and tasks, the most essential step of the process, identifying information flows according to activities, is conducted. These information flows are of such importance, as they affect other CIs' states due to cascading effects. For example, if there is an area-wide power outage, which may lead to traffic accidents due to failures in traffic lights, emergency services have to secure these accidents sites, which in turn affects the capacity of available emergency response units. In case of another emergency, there might be bottlenecks.

Identifying information flows between stakeholders includes thoroughly reading the given textual use case and extracting all information flows predefined in the description. Additionally, information flows can be identified by perusing every identified task and deepen the knowledge relating to each task by conducting background research or seek for additional input from the stakeholder group, as suggested by [6] and [1]. This is especially relevant in the case of cascading failures, where only the perspective of some elements of the failure chain has been initially captured, and additional input from potentially affected stakeholders is required. Other information flows may have been revealed by end-users intentionally or unintentionally during the conducted workshop. Once all information from the textual form is extracted, the actual model can be built.

In order to ensure the practical relevance of the constructed activity diagram, established notations, such as BPMN, were applied. BPMN allows to demonstrate process sequences within one layer as well as information exchange between different layers. For facilitating the activity diagram, a layered design is recommended, where one infrastructure is visualized by a pool corresponding to the BPMN standard. Within one pool, the sequence flow of processes is modelled for one infrastructure. Tasks can be either activities that do not impact other infrastructures, or activities that send information to other infrastructures. To emphasize the differentiation between the two forms of tasks, we suggest using different coloring, as presented in Figure 1.

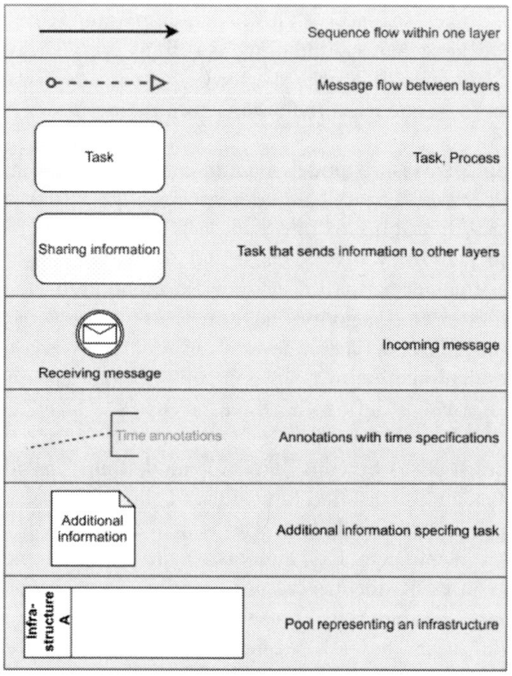

Fig. 1. Notation for Activity Diagram

Receiving information from other infrastructures is demonstrated by Intermediate Message Events, according to the BPMN concepts. Information flows are demonstrated by dashed blue lines with an arrow, which demonstrates information exchange from one infrastructure to another one. Information flows included in the model are unidirectional, which means that information is exchanged only in one way, namely from the sending to the receiving infrastructure. If information should be shared in both ways, it is necessary to model information flows separately, by utilizing an individual information flow in each direction. Sequence flows within one infrastructure are represented by a black line with an arrow at one end. Furthermore, we would emphasize to use different coloring for information and sequence flows, to distinctly differentiate those two flows. Additionally, the modelling entities provide the option to add time annotations and other additional information, if required.

C. Modelling Scenario Parameters in Object Diagrams

The designed activity diagram allows to develop an advanced information flow model and to identify objects and parameters needed for simulating behaviors and information flows in CIs in the context of the described threat scenarios. This step requires close cooperation with simulation experts, as they offer input regarding requirements and limitations of simulation environments.

The first step of developing an object diagram is to identify and specify the objects that are relevant for the specified threat scenario. This requires a closer look at the CIs and other assets identified in the context of the activity diagram, and extract the objects that are actually affected by it. When considering the scenario of a blackout, which results in failure of traffic lights, traffic light represents an object of the transport CI. For consistency and simple representation, a layered design is suggested, where all objects of one infrastructure are combined in one layer.

Necessary objects that describe the use case can be revealed by considering questions like "Which objects present the infrastructure in general?", "Which objects are necessary for processing the tasks presented in the activity diagram?" or "Which objects are required for processing information flows from other infrastructures?".

Once the objects are identified, parameters for each item are defined, whereby only descriptive parameters are considered, as values will be assigned in another phase of the project. Distinguishing between descriptive parameters and their values is important, as the value changes depending on the simulation environment, while the descriptive parameter remains the same. However, it can be helpful to consider values at this point for determining descriptive parameters [14]. Declaring parameters can be facilitated by dividing them into the following subcategories:

- Private: Parameters that are predefined
- Public: Parameters that are set during simulation
- Derived: Parameters derived from other parameters' values

The suggested categories are based on the UML standard attribute categories, but their meaning is adapted to the needs of the domain. After considering all parameters, relationships between objects are specified by considering relations between objects within a layer and information flows between objects of different layers, according to the activity diagram. For completing the technical view, parameters that are shared between infrastructures need to be identified, for allowing correct simulation of information flows.

For visualizing the object diagram, we suggest UML class diagram representation, since it offers entities relevant for our method. Small adaptions were made to support the domain's requirements, as presented in Figure 2. As UML class diagrams do not provide modelling entities for representing information flows, a notation for this concern was added. Through this notation it is possible to represent information shared between infrastructures involved in the use case, which is especially required for simulation purposes. In this context, UML also does not have a notation for representing parameters that are shared between entities according to information flows. A notation to represent shared parameters within a blue rectangle as an annotation to the information flows was added.

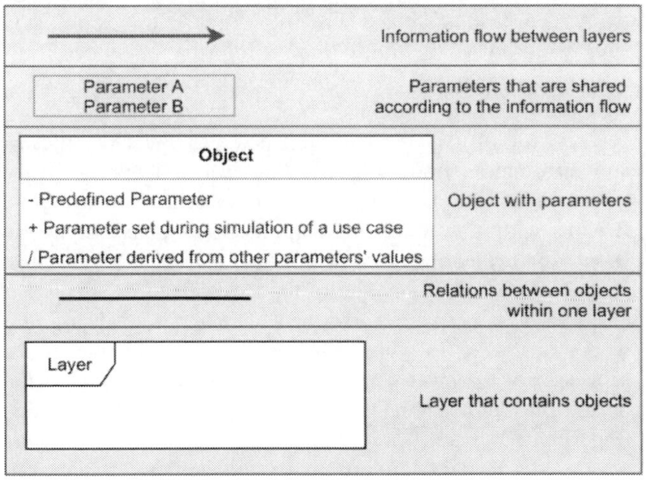

Fig. 2. Notation for Object Diagram

Similar to the activity diagram, we recommend to use layers for representing infrastructures. An object is represented by the UML entity of a class and contains parameters presented according to their characteristics. For specifying the type of the parameter, the standard notation from UML was used but semantically adapted to the domain's needs. According to UML, the symbol "-" preceding the name of an attribute classifies the visibility as private and "+" defines it as public [10]. For the presented domain the semantics of the symbols are adapted. The symbol "-" before the parameter classifies that the parameter's value is specified prior to the simulation start, "+" however classifies parameter values that are initiated during the simulation and "/" specifies a value that is derived from other parameters' values.

Relations between objects can either represent relations within one infrastructure, or information flows between objects owned by different stakeholders. Information flows in this context are only unidirectional, with the arrow on one end indicating the receiving object. For an easy distinction between the two types of relations, it is also suggested to use different coloring.

D. *Iterative Refinement of Modelling Results*

Once the diagrams are established, it is vital to hold additional workshops in the stakeholder group in order to gather additional feedback from domain experts and evaluate information captured in the diagrams. This is in line with the design-science methodology [3] as well as the SSM [4] presented in Section II, which both include iterative refinement of the established models of the studied domain as a core principle of the methodology. Reviewing the results together with the stakeholders allows to identify inaccuracies or wrong representation of events and allows to refine modelled information flows between CIs. Furthermore, it enables to substantiate specific aspects of objects or behaviors with more detail, until the desired level of detail is reached to derive a meaningful and realistic simulation.

The goal of further workshops is to reveal information regarding every-day processes, threats which can lead to failures in the CI's services, how such a failure would affect other infrastructures, how the CI can be affected by failures of other stakeholders and to assign realistic values to identified parameters in the context of the threat scenarios. Workshops should support revealing such dependencies, which can be further analyzed within the simulations. Additionally, information on communication and collaboration with other stakeholders can be revealed.

After such workshops the activity diagrams and possibly also the textual description can be adapted to obtain realistic use cases that capture all relevant information for modelling processes during a threat. The visual models enforce feedback and discussion in workshops as information is presented more clearly and organized than it is in a purely textual representation.

IV. Case Study

In the context of the ODYSSEUS project [2], a case study was conducted with domain experts ranging from research partners to employees from various CIs including experts from the field of cyber security, operations, and business continuity. The following section provides an in-depth overview of the case study and the evaluation process.

The project's goal is to identify and simulate cascading effects between CIs in an urban area to improve procedures and reactions in case of a threat scenario. Therefore, main end-users in this context are CI providers and emergency services, who participated in multiple workshops and offered insights into the procedures of their domain.

According to the approach introduced in this paper, use cases representing threat scenarios in urban areas were designed and evaluated in the context of end-user workshops. The workshops were held in form of a world cafe, where use cases were evaluated by the relevance for providers of CIs. Due to their profound feedback, only three out of four initially defined use cases were considered as relevant enough to be further elaborated.

Once the newly gained information was applied to adapt the use cases, the textual form was converted into an activity diagram. Figure 3 shows an excerpt of the created activity model with information flows between CIs. The activity diagram shows the case of a power failure. The CIs involved and presented in the diagram are power supply, private transport and police forces represented as pools. The yellow tasks are activities within the CI with no influence on other ones. The blue tasks represent activities that send information to other CIs. For instance, activity P2.3 "Serious traffic accidents" sends a message to police forces, as they receive emergency calls due to these accidents. In consequence of these received emergency calls, police forces have to secure accident sites as stated in task P3.2, sending a message flow to private traffic indicating that traffic will be regulated.

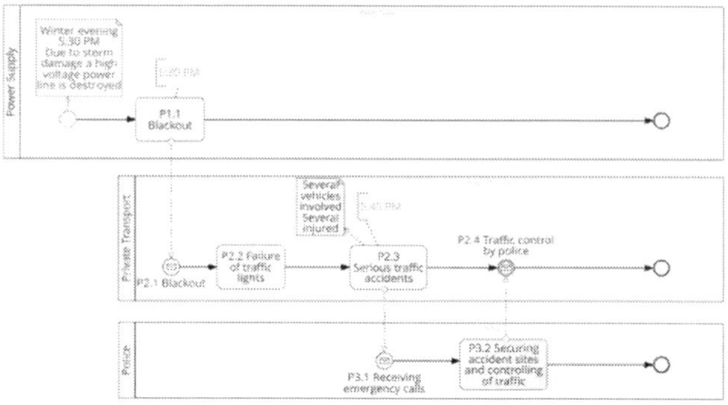

Fig. 3. ODYSSEUS Activity Diagram - Snapshot

Additional information that is not part of the actual information flow, but can provide useful annotations for the scenario or the users of the scenario, can be annotated to each node via a comment, as can be seen in the context of node P2.3.

Figure 4 presents an excerpt of the resulting object diagram in the project's context, created according to Section III-C.

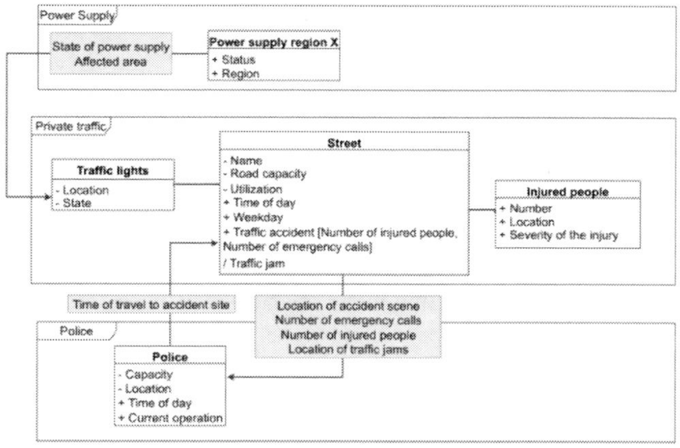

Fig. 4. ODYSSEUS Object Diagram - Snapshot

The model presents each CI and its main objects relevant for simulating the defined use cases. Each object includes parameters that are necessary for presenting the infrastructure and indicating its actual state, e.g., infrastructure private traffic is presented by the objects traffic lights, street and injured people. Each object is further depicted by parameters that are additionally classified due to their behavior. The object "Police" for example is presented by the predefined parameters "Capacity" and "Location", which indicates that these parameters do not change during simulation. "Time of day" and "Current operation" on the other hand are parameters, which change during simulation, according to inputs from other infrastructures or the simulation environment itself. Most of the objects include a parameter "Capacity" to capture whether the object should change its state, if the maximum capacity is reached.

The first draft of the diagram included objects, parameters and information flows, but after evaluation with project partners, it was decided to additionally include parameters exchanged by information flows. Information flows are presented by blue lines, where the arrow states the receiving infrastructure. Parameters exchanged during an information flow are represented by blue rectangles including the parameter names. For instance, there is an information flow from "Power supply region X" to "traffic lights". Information shared in this example is the state of the power supply and which area is served by the power supply.

The aim of the created models is to present processes and information flows between CIs executed during a given threat event and to provide a basic model for simulation. In line with the modelling approach presented in Section III-D, for evaluating the current state of the use cases and according models, workshops with experts of each area of CIs individually were performed. The main goals of these workshops were to gain more insight regarding the general processes of the infrastructure, as well as processes happening during our defined threats. With each workshop, we obtained important feedback from participating domain experts, which was used to adapt the use cases and activity diagrams, to provide a more realistic view of behaviors during a threat.

V. Discussion of Results

The paper presents an information flow modelling approach to support simulating cascading effects in CIs by achieving the following objectives:

- *Modelling cascading effects through CIs in a structured form*
  The resulting activity diagram demonstrates how cascading effects and information flows through CIs during threat scenarios can be transformed from a textual description into a structured visual form. The output is able to adequately model the activities depicted in the threat scenarios, and is especially helpful in outlining the potential cause and effect relationships of cascading failures. Additionally, the created model supports evaluating the realistic representation of events and information flows with experts during information gathering workshops.
- *Establishing a basis for subsequent simulation*
  The model has shown to be a valid basis for subsequent simulation, as it provides a process view of the threat scenarios including information flows and the objects needed for establishing a simulation environment. The activity diagram represents the process view of behaviors and events, while the object diagram provides the technical view including assets and parameters needed for simulation.
- *Supporting discussion with and between CI providers and emergency services*
  During the expert workshops, we observed that the activity diagram supported stakeholders in easier following our intention of providing scenario based CI interdependency models, and the activities observed in the involved CIs

during those scenarios. The subsequent discussions with stakeholders in the context of iterative refinement of the model have shown that many of the relationships presented in the activity diagram were not adequately considered and understood by CI operators. In this sense, the activity diagram has proven to add value in adding to the holistic understanding of threat scenarios for CI providers. The stakeholders have shown particular interest in those findings during our workshop sessions.

- *Supporting emergency services to prepare emergency plans*
  The activity diagram and subsequent simulation outputs should support emergency services for establishing emergency plans in case such threat scenarios occur. At this point we are not yet able to provide an evaluation of this aspect, since the validation will be part of a later phase of the currently ongoing ODYSSEUS project. Thus, a final conclusion regarding the aspect of communication and collaboration between CIs and emergency services cannot yet be made.

VI. Conclusion and Future Work

The presented modelling approach demonstrates how textual descriptions of threat scenarios can be transformed into a process view and a technical view to support simulating cascading effects in CIs. With this method cascading effects through CIs can be modelled in a structured form, to support discussions in workshops with stakeholders and to provide a comprehensible basis for establishing communication and collaboration between CIs and emergency services. The modelling approach consists of multiple steps from analyzing the requirements on threat scenarios, reviewing the defined scenarios in end-user workshops on the basis of established activity diagrams and finally designing a technical view by creating object diagrams. The textual descriptions and the constructed diagrams serve as a core enabler for specifying an environment for simulation of the scenarios, which can be to a large extent directly based on this model. The modelling approach was used in the context of the ODYSSEUS project, where the method has proven to be quite helpful in building a common understanding of the basic foundations for all partners involved in the project, especially for the simulation experts. Additionally, the designed activity diagrams supported the evaluation of the defined threat scenarios in the end-user workshops, which resulted in substantial feedback based on the realistic representation of behaviors in threat scenarios. Future work on this approach within the ODYSSEUS project includes obtaining values for identified objects' parameters and further evaluation with end-users.

Acknowledgments

This work was partially funded by the Austrian FFG research program KIRAS in course of the project ODYSSEUS ("Simulation und Analyse kritischer Netzwerk-Infrastrukturen in Städten") under Grant No. 873539.

References

[1] I. B. Utne, P. Hokstad, and J. Vatn, "A method for risk modeling of interdependencies in critical infrastructures," *Reliability Engineering & System Safety*, vol. 96, no. 6, pp. 671–678, 2011.

[2] KIRAS Sicherheitsforschung, "ODYSSEUS - simulation and analysis of critical network infrastructures in cities," [retrieved: October, 2020]. [Online]. Available: https://www.kiras.at/en/financed-proposals/detail/d/odysseus-simulation-und-analyse-kritischer-netzwerk-infrastrukturen-in-staedten/

[3] A. R. Hevner, S. T. March, J. Park, and S. Ram, "Design science in information systems research," *Management Information Systems Quarterly*, vol. 28, pp. 75–, 03 2004.

[4] P. Checkland, *Systems Thinking, Systems Practice: Includes a 30-Year Retrospective*. Chichester, England, UK: Wiley, Jun 1981.

[5] The World Café Community Foundation, "The World Cafe," [retrieved: October, 2020]. [Online]. Available: http://www.theworldcafe.com

[6] V. Kupfersberger, T. Schaberreiter, and G. Quirchmayr, "Security-driven information flow modelling for component integration in complex environments," in *Proceedings of the 10th International Conference on Advances in Information Technology, IAIT 2018, Bangkok, Thailand, December 10-13, 2018*. ACM, 2018, pp. 19:1–19:8. [Online]. Available: https://doi.org/10.1145/3291280.3291797

[7] "A cybersecurity situational awareness and information sharing solution for local public administrations based on advanced big data analysis CS-AWARE," Sep 2020, [retrieved: October, 2020]. [Online]. Available: https://cordis.europa.eu/project/id/740723

[8] OMG, "Business process model and notation (bpmn)-version 2.0.2," 2013, [retrieved November, 2020]. [Online]. Available: http://www.omg.org/spec/BPMN/2.0.2/

[9] M. Chinosi and A. Trombetta, "Bpmn: An introduction to the standard," *Computer Standards & Interfaces*, vol. 34, no. 1, pp. 124–134, 2012.

[10] OMG, "Unified modeling language (uml 2.5.1.)," 2017, [retrieved: October, 2020]. [Online]. Available: https://www.omg.org/spec/UML/2.5.1

[11] S. M. Rinaldi, J. P. Peerenboom, and T. K. Kelly, "Identifying, understanding, and analyzing critical infrastructure interdependencies," *IEEE control systems magazine*, vol. 21, no. 6, pp. 11–25, 2001.

[12] Bundesamt für Bevölkerungsschutz (BABS), "Catalog of threats, disasters and emergencies Switzerland," 2019, [retrieved: October, 2020]. [Online]. Available: https://www.babs.admin.ch/de/aufgabenbabs/gefaehrdrisiken/natgefaehrdanalyse/gefaehrdkatalog.html

[13] B. C. Hungerford, A. R. Hevner, and R. W. Collins, "Reviewing software diagrams: A cognitive study," *IEEE Transactions on Software Engineering*, vol. 30, no. 2, pp. 82–96, 2004.

[14] J. Sokolowski, C. Turnitsa, and S. Diallo, "A conceptual modeling method for critical infrastructure modeling," in *41st Annual Simulation Symposium (anss-41 2008)*. IEEE, 2008, pp. 203–211.

A Gap Analysis of Visual and Functional Requirements in Cybersecurity Monitoring Tools

Christian Luidold, Thomas Schaberreiter
Faculty of Computer Science
University of Vienna
Vienna, Austria
email: christian.luidold@univie.ac.at, thomas.schaberreiter@univie.ac.at

***Abstract*—In order to access valuable indicator information in the field of cybersecurity, domain experts tend to use visualizations to quickly gain an overview of a given situation, even more so in the age of big data where initially following visual summaries tends to be more efficient before diving into raw data. For this purpose, researchers analyze the visual and functional requirements of systems to facilitate data exploration. In this paper, we conduct a trend analysis of latest research contributions presented in VizSec symposia in terms of visualization techniques and functional requirements. Additionally, an international and a currently ongoing national project, focusing on Local Public Administrations (LPAs) and Critical Infrastructures (CIs) are analyzed and compared to current state-of-the-art research in terms of requirements of real users in the field of CIs and LPAs. Particularly, a deficiency concerning the requirements of collaboration, enhanced situational awareness, multi-stakeholder involvement, and multi-stakeholder visualization were identified and are discussed in the context of the utilization of cybersecurity visualizations in their work environments.**

Index Terms*—*requirements analysis; collaboration; situational awareness; multi-stakeholder; visualization.

I. Introduction

Monitoring tools are meant to provide users with processed data and, regarding human computer interaction, preferable visualizations of various granularities. Tools evolved in terms of functionality and monitored scope, trying to provide the best possible user experience in times of big data and dynamic environments. This is especially true in the field of cybersecurity, where in an environment of increasing complexity a continuous stream of potentially massive data needs to be automatically preprocessed and classified for increased human comprehension.

Despite the increased sophistication of cybersecurity monitoring tools, current state-of-the-art research mainly focuses on the concept of visualization for analyses and neglecting additional needs of users regarding collaboration, enhanced situational awareness, multi-stakeholder involvement, and multi-stakeholder visualization. These additional capabilities are especially valuable in the context of Critical Infrastructure Protection (CIP).

As the main point of monitoring tools focusing on dynamic environments lies in the provision of real-time data visualizations, the core work mostly focuses on which types of visualizations are used and how data can be interacted with in order for the user to facilitate a deeper understanding of the underlying data. In an organizational context, especially when dealing with CI, it might not be sufficient to determine the state of a given situation and provide assistance in terms of CI-related decision making on a purely technical level. The socio-technical and social dimension within an organization is a key factor for decision making: In order to implement a solution to a cybersecurity problem, it is often necessary to collaborate within the organization to decide on an appropriate course-of-action. The decision making process includes employees with different backgrounds on different levels of the organizational hierarchy. Yet the representation of the data describing the issues is geared towards employees with a technical background. In order to facilitate collaboration and informed decision making on all levels, data representations that are more suitable to employees without a technical background should be investigated as well.

This shows that data driven cybersecurity requires significant consideration regarding data provision and visualization for a wide range of stakeholders, e.g., technical personnel, managers, first responders, authorities, and the general public. Crucial information needs to be tailored to user groups according to their needs and ensuring irrelevant data is filtered out.

The main objective of this work is to analyze aspects of functionalities and visualization used in state-of-the-art research regarding cybersecurity monitoring tools, as well as comparing their potential for integration in existing workflow processes of LPAs and CIs. The central research questions addressed in this research paper are:

- What are current trends in state-of-the-art research for administrations and organizations in terms of visual and functional requirements?
- What are identified gaps between presented research contributions and the needs of organizations?

After this introduction, this paper continues with Section II describing the related work, providing mentions and evaluations from different domains (including CIP) regarding visualizations and similar trend analyses. Section III inspects core requirements analyzed in the context of the international research project CS-AWARE [1] in the field of cybersecurity for LPAs, and the currently ongoing national research project ODYSSEUS [2] aimed at creating a multi-layered risk model in the CI sector. In Section IV, an additional analysis of state-of-the-art research of visualization and functional concepts in the domain of cybersecurity was conducted, followed by a comparison with findings from the previous section. Section VI provides a conclusion and outlook on future work.

II. Related Work

Concerning detection and analysis of cyber incidents, the human factor plays an essential role in the continuously evolving environment of cybersecurity. A variety of tools with different focus areas keep on emerging and all of them bring their own techniques and visualizations to address the specific problems at hand in that area.

According to D'Amico et al. [3], who conducted a survey on cyber operators in terms of cybersecurity visual presentations, the human factor is regarded as a critical part in assessing various situations and consequential decision making. The major issue being addressed is the fluctuant effectiveness of data visualization due to subjectivity, different levels of experience, as well as different goals of respective user groups. Their findings concerning visualizations concluded that visualizations are becoming increasingly more important than regular text-based analyses, although they should still be provided for deeper inspection. The greatest focus of the researchers with respect to the questions asked was whether hours worth of time and effort to learn discerning visualizations would pay off, to which 10 out of 15 participants agreed.

Regarding the facilitation of decision making cited by Wagner et al. [4], one of the major issues lies in the fact that a diagnostic routine in a continuously evolving environment such as cybersecurity is virtually impossible. Generally, extensive domain knowledge is necessary to derive valid assumptions. Current trends show that instead of automating the process of decision making, the existing data has to be automatically analyzed and interactive visualizations as a basis for decision making need to be generated from those results. To facilitate comprehension, the output has to take the granularity of information into account. Despite the advantage of visualizing additional dimensions using 3D visualization techniques, a majority of tools and research contributions avoid their inclusion. Concerning the overall type of visualizations used, 24 out of 25 proposed systems support 2D visualizations, whereas only 4 out of 25 proposed systems either only support 3D visualizations or use it to complement their 2D visualizations.

Focusing on CI and CIP, Merabti et al. [5] explore major challenges regarding CIP, differentiating between system modelling, system of systems design (addressing the problem of a complex internal heterogeneous ecosystem), (cyber-) security, and crisis management. Concerning crisis management, the authors developed a tool facilitating the discovery of vulnerabilities and study cascade effects of crisis management processes. The user interface mainly relies on a 2.5D geographical map with a node-link diagram overlay.

Nukavarapu and Durbha [6] present a dynamic simulation model for real-time situational awareness for operational risk management in CIs during disasters. By employing a colored petri net visualizing data provided through a Geographic Information System (GIS) cascading effects can be simulated. The usage of the model aims to provide assistance regarding decision making and response planning for disaster response personnel. Although use case scenarios were provided regarding the motivation of the model's usage, there were no domain experts involved in the design or evaluation cycles.

Lee et al. [7] present a dynamic monitoring and analysis system incorporating multiple CI and GIS datasets. The system includes data processing and analysis capabilities regarding efficiency and vulnerabilities, as well as simulation of "what-if" scenarios in the context of CI incidents. The visualizations include node-link diagrams over geographical maps, line charts and textual representations. Follow-up work by Tabassum et al. [8] provides demonstration scenarios based on the previous work.

As part of communication and enhanced situational awareness analysis, Thom et al. [9] [10] conducted user interviews comprising of 29 domain experts from disaster response and CI management regarding the results of a social media analysis on a real world Twitter data set during the German flood 2013. While the results and the subsequent discussion with participating stakeholders provided various insights concerning data provision and data processing, e.g., included media support and classification, the domain experts stated fake news as a major concern.

Similarly, Mittelstädt et al. [11] introduce a visual analytics system for CIs with simulation features for cascading effects. The system facilitates enhanced situational awareness by analyzing Twitter messages linked to a given incident. The targeted users consist of various stakeholders from different domains, i.e., analytics experts and police, grouped into crisis managers, site commanders, or first responders. User evaluations and interviews conducted with domain experts from CIs and government provided positive feedback. A significant limitation stated during interviews was the aspect of fake news regarding analyzed Twitter messages.

Puuska et al. [12] present a CI simulation system focusing on the aspects of situational awareness and collaboration regarding data sharing. They conducted user interviews with domain experts and stakeholders from different CIs, mobile network operators, and rescue service providers (e.g. police force) resulting in a set of requirements covering collaboration, interoperability, multi-stakeholder needs, visualization, as well as general system requirements. The applied visualization techniques focus on node-link diagrams over a geographical map and line charts displaying the impact of natural disasters on CI.

III. Analysis of User Requirements in the CI and LPA Sectors

The following section analyzes requirements of nationally and internationally funded projects in the field of security, including the CS-AWARE project [1], and the currently ongoing ODYSSEUS project [2]. Special attention is given to the concept of enhanced situational awareness to extend the regular scope.

A. Requirements Analysis in CS-AWARE

In the context of the CS-AWARE project [1], which focuses on the concepts of enhanced situational awareness and information sharing for LPAs, multiple end-user workshops organized in form of focus group interviews were conducted during the design cycles with cybersecurity and representatives from various LPA user groups (including executives, operations, and external stakeholders, i.e., the general public). During the evaluation cycles, a set of technical evaluations in form of user studies and UX interviews were conducted followed by the completion of questionnaires, if applicable.

1) User Requirements: The user requirements were acquired during the design cycle's workshops types with the project's end-user partners, the cities of Rome and Larissa. The workshops provided insights into internal processes, structure, and limitations of LPA operations. In the workshops, the domain experts reported their experience in form of stories in collaborative groups starting with individual experiences and afterwards broadening them by adding more details about the context, issues, and the outcome of events. Stories included various topics ranging from fake news to sharing potentially sensitive data through web conferencing tools. The involved user groups consisted of managers (n=5), system administrators (n=6), and local service users (n=2) in Rome, and manager (n=1), system administrators (n=3 + 1 unit manager) and local service users (n=2) in Larissa. The results of the workshops allowed to derive requirements based on each user groups objectives, including "reduction of time for threat understanding" and "more effective relation with service providers in handling cybersecurity", system artifacts, i.a., "report of information shared by other LPAs" and "weekly incident reports", and the desired behavior, i.a., "Regular communication with technical team and internal users" and "collaboratively discussing solutions", during the deployment of the system.

2) Visual Requirements: Regarding the visual components used, the CS-AWARE system primarily focuses on tabular views and the provision of raw data. Used visualization techniques belong to the 2D display and geometrically transformed displays category, including a dartboard chart and a node-link diagram. The system focuses on textual representations of information and provides the users with a high degree of interaction including searching and filtering textual and visual representations, as well as zooming and panning the interface elements.

3) Functional Requirements: The main concepts of the CS-AWARE project are, i.a., collaboration and an extended aspect of situational awareness, as the latter focuses on the gathering of data from a multitude of external sources, as well as building a threat sharing community consisting of CS-AWARE users. Kupfersberger et al. [13] describe the information flow model of the CS-AWARE project providing an in-depth analysis regarding its functional requirements. One of the major requirements of the domain experts was the functionality of interoperability, specifically to seamlessly support the integration of the system into the existing work environment. This includes the sharing of findings between applications, i.e., data import / export and email notifications.

B. Requirement Analysis in ODYSSEUS

During the ODYSSEUS project [2], which focuses on the analysis of cascading effects between critical supply networks in cities, the domain experts from various CIs stated collaboration and enhanced situational awareness to be critical factors concerning the life cycle of threats.

While the core functionality of CIs (i.a., power supply or water supply) work independently from external networks and therefore generally remain unaffected by external outages, problems stated by the domain experts may arise from outside their field of activity, i.a., panic reactions from the population and fake news. These erroneously undermine public trust and pose a security risk for public administrations and the population. The identified requirements include:

1) Project Environment: The project environment consists of internal project partners encompassing research facilities, industry, and federal ministries. After creating a set of use case scenarios, multiple end-user workshops were conducted to evaluate the assumptions. The first workshop had the form of focus group interviews with domain experts from different CIs. After an initial assessment and adaptions of the use case scenarios, a set of subsequent workshops were conducted focusing on various domain experts regarding business continuity, and security from each CI involved.

2) Functional Requirements: In order to cope with potential problems, which is largely done in collaboration with other public administrations, a reliable flow of communication between these administrations and the CIs has been identified as essential.. In this regard, the requirement of information sharing is to be underlined, as it facilitates timely reactions of involved parties both in terms of communicating valuable information, and in terms of collaboration regarding mitigation actions and next steps.

Additional paths of information flows concerning information sharing facilitate enhanced situational awareness. While this constitutes a favorable advantage for CIP and other organizations, the domain experts stated the need for increased assessment of public resources regarding trustworthiness, duplicates, and accuracy in order to correctly assess the situation.

IV. Focus, Gaps of Major Trends Identified in Literature

In order to objectively evaluate the work presented in the Symposium on Visualization for Cyber Security (VizSec) during the years 2017 to 2019, a set of different categories were chosen ranging from visualization techniques to user involvement. Additionally, as not all papers focus on the demonstration of applications, general categories described by Liu et al. [14] were used for the classification of research contributions.

A. Dimensions Evaluated

The following subsection describes new dimensions evaluated in this paper, derived from or complementing existing categories.

1) Category of Contribution: Liu et al. [14] provide an analysis of submitted research in Information Visualization (InfoVis) concerning future trends, major goals, recent trends, and state-of-the-art approaches. The authors classify these works into four main categories: Empirical methodologies, Systems & Frameworks, Applications, and Interactions. In the context of this work the last category will be removed.

The category of contribution selects the main contribution type presented by the authors. If authors use an application to demonstrate their proposed model, then the contribution will be assigned to the empirical methodology category, despite also including an application.

2) Visualization techniques: Regarding visualization techniques, a subset of categories identified by Keim [15] and used by Wagner et al. [4] was selected consisting of: Standard 2D/3D Displays, Geometrically Transformed Displays, Iconic Displays, Dense Pixel Display, and Stacked Display. Additionally, as the VizSec specializes in the collaboration between academia, government, and industry, the following categories have been added or underlined form the list above:

- **Maps** as geographical visualizations. This category is part of the **Standard 2D/3D Displays** category, but due to the coverage of specific use cases, this subcategory will be treated separately.
- **Tabular View** as a textual representation of summarized or derived information, generally displayed as, but not limited to, tabs.
- **Raw Data** as supporting the display to raw data regarding the data source. This category is especially valuable to gain an in-depth understanding after an initial analysis in order to facilitate decision making.

Multiple categories can be selected due to a range of use cases applicable.

3) Interactivity and Mapping: The functionality of contributed applications is evaluated in part according to the presence of interaction and distortion techniques by Keim [15] and categorization by Wagner et al. [4]. The selected subset consists of different degrees of Interactivity, Filtering, and Dynamic or Static Mapping.

In addition to the categories listed in related work, we identified several additional categories relevant for interactivity and mapping, which is based on practical experience with user requirements from the CI and LPA field:

- **Interactivity Low** describes basic interactive features between the user and the application, e.g., viewing static visualizations.
- **Interactivity High** describes advanced interactive features between the user and the application, e.g., inspecting selections and applying filters.
- **Collaboration** as the functionality of collaboration between users using one application and external targets, or between multiple instances of the same application.
- **Customization** as the functionality to adapt the application view according to various parameters, i.a., color palette.

4) User Involvement: The categories for user involvement differentiates between the level of expertise of people involved either in form of user interviews before or during the initial design processes, or user studies during the design or evaluation processes of the contributed research. The categorization follows adapted user types described by [16] and consists of:

- **No Users** describes a research contribution with no involved individuals during the design or evaluation cycles. Use case scenarios exemplifying the usage of the provided contribution without actual real user involvement also fall into this category.
- **Lay Users** are users without required domain knowledge.
- **Novices** are users with beginners knowledge of the domain, e.g., students in the required field.
- **Experts** are users with extensive domain knowledge generally working in the industry.

5) Included Content: The included content category provides an overview of all aspects involved comprising the individual research contributions as follows:

- **Tool, Prototype, etc.** describes the usage of a technical application either as the main contribution, or to support the main contribution.
- **Model, Approach, etc.** describes the usage of novel methods in order to tackle unique problem spaces through new visualization techniques.
- **User Study** describes the involvement of real domain experts for evaluation purposes.
- **User Story/ Interview** describes the involvement of real domain experts for the purpose of gathering information about the problem space being tackled.

B. Analysis of VizSec symposia 2017-2019

In the context of this work, we analyzed the years 2017 - 2019 of the VizSec symposia according to the categories described above. The VizSec symposium constitutes a forum of research contributions encompassing academia, government, and industry, which provides a meaningful insight into current trends. The results regarding relevant contributions might differ according to the authors intent. The outcome of the analysis is presented in Tables I to V, and are discussed in Section IV-B4 and Section V.

1) VizSec 2017: In terms of visualization techniques used, a majority of authors focus on simple 2D displays with additional techniques, if their usage would support the purpose of the work, i.a., dense pixel displays. Concerning interactivity, nearly every proposed tool includes a form of high interactivity characterized by the possibility to manipulate rendered visualizations, i.a., by applying filters, panning, or zooming.

A major gap identified of the VizSec 2017 papers is the functionality in terms of collaboration. Only two [17] [18] out of ten papers addressed this topic, although Sethi and Wills [18] only conducted expert interviews resulting in those experts stating the need for collaboration without going into further detail on how to ensure this functionality, or proposing ways on the implementation. On the other hand, Franklin et al. [17] designed a prototype specifically supporting a collaborative process by implementing a shared space to "brainstorm, share notes and hold [their] brains during interruption".

2) VizSec 2018: All authors include a form of 2D displays as visualization techniques in their work with only Krokos et al. [19] additionally using 3D display visualization techniques. Apart from this aspect, nearly every author included another visualization technique in order to complement their work.

In terms of interactivity, seven out of nine papers proposing a tool or prototype implemented additional functionality for increased interactivity of the system.

Again, the major scientific gap identified in the VizSec 2018 papers is the aspect of collaboration, as none of the eleven papers discussed the importance of collaboration or incorporated collaborative functionality into their prototypes.

3) VizSec 2019: Every author with focus on a presented application included a form of 2D display into their research, with four out of seven authors including another visualization technique to complement their work.

The major gap identified in the VizSec 2019 papers is again the aspect of collaboration, as none of the eleven papers discussing or supporting the implementation of collaborative functionality. Ulmer et al. [20] discuss collaboration as part of future work.

4) Current Trends: In terms of evaluation techniques, Barkhuus et al. [21], is analyzing papers submitted to the CHI conference and found that those techniques commonly used in industry are generally unsuitable for academia as they are specifically designed to meet the needs of businesses. In terms of empirical evaluations, a strong shift in favor of qualitative evaluations was detected.

Staheli et al. [16] analyzed the research submitted to the IEEE VizSec symposia over a time period of ten years from 2004 - 2013. Their goal was to identify gaps in evaluation approaches regarding information visualization. Concerning the statement of Barkhuus et al. [21], the authors express that the research provided in VizSec papers are designed to be used in practical situations regarding real world use cases. The core findings in terms of trend analysis showed a rise regarding feature set utility, insight generation, and usability, while the aspect of collaboration was barely present (2 out of 119 research contributions).

Current trends in the context of VizSec research contributions show that a majority of submissions tend to focus on the presentation of novel applications or prototypes for visualization, as shown in Table I, while empirical methodologies (i.a. novel models or evaluations) fluctuate between years.

In contributions focusing on the presentation of applications or prototypes, or using them to visualize underlying models, a majority of research contributions use simple 2D charts as visualization technique, as depicted in Table II.

TABLE I. . RESEARCH CONTRIBUTIONS CLASSIFIED ACCORDING TO THE MAIN FOCUS OF THE CONTRIBUTION.

Category	VizSec 2017	VizSec 2018	VizSec 2019
Empirical methodology	[22]	[23], [24], [25], [26], [19], [27]	[28], [29], [30]
Systems and Frameworks			[31], [32]
Applications	[33], [34], [35], [36], [37], [38], [39], [17], [40]	[41], [42], [43], [44], [45]	[46], [47], [48], [20], [49], [50]

Additional provision of textual representations or access to raw data proves especially advantageous for domain experts in conducted evaluations. Visualization techniques using iconic displays or dense pixel displays tend to be part of empirical methodologies to underline alternative aspects of data, which consequently provides valuable input for further research.

TABLE II. . RESEARCH CONTRIBUTIONS CLASSIFIED ACCORDING TO VISUALIZATION TECHNIQUES USED.

Category	VizSec 2017	VizSec 2018	VizSec 2019
2D Display	[33], [34], [37], [38], [39], [17], [40]	[23], [24], [41], [42], [43], [44], [25], [45], [26], [19], [27]	[46], [31], [28], [47], [48], [32], [20], [49], [50]
3D Display	[35]	[19]	[20]
Geometrically Transformed	[35], [36], [37], [39], [40]	[42], [44], [27]	[28], [32], [20], [49], [50]
Iconic Display		[25], [45]	
Dense Pixel Display			[29]
Stacked Display	[38], [39], [40]	[41], [42], [19]	[29], [48]
Maps	[39]	[42], [45], [32]	
Tabular View	[37], [38], [39], [17], [40]	[24], [41], [42], [44], [26],	[31], [48], [20], [49], [50]
Raw Data	[37], [38], [39], [17], [40]	[41], [43], [44], [45], [26]	[20]

As the main contribution of visualizations in cybersecurity is related to data exploration and insight creation, applications are bound to provide a high degree of interactivity - like the functionality of brushing and linking for the purpose of filtering data. The category Dynamic Mapping is especially relevant in this evaluation, as it constitutes an essential part of situational awareness. Detailed results are provided in Table III. The category of collaboration shows a significant gap in the cybersecurity ecosystem, despite a critical need for increased increased cooperation and collaboration between cybersecurity actors, as highlighted by the European cybersecurity strategy of 2013 [51] and the Network and Information Security (NIS) directive [52]. Although a few research contributions mention the aspect of collaboration as part of related work, it is generally not implemented by the presented conceptions.

Regarding user involvement in terms of interviews with domain experts and evaluation processes, the results seem to reflect the findings of Staheli et al. [16], as a majority of users in presented research contributions were domain experts vs. users with differing experience levels. Despite most contributions include tools or use case scenarios, about one third did not provide any end-user involvement (e.g. interviews

TABLE III. . Research contributions classified according to interactivity and mapping used.

Category	VizSec 2017	VizSec 2018	VizSec 2019
No Interactivity			
Interactivity Low	[33], [34], [17]	[41],	
Interactivity High	[35], [36], [37], [38], [40]	[24], [42], [43], [44], [25], [45], [26], [19],	[46], [31], [47], [48], [32], [20], [49], [50]
Customization	[38]	[41], [47]	
Sorting/Filtering	[37], [38], [39], [17], [40]	[24], [41], [42], [43], [44], [45], [26], [19]	[46], [31], [47], [48], [32], [20], [49], [50]
Dynamic Mapping	[39], [17]	[19]	[47], [20], [50]
Static Mapping	[33], [34], [35], [36], [37], [38], [40]	[23], [24], [41], [42], [43], [44], [25], [45], [26]	[46], [31], [48], [32], [49]
Collaboration	[22], [17]		

or evaluations). The detailed evaluation results are shown in Table IV.

TABLE IV. . Research contributions classified according to users involved during design cycles or user studies.

Category	VizSec 2017	VizSec 2018	VizSec 2019
No Users	[34], [35], [39], [40]	[24], [44], [26]	[31], [28], [29], [32], [30]
Lay Users		[25], [27]	[47]
Novices	[37], [38]	[45]	[46], [20], [50]
Experts	[33], [22], [36], [37], [38], [17]	[41], [42], [43], [19]	[47], [48], [20], [49]
Not disclosed		[23], [25]	

An overall analysis of the provided content of the research contributions includes either a tool or a user study to evaluate their findings. Initial user interviews provide the advantage of receiving in-depth experiences of domain experts on which research contributions can be build upon, despite opportunities for their implementation are often limited. A detailed table displaying the categorizations is provided in Table V.

TABLE V. . Research contributions listed according to provided content.

Category	VizSec 2017	VizSec 2018	VizSec 2019
Tools	[33], [34], [35], [36], [37], [38], [39], [17], [40]	[23], [24], [41], [42], [43], [44], [45], [26], [19]	[46], [31], [47], [48], [32], [20], [49], [50]
Algorithm/ Approach/ etc.	[34]	[23], [24]	[28], [29], [30]
User Study	[33], [22], [37], [38]	[23], [41], [42], [43], [25], [45], [19], [27]	[46], [47], [20], [49], [50]
User Story/ Interviews	[22], [36], [17]		[47], [48]

V. Discussion of Identified Gaps

In the context of discussing gaps, the aspects of collaboration, enhanced situational awareness, multi-stakeholder involvement, and multi-stakeholder visualization are discussed, as we have identified a need for cybersecurity visualizations in this context from user feedback in the context of the two research projects presented in Section III.

The analysis shows that collaboration is rarely a factor in current state-of-the-art cybersecurity visualization research. The benefits of a collaborative approach include the facilitation of information sharing between CI stakeholders and government authorities during incidents and enhance mitigation and response actions, as shown by Puuska et al. [12], and in the context of CS-AWARE.

Regarding enhanced situational awareness, the current state-of-the-art focuses on situational awareness within an organization rarely exceeding the boundaries of a given organization. A growing trend to CIP research can be observed in the context of evaluations of Twitter posts as analyzed by Thom et al. [9] [10] and Mittelstädt et al. [11]. The expectations of enhanced situational awareness incorporate the analysis of external data, i.a., social media or distinct information sharing communities, in order to gather more knowledge regarding active threats to facilitate responsive measures. Domain experts involved in CS-AWARE and ODYSSEUS stated an increased need for data analysis outside the organizational scope of LPAs and CIs.

Regarding multi-stakeholder involvement in the design and evaluation cycles of a project, the general trend in state-of-the-art analysis only incorporates the views of a single stakeholder group at most. Puuska et al. [12] and Mittelstädt et al. [11] incorporate views and processes of multiple user groups ranging from analysts to first responders. The expectations include an increased incident handling capability to account for multiple interdependent processes (i.a. supported incident handling & data sharing across departments and increased coordination with external organizations and authorities). During ODYSSEUS the need for the evaluation and adaption of created use case scenarios arose, after which different stakeholders were interviewed to gain insight into dependent processes including domain experts from CIs and LPAs.

Regarding multi-stakeholder visualizations, the current state of state-of-the-art research generally focuses on single use cases for technical personnel to alleviate readability of processed raw data. A majority of CIP related work provides visualizations encompassing at least technical user groups and facilitates coordination with other groups like, e.g., first responders, for which individual views need to be created. The expectations of incorporating multi-stakeholder visualization lies in the increased homogeneity of the ecosystem facilitating interoperability and collaboration. In the context of CS-AWARE, the need for accommodating different user groups (e.g. management, technical personnel) by representing data to suit their specific requirements was clearly expressed during the end-user workshops.

In order to meet those expectations, an initial assessment of involved stakeholder groups is essential, highlighting individual needs and desirable outcomes in terms of visual and functional requirements. Furthermore, the results may expose dependencies previously not taken into consideration. As a recommendation, we propose:

- Using workshops and user interviews during early stages of a project's life cycle to assess and define the desired outcomes for each user group. This includes the assessment of what information is required by each user group, and how data needs to be represented to meet those requirements.

- Additionally, proposed systems need to take collaboration and coordination efforts between multiple user groups into account, including domain-independent stakeholders. Notably, the functionality of supporting data/information sharing provides stakeholders with the capability of efficient incorporation of a system into an existing environment.

VI. Conclusion and Future Work

In this work a gap analysis in the current state-of-the-art of cybersecurity related visualizations is presented. The requirements for cybersecurity visualizations of end users from the LPA and CI sectors are analyzed, based on results achieved during the two research projects CS-AWARE and ODYSSEUS. A gap analysis with respect to the requirements identified is conducted based on an in-dept analysis and categorization of the VizSec symposia from 2017-2019.

The findings show a gap between the state-of-the-art research and the extended requirements of LPAs and CIs specifically in the context of collaboration, enhanced situational awareness, multi-stakeholder involvement, and multi-stakeholder visualization. For each gap, we analyze the current trend, as well as expectations resulting from the implementation of these aspects. Finally, we propose recommendations aimed at increasing the efficiency of realization of projects including multiple domain-interdependent stakeholders.

Future work encompasses the evaluation of analyzed aspects and requirements to be included during the progress of the ODYSSEUS project, and providing a proof-of-concept implementation of cybersecurity related visualizations that take the aspects of cooperation/collaboration and optimization of visualizations for different user groups within the organization into account.

Acknowledgments

This work was partially funded by the Austrian FFG research program KIRAS in course of the project ODYSSEUS ("Simulation und Analyse kritischer Netzwerk-Infrastrukturen in Städten") under Grant No. 873539.

References

[1] "A cybersecurity situational awareness and information sharing solution for local public administrations based on advanced big data analysis CS-AWARE Project H2020 CORDIS European Commission," Sep 2020, [retrieved: September, 2020]. [Online]. Available: https://cordis.europa.eu/project/id/740723

[2] "Kiras - sicherheitsforschung," Aug 2020, retrieved: August, 2020]. [Online]. Available: https://www.kiras.at/en/financed-proposals/detail/d/odysseus-simulation-und-analyse-kritischer-netzwerk-infrastrukturen-in-staedten

[3] A. D'Amico, L. Buchanan, D. Kirkpatrick, and P. Walczak, "Cyber operator perspectives on security visualization," in *Advances in Human Factors in Cybersecurity*, D. Nicholson, Ed. Cham: Springer International Publishing, 2016, pp. 69–81.

[4] M. Wagner, F. Fischer, R. Luh, A. Haberson, A. Rind, D. A. Keim, and W. Aigner, "A survey of visualization systems for malware analysis," in *EuroVis*, 2015.

[5] M. Merabti, M. Kennedy, and W. Hurst, "Critical infrastructure protection: A 21st century challenge," in *2011 International Conference on Communications and Information Technology (ICCIT)*, 2011, pp. 1–6.

[6] N. Nukavarapu and S. Durbha, "Geo-visual analytics for healthcare critical infrastructure simulation model," in *2017 IEEE International Geoscience and Remote Sensing Symposium (IGARSS)*, 2017, pp. 6106–6109.

[7] S. Lee, L. Chen, S. Duan, S. Chinthavali, M. Shankar, and B. A. Prakash, "Urban-net: A network-based infrastructure monitoring and analysis system for emergency management and public safety," in *2016 IEEE International Conference on Big Data (Big Data)*, 2016, pp. 2600–2609.

[8] A. Tabassum, S. Chinthavali, S. Lee, L. Chen, and B. Prakash, "Urban-net : A system to understand and analyze critical infrastructure networks for emergency management," 2019.

[9] D. Thom, R. Krüger, T. Ertl, U. Bechstedt, A. Platz, J. Zisgen, and B. Volland, "Can twitter really save your life? a case study of visual social media analytics for situation awareness," in *2015 IEEE Pacific Visualization Symposium (PacificVis)*, 2015, pp. 183–190.

[10] D. Thom, R. Krüger, and T. Ertl, "Can twitter save lives? a broad-scale study on visual social media analytics for public safety," *IEEE Transactions on Visualization and Computer Graphics*, vol. 22, no. 7, pp. 1816–1829, 2016.

[11] S. Mittelstädt, X. Wang, T. Eaglin, D. Thom, D. Keim, W. Tolone, and W. Ribarsky, "An integrated in-situ approach to impacts from natural disasters on critical infrastructures," in *2015 48th Hawaii International Conference on System Sciences*, 2015, pp. 1118–1127.

[12] S. Puuska, S. Horsmanheimo, H. Kokkoniemi-Tarkkanen, P. Kuusela, L. Tuomimäki, and J. Vankka, "Integrated platform for critical infrastructure analysis and common operating picture solutions," in *2017 IEEE International Symposium on Technologies for Homeland Security (HST)*, 2017, pp. 1–6.

[13] V. Kupfersberger, T. Schaberreiter, and G. Quirchmayr, "Security-driven information flow modelling for component integration in complex environments," in *Proceedings of the 10th International Conference on Advances in Information Technology, IAIT 2018, Bangkok, Thailand, December 10-13, 2018*. ACM, 2018, pp. 19:1–19:8. [Online]. Available: https://doi.org/10.1145/3291280.3291797

[14] S. Liu, W. Cui, Y. Wu, and M. Liu, "A survey on information visualization: recent advances and challenges," *The Visual Computer*, vol. 30, no. 12, pp. 1373–1393, Dec 2014. [Online]. Available: https://doi.org/10.1007/s00371-013-0892-3

[15] D. A. Keim, "Information visualization and visual data mining," *IEEE transactions on Visualization and Computer Graphics*, vol. 8, no. 1, pp. 1–8, 2002.

[16] D. Staheli, T. Yu, R. J. Crouser, S. Damodaran, K. Nam, D. O'Gwynn, S. McKenna, and L. Harrison, "Visualization evaluation for cyber security: Trends and future directions," in *Proceedings of the Eleventh Workshop on Visualization for Cyber Security*, ser. VizSec '14. New York, NY, USA: ACM, 2014, pp. 49–56. [Online]. Available: http://doi.acm.org/10.1145/2671491.2671492

[17] L. Franklin, M. Pirrung, L. Blaha, M. Dowling, and M. Feng, "Toward a visualization-supported workflow for cyber alert management using threat models and human-centered design," in *2017 IEEE Symposium on Visualization for Cyber Security (VizSec)*, Oct 2017, pp. 1–8.

[18] A. Sethi and G. Wills, "Expert-interviews led analysis of eevi — a model for effective visualization in cyber-security," in *2017 IEEE Symposium on Visualization for Cyber Security (VizSec)*, Oct 2017, pp. 1–8.

[19] E. Krokos, A. Rowden, K. Whitley, and A. Varshney, "Visual analytics for root dns data," in *2018 IEEE Symposium on Visualization for Cyber Security (VizSec)*, Oct 2018, pp. 1–8.

[20] A. Ulmer, D. Sessler, and J. Kohlhammer, "Netcapvis: Web-based progressive visual analytics for network packet captures," in *2019 IEEE Symposium on Visualization for Cyber Security (VizSec)*, 2019, pp. 1–10.

[21] L. Barkhuus and J. Rode, "From mice to men - 24 years of evaluation in chi," in *Proceedings of the SIGCHI Conference on human factors in computing systems*, ser. CHI '07. ACM, 2007.

[22] A. Sethi, F. Paci, and G. Wills, "Eevi - framework for evaluating the effectiveness of visualization in cyber-security," in *2016 11th International Conference for Internet Technology and Secured Transactions (ICITST)*, Dec 2016, pp. 340–345.

[23] Y. Yang, J. Collomosse, A. K. Manohar, J. Briggs, and J. Steane, "Tapestry: Visualizing interwoven identities for trust provenance," in *2018 IEEE Symposium on Visualization for Cyber Security (VizSec)*, Oct 2018, pp. 1–4.

[24] R. Gove and L. Deason, "Visualizing automatically detected periodic network activity," in *2018 IEEE Symposium on Visualization for Cyber Security (VizSec)*, Oct 2018, pp. 1–8.

[25] D. L. Arendt, L. R. Franklin, F. Yang, B. R. Brisbois, and R. R. LaMothe, "Crush your data with vic2es then chissl away," in *2018 IEEE Symposium on Visualization for Cyber Security (VizSec)*, Oct 2018, pp. 1–8.

[26] B. C. M. Cappers, P. N. Meessen, S. Etalle, and J. J. van Wijk, "Eventpad: Rapid malware analysis and reverse engineering using visual analytics," in *2018 IEEE Symposium on Visualization for Cyber Security (VizSec)*, Oct 2018, pp. 1–8.

[27] J. Chou, C. Bryan, J. Li, and K. Ma, "An empirical study on perceptually masking privacy in graph visualizations," in *2018 IEEE Symposium on Visualization for Cyber Security (VizSec)*, Oct 2018, pp. 1–8.

[28] A. Dasgupta, R. Kosara, and M. Chen, "Guess me if you can: A visual uncertainty model for transparent evaluation of disclosure risks in privacy-preserving data visualization," in *2019 IEEE Symposium on Visualization for Cyber Security (VizSec)*, 08 2019.

[29] S. O'Shaughnessy, "Image-based malware classification: A space filling curve approach," in *2019 IEEE Symposium on Visualization for Cyber Security (VizSec)*, 10 2019.

[30] M. Varga, C. Winkelholz, and S. Träber-Burdin, "An exploration of cyber symbology," in *2019 IEEE Symposium on Visualization for Cyber Security (VizSec)*, 2019, pp. 1–5.

[31] B. Laughlin, C. Collins, K. Sankaranarayanan, and K. El-Khatib, "A visual analytics framework for adversarial text generation," *arXiv*, Sep 2019. [Online]. Available: https://arxiv.org/abs/1909.11202

[32] S. Subramanian, P. Pushparaj, Z. Liu, and A.-d. Lu, "Explainable visualization of collaborative vandal behaviors in wikipedia," in *2019 IEEE Symposium on Visualization for Cyber Security (VizSec)*, 08 2019.

[33] M. Angelini, S. Lenti, and G. Santucci, "Crumbs: A cyber security framework browser," in *2017 IEEE Symposium on Visualization for Cyber Security (VizSec)*, Oct 2017, pp. 1–8.

[34] A. P. Norton and Y. Qi, "Adversarial-playground: A visualization suite showing how adversarial examples fool deep learning," in *2017 IEEE Symposium on Visualization for Cyber Security (VizSec)*, Oct 2017, pp. 1–4.

[35] L. Leichtnam, Totel, N. Prigent, and L. Mé, "Starlord: Linked security data exploration in a 3d graph," in *2017 IEEE Symposium on Visualization for Cyber Security (VizSec)*, Oct 2017, pp. 1–4.

[36] H. Kim, S. Ko, D. S. Kim, and H. K. Kim, "Firewall ruleset visualization analysis tool based on segmentation," in *2017 IEEE Symposium on Visualization for Cyber Security (VizSec)*, Oct 2017, pp. 1–8.

[37] G. R. Santhanam, B. Holland, S. Kothari, and J. Mathews, "Interactive visualization toolbox to detect sophisticated android malware," in *2017 IEEE Symposium on Visualization for Cyber Security (VizSec)*, Oct 2017, pp. 1–8.

[38] R. Romero-Gomez, Y. Nadji, and M. Antonakakis, "Towards designing effective visualizations for dns-based network threat analysis," in *2017 IEEE Symposium on Visualization for Cyber Security (VizSec)*, Oct 2017, pp. 1–8.

[39] M. Angelini, L. Aniello, S. Lenti, G. Santucci, and D. Ucci, "The goods, the bads and the uglies: Supporting decisions in malware detection through visual analytics," in *2017 IEEE Symposium on Visualization for Cyber Security (VizSec)*, Oct 2017, pp. 1–8.

[40] R. Theron, R. Magán-Carrión, J. Camacho, and G. M. Fernndez, "Network-wide intrusion detection supported by multivariate analysis and interactive visualization," in *2017 IEEE Symposium on Visualization for Cyber Security (VizSec)*, Oct 2017, pp. 1–8.

[41] A. Sopan, M. Berninger, M. Mulakaluri, and R. Katakam, "Building a machine learning model for the soc, by the input from the soc, and analyzing it for the soc," in *2018 IEEE Symposium on Visualization for Cyber Security (VizSec)*, Oct 2018, pp. 1–8.

[42] S. Chen, S. Chen, N. Andrienko, G. Andrienko, P. H. Nguyen, C. Turkay, O. Thonnard, and X. Yuan, "User behavior map: Visual exploration for cyber security session data," in *2018 IEEE Symposium on Visualization for Cyber Security (VizSec)*, Oct 2018, pp. 1–4.

[43] M. Angelini, G. Blasilli, P. Borrello, E. Coppa, D. C. D'Elia, S. Ferracci, S. Lenti, and G. Santucci, "Ropmate: Visually assisting the creation of rop-based exploits," in *2018 IEEE Symposium on Visualization for Cyber Security (VizSec)*, Oct 2018, pp. 1–8.

[44] G. Bakirtzis, B. J. Simon, C. H. Fleming, and C. R. Elks, "Looking for a black cat in a dark room: Security visualization for cyber-physical system design and analysis," in *2018 IEEE Symposium on Visualization for Cyber Security (VizSec)*, Oct 2018, pp. 1–8.

[45] A. Ulmer, M. Schufrin, D. Sessler, and J. Kohlhammer, "Visual-interactive identification of anomalous ip-block behavior using geo-ip data," in *2018 IEEE Symposium on Visualization for Cyber Security (VizSec)*, Oct 2018, pp. 1–8.

[46] J. Torres, E. Veas, and C. Catania, "A study on labeling network hostile behavior with intelligent interactive tools," in *2019 IEEE Symposium on Visualization for Cyber Security (VizSec)*, 2019, iEEE Symposium on Visualization for Cyber Security, VIZSEC ; Conference date: 20-10-2019 Through 25-10-2019. [Online]. Available: http://ieeevis.org/year/2019/welcome

[47] A.-P. Lohfink, S. Duque Antón, H. D. Schotten, H. Leitte, and C. Garth, "Security in process: Visually supported triage analysis in industrial process data," in *Proceedings of the IEEE Symposium on Visualization for Cyber Security 2019, IEEE Symposium on Visualization for Cyber Security (VizSec-2019), October 20-25, Vancouver, British Columbia, Canada*, IEEE. IEEE, 2019.

[48] M. Angelini, G. Blasilli, L. Borzacchiello, E. Coppa, D. C. D'Elia, C. Demetrescu, S. Lenti, S. Nicchi, and G. Santucci, "Symnav: Visually assisting symbolic execution," in *2019 IEEE Symposium on Visualization for Cyber Security (VizSec)*, 10 2019.

[49] B. Fouss, D. M. Ross, A. B. Wollaber, and S. R. Gomez, "Punyvis: A visual analytics approach for identifying homograph phishing attacks," in *2019 IEEE Symposium on Visualization for Cyber Security (VizSec)*, 2019, pp. 1–10.

[50] R. Ošlejšek, V. Rusňák, K. Burská, V. Švábenský, and J. Vykopal, "Visual feedback for players of multi-level capture the flag games: Field usability study," in *2019 IEEE Symposium on Visualization for Cyber Security (VizSec)*, 2019, pp. 1–11.

[51] "Eu cybersecurity plan to protect open internet and online freedom and opportunity - cyber security strategy and proposal for a directive - shaping europe's digital future - european commission," Mar 2020, [retrieved: September, 2020]. [Online]. Available: https://ec.europa.eu/digital-single-market/en/news/eu-cybersecurity-plan-protect-open-internet-and-online-freedom-and-opportunity-cyber-security

[52] E. P. Council of the European Union, "Directive (eu) 2016/1148 of the european parliament and of the council of 6 july 2016 concerning measures for a high common level of security of network and information systems across the union," *Publications Office of the European Union*, Jul 2016. [Online]. Available: https://op.europa.eu/en/publication-detail/-/publication/d2912aca-4d75-11e6-89bd-01aa75ed71a1/language-en

Trust Through Origin and Integrity: Protection of Client Code for Improved Cloud Security

Anders Fongen, Kirsi Helkala and Mass Soldal Lund
Norwegian Military University College, Cyber Defense Academy
Lillehammer, Norway
Email: anders@fongen.no

***Abstract*—Military computing is migrating to cloud architecture for several reasons, one of them is the opportunities for improved security management. One opportunity is to ensure that cloud clients are running approved and untainted program code, provided as a proof presented to the cloud service. Such proofs can extend the trust in the client's integrity further than what traditional access control protocols can provide. While access control protocols can ensure that a computer is operated by authorized and trained personnel, they cannot ensure that the client computer is unaffected by malware or poor software control. Problems related to illegitimate program code cannot, in general, be solved by traditional security protocols. The contribution of this paper is an arrangement whereby proof of software approval and integrity can be established, exchanged and validated during service invocations. The demonstration program is a chat forum where the exchanged messages are signed and validated in the client computers, a typical use case which may benefit from our contribution. Two different client-server protocols were tested in order to study the applicability of our contribution.**

***Keywords*—cloud security; integrity attestation; trusted computing; Google ChromeOS**

I. Introduction

Military computing applications are being migrated to cloud architecture due to a number of advantages, including those related to security management [1] [2].

The integrity of client code is important in most cloud application, but of particular importance where sensor readings and cryptographic operations are involved. Cloud computing relies on mutual trust between client and the service, trust in that the transactions between them take place in a *bona fide* manner. The service offers its interface to a client which is presumed to operate through it in a responsible manner. The mutual trust is usually derived from *authentication* of the person who is operating the client computer, together with personnel management procedures that ensure the loyalty and competence of this person.

Authentication does not extend the trust to the software in use, however. Malware, version mismatch, unauthorized modification and updates may cause the interface to be operated in a harmful manner, causing leaked or falsified information and loss of trust in the system. What is needed is a proof of untainted client software which can be verified by the service during the authentication process. For the remainder of this paper this proof will be called an *integrity attest*. Likewise, the service may attest its software integrity to the client, but we are less concerned about the software integrity in a tightly controlled server environment. Military use cases for integrity attests include sensor readings and cryptographic operations, where client malware may modify, leak or spoof information sent to an unsuspicious server.

This paper will discuss and demonstrate schemes for integrity attestation and how they may be combined with personal credentials in trust management operations. A demonstrator application will be briefly presented. The application will employ the properties of ChromeOS together with the *Cross-origin resource sharing* (CORS) protocol and client-authenticated *Transport Layer Security* (TLS) connections to provide the necessary guarantees for browser based client programs written in Javascript. This demonstrator application employs the *Web Cryptography API* (WCA) [3] which also gives useful insight in the cryptography operation and key management in this environment. The novelty of the contribution is a new application of existing security protocols in order to offer protection of client integrity.

A. Desired security properties

The goal for any computer program is that it behaves as expected and conducts its transactions in a "bona-fide" manner. Since this property cannot be assessed in general, we choose to replace it with the following requirement:

"Only approved client code may access a given service"

This requirement entails that software running in the client has been inspected and approved during development, and protected from hostile modifications during deployment and execution. If adequate procedures for development and deployment of client code are in effect, this requirement will be equivalent to the required "bona-fide" operation of the client.

The technology elements taken into regard in this paper for establishing the required trust are:

1) Platform integrity protection
2) Hardware bound keys and certificates
3) The Cross Origin Resource Sharing (CORS) protocol
4) *Indication of Origin* in the HTTP headers
5) Device Security Policy Management
6) Mutually authenticated TLS connections

B. Related work

The protection of software integrity has been a prominent research field for decades. Oldest is likely to be the *process separation* found in any operating system, and the *virus detection* programs that aim to recognize binary fingerprints of well known malware types. *Code signing* is used to authenticate the software creator and to detect any changes to the software since release. The introduction of *Application Stores* in recent operating systems offers code signing as well as life-cycle management of the distribution, deployment, upgrading and removal of software. These research areas are distantly related to the presented research efforts, but they all fail if the protection mechanisms themselves are attacked. Hardware assisted protection mechanisms are needed, as operating systems designers have known for 50 years.

A combination of hardware assisted integrity protection and identity management is shown in [4], but the solution presented there does not protect software above the platform level. To the authors' best knowledge, no other platform than ChromeOS offer hardware-assisted integrity protection of the entire software stack, and the protection arrangements presented in this paper is believed to be novel.

The remainder of the paper is organized as follows: In Section II a discussion on the technology elements used in the presented protection scheme will be presented, followed by a model for the client code protection in Section III. A proof-of-concept prototype for evaluation of the protection model is presented in Section IV, follows by a conclusion in Section V.

II. Technology Discussion

This section provides a more detailed discussion of the technology elements involved in the aforementioned protection scheme.

A. *Platform integrity protection*

The integrity of the software stack can be protected through inspection techniques, where either (1) patterns of known malware is detected or (2) through detection of any modifications from an approved/correct state through the verification of hash values. For the latter approach, the Trusted Platform Module (TPM) [5] offers a range of services for boot-time software inspection, which also aids the protection of non-volatile storage in case the platform has been compromised.

Other techniques include the verification of a digital signature created over the software image, to verify the integrity of the software as well as its source. This approach is taken by Google ChromeOS [6], where Google's public key and signature verification code is located in ROM and executed during bootstrap. ChromeOS will not operate unless the verification stage has completed successfully, and it cannot be booted from USB memory. Likewise, the ARM processor architecture may use its *TrustZone* mode to establish a verified boot in a step-wise process similar to the TPM [7].

Two limitations are apparent in this arrangement: (1) The platform code is inspected only during bootstrap, and (2) the application programs are not inspected. Limitation no. 1 is due to feasibility reasons. Software inspection must be an atomic operation so task switching and interrupt handling must be disabled for the duration of the operation. It is therefore executed during bootstrap in order not to disturb other activities in the computer. Limitation no. 2 is probably due to the dynamicity and multi-vendor nature of the application programs in use. However, limitation no.2 is also the reason for concern over how malware can enter into the application software and challenge the integrity of the entire platform through exploits of vulnerabilities in its process separation and access control.

Among the well known and current platforms, only ChromeOS verifies the entire software stack, including the applications (which are limited to the Chrome browser, a file manager and a media player). Application code running as Javascript in the web browser is not integrity checked since it is loaded after boot-time, but Section II-C will show how loaded Javascript can be trusted both by its integrity and its origin. For other platforms, device security policy management may offer some protection from malware inside application code (cf. Sect II-E).

B. *Hardware bound keys and certificates*

Private keys are used to authenticate users or devices. In the former case, the private key should be accessible from all devices operating on behalf of this user. Such private keys can successfully be stored in USB dongles, smart cards, etc. In the latter case, the private key should be bound to the device hardware in a manner where it cannot be exported elsewhere. The typical hardware solution for private key storage is the TPM. For the protection arrangement presented in this paper, the binding of a key (and its certificate) to a device is crucial in order to establish the identity of the device and its associated properties.

Several platforms allow certificates and keys to be installed and bound to the hardware device, e.g., Windows 10, Android and ChromeOS. Certificates can be designed to authenticate both the user and the device, and allow the other party to make assumptions about the identity of the user as well as the properties of the software platform of the device. The presentation of a device-bound certificate during a transaction may (depending on platform) indicate a successful bootstrap integrity control. Within the limitations identified in Section II-A, the combination of integrity control and device bound keys provides *integrity attestation*.

Among the well known platforms, ChromeOS has the most complete assurances, since its bootstrap integrity control also includes the application software: When a client proves the ownership of a user certificate known to be bound to a ChromeOS device, e.g., during establishment of a client-authenticated TLS connection, the service can safely assume that the client device is free of malware and operates as expected (disregarding potential software bugs for the moment). The assumption relies on key management procedures where trusted personnel install the correct keys and certificates in the device during the device deployment phase, and later as certificates expire.

C. *The CORS protocol*

Inside a browser there are restrictions on where the Javascript code can set up network connections. Originally, there was a *same origin policy* in effect, i.e., connections could only be made using the same scheme, IP address and port as was used to load the web page [8]. Although originally designed to inhibit rogue Javascript programs from leaking information to arbitrary receivers, the restriction also protects the service from access from unauthorized clients; only Javascript loaded from the same server could access the service, which allowed the content of the client code to be

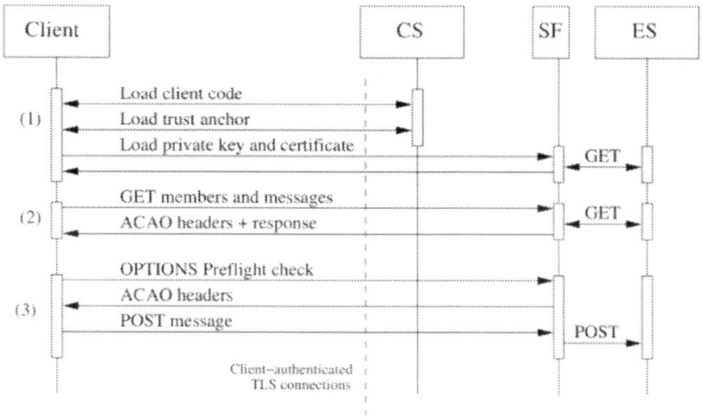

Fig. 1. The protocol elements of the Forum application, CS is the Code Service, ES the Execution Service and SF the Servlet Filter. Details are explained in Section IV.

closely inspected and protected. The use of *Content-Security-Policy* (CSP) directives in the code adds to the robustness of this arrangement [9].

The *same origin policy* has since been relaxed to allow Javascript access to services which explicitly permit connections from designated origins. Termed *Cross Origin Resource Sharing* (CORS), this protocol adds new HTTP headers for the client to request a list of *allowed origins* from the service [10]. These headers are termed *Access-Control-Allow-Origin* (ACAO), as shown in Figure 1. A POST method requires a "preflight-check" in the form of an OPTION method to obtain the ACAO headers prior to the actual POST method, which is not necessary for a GET method. In both cases, the operation is aborted if the ACAO headers do not contain the necessary values.

It is the responsibility of the web browser to enforce these rules, and in order to use the CORS protocol to protect the service from rogue client code, it must be evident that the browser is in fact obeying the CORS rules. Integrity attestation may provide such evidence if the mechanism also verifies this particular property of the browser in use. Only ChromeOS verifies the integrity of the Chrome browser (which is the only browser allowed), while other platforms will need additional measures to obtain the necessary proofs.

D. Indication of Origin HTTP header

As an alternative to the CORS protocol mechanisms, the browser may include a HTTP header to indicate the origin (the URL of the requesting web page, not the IP address of the client computer) of the HTTP request. The service may use this information to complete or abort the operation. The access approval decision takes place in the service, which would need to return an HTTP status code `403 Forbidden` if the origin value indicates an unauthorized source. Error handling in the client is therefore different from CORS use, where the error would be handled in a `catch` block. The use of the Origin header is a fall-back strategy when the client-server communication uses the WebSocket protocol, which does not obey the CORS protocol.

E. Device Security Policy Management

Devices can be subject to mandatory security policy management through installation of software for *Mobile Device Management* (MDM). Allowing only "whitelisted" applications to be installed ensures that only approved web browsers can be used. MDMs are comprehensive frameworks and have not been investigated for the purpose of this paper, but it is possible that MDMs can compensate for the lack of application-level integrity inspection in, e.g., Android.

MDMs can also be used to further reduce the risk coming from disloyal, untrained or careless users, who may change the network configuration to use a different DNS service, install new trusted root certificates, bypass the certification validation during TLS connections, etc. An MDM may enforce a policy that such actions require elevated user privileges. In particular, ChromeOS devices can be subject to *Chrome Device Management* to reduce the risk from these actions [11].

III. Suggested Model for Protection of Client Code

The desired property for a client is that it only runs code approved for the given service. This property should be validated by the service itself, which will deny any access from unauthorized code. The presented protection model is targeting browser based client code written in Javascript. The validation relies on a chain of trust elements:

1) During the establishment of a client-authenticated TLS connection to the service, the client presents a certificate that is known to belong to a computer with integrity protection of both platform and browser. In the presented implementation, specific values in the Distinguished Name *OU* element are used to indicate this property.
2) A carefully implemented device administration procedure is in effect to ensure that correct certificates are bound to the respective hardware devices, cf. Section II-B.
3) An uncompromised operating system and web browser will obey the CORS protocol rules, and the service will know that Javascript calls only come from approved software. Alternatively, the `Origin:` HTTP header value may be trusted to determine the source of the client code. By system management procedures, the approved software source will be trusted to contain only well inspected and verified code.
4) Javascript program code is always loaded through TLS (HTTPS) connections, which protect the integrity of the code during transport.

This chain of trust does not become stronger than its weakest link, so a number of reservations apply:

1) The CORS protocol/Indication of Origin relies on correct IP address values from the DNS service. The DNS service never authenticates itself to its clients, and the IP address of the DNS service can be forged, e.g., through manipulation of the DHCP (Dynamic Host Configuration Protocol) service, or by overriding the network configuration on the client

computer. If the connection is TLS protected, a falsified certificate would also be needed for a successful CORS attack, see no.3 below.

2) There are several known attacks on the TLS protocol, as summarized in RFC7457 [12] as well as the more recent Heartbleed and Robot attacks.
3) There is an excessive number of trusted root certificates in the default configuration of the main web browsers. If any of these roots are compromised, they may sign fake certificates that will be validated by the browser and jeopardize the authentication operation in either direction.
4) The standard configuration of a browser allows the user to override an unsuccessful certificate validation during a TLS connection establishment (although trusted not to), so the connection may be completed despite the invalid certificate.

IV. Experimental Evaluation of the Model

For demonstration purposes, and for a detailed investigation on the feasibility of the presented model, a message chat forum application was programmed. Figure 2 contains a screen shot from the Forum application. The application requirements were as follows:

- All clients fetch their client code from the *Code Service* (abbreviated CS).
- All clients connect to the *Execution Service* (ES) for services using client-authenticated TLS.
- The browsers need to install keys and certificates issued by one specific Certificate Authority.
- A client posts messages with a digital signature. They will be received by all other connected clients.
- Received messages will be validated for correct signature and a valid certificate, and given a trust rating.
- Received messages will be listed on the user interface.
- A list of the names of connected clients will be shown on the user interface.

Digital signatures on messages were created and validated for the reason to explore end-to-end security mechanisms in Javascript. The *Web Cryptography API* [3] was used and provided the authors with useful experience with WCA and related libraries for key management and cryptographic operations.

Figure 1 shows the protocol elements of the Forum application in three blocks: (1) is executed as the client program starts, (2) is executed at regular intervals as a polling operation, (3) is executed each time the user sends a message to the forum. Since the client code is not loaded from ES (Execution Service), all accesses to ES must obey the CORS rules. During a GET operation, the ACAO headers are returned with the returned value (block 2), whereas a POST operation requires a preflight check as shown in block 3. Note how the Servlet Filter (SF) handles the ACAO headers isolated from the application code in ES.

Two alternative implementations of the applications were programmed, based on HTTP and WebSocket protocols, respectively. (1) The use of HTTP protocol allows for a straightforward Servlet implementation on the service side and invoking the `XMLHttpRequest` object on the client side. The CORS protocol will be used together with the inspection of the TLS client certificate to enforce the desired access policy. (2) The WebSocket protocol does not employ the CORS protocol, so inspection of the `Origin:` HTTP header value will serve as a replacement. The TLS client side certificate will still need to be inspected by the service. Details related to the two implementations are described in Sections IV-B and IV-C, respectively.

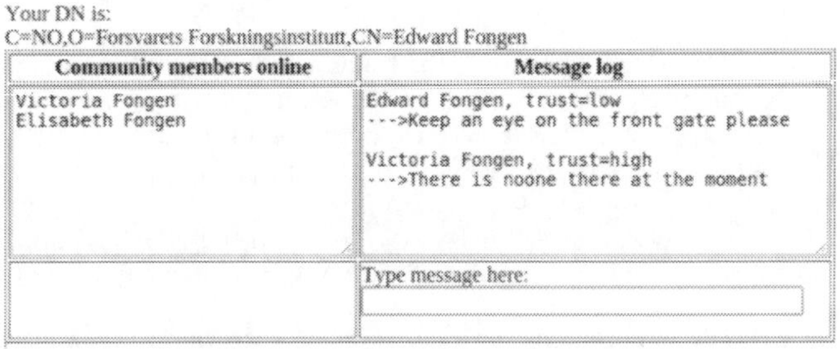

Fig. 2. A screen shot from the chat forum application. Messages from "Victoria" are sent from a ChromeOS device and are marked `trust=high`. Messages from "Edward" are sent from a MacBook.

A. *Loading of keys and certificates*

The Javascript environment does not have access to the browser's keystore, so the necessary public and private keys will need to be loaded from elsewhere. The chosen solution was to load the private key and certificate from the Execution Service (ES) over a client-authenticated TLS connection. ES returns the private key corresponding to the certificate used for TLS authentication, effectively copying the keys from the browser's keystore to the Javascript environment, where they are imported into the WCA for subsequent signature and validation operation. This solution appeared to be the best of only poor options, but a private key needs better protection than this. The trust anchor is loaded from the Code Service (CS) and also imported into WCA.

The service (ES) does not validate any signatures on the message traffic, and does not need any other keys than what is necessary for the TLS protocol. Signatures are validated by the clients, while ES is merely relaying messages.

B. *Managing CORS protocol and client certificate*

The service program was implemented as a Java Servlet, and during a client-authenticated TLS connection the client certificate is made available to the invoked servlet through the `HttpServletRequest` object. This certificate may be inspected for any access control purposes, i.e., to allow only clients with attested integrity to invoke services. Although the Java Servlet interface does handle HTTP OPTION methods, the processing of the CORS "preflight checks" is done by a Servlet Filter for reasons of loose coupling between protocol handling and application logic. The Servlet Filter manages both the certificate inspection as well as the CORS protocol, decoupled from the Servlet application logic. The certificate inspection only accepts one specific issuing CA. Parts of the code in the Servlet Filter is shown in Figure 3.

Being able to inspect the client TLS certificate is essential for the protection arrangement based on attested integrity. Java Servlets (and PHP to some extent) appears to be the only widespread server technologies to offer this opportunity.

C. Inspection of the Origin header in WebSocket communication

The WebSocket protocol is an asynchronous communication protocol, which allows for push-based information exchange. Push-based dissemination offers lower latency and better scalability than polling operation through HTTP. A WebSocket service is easily implemented in Java through annotations described in JSR356 - "Java API for WebSockets" [13]. The server class does not inherit from `HttpServlet` and the client certificate is therefore not readily accessible since the `HttpServletRequest` object is not within scope.

The WebSocket service is (possibly through annotation processing) still running as a Servlet and some servlet containers (i.e., Tomcat and Glassfish) will allow Servlet Filters to be inserted in front of it, giving access to the `HttpServletRequest` object from there. Furthermore, the `HttpSession` object can be used to convey information into a `ServerEndpointConfig.Configurator` object, which can move the desired information into the `UserProperties` object (found through the `ServerEndpointConfig` object). The WebSocket server class can pick up this information in the `@OnOpen` method through the `EndpointConfig` object.

Quite a few problems arose during the WebSocket based experiment. Setting up the TLS configuration on Glassfish revealed that the configuration console is not working properly, and manual editing of configuration files (a poorly documented process) was necessary. The Glassfish server has a large installation footprint but worked otherwise as expected with regards to the arrangement presented in the previous paragraph.

The Jetty server (version 9.3.8) supports WebSocket through the JSR356 API and is easily configured for client authenticated TLS. It is, however, not possible to insert a Servlet Filter in front of the WebSocket server object, and no other way to access the client certificate was found. Additionally, Jetty refuses to set up TLS protected WebSocket connections (through the `wss://` protocol prefix) from a Javascript client running in Chrome (contrary to Firefox). Jetty was therefore deemed unsuited for our demonstrator application.

The Tomcat server (version 8) also implements WebSocket JSR356 API, and supported the presented arrangement for retrieval of the client certificate. The installation footprint is smaller than Glassfish (since this is not a full J2EE server) and a standalone configuration with automatic WAR-file deployment was quite easy to set up. Tomcat is therefore regarded as the best alternative for applications that seek to employ the presented security arrangement for WebSocket communication.

For the selection of a client certificate during the establishment of a TLS connection initiated by the `XmlHttpRequest` object or an ordinary page loading operation, all the browsers used in this experiment have prompted the user with a list of available certificates to choose from. For subsequent connections, this certificate will be used for the same server, also for connection made through the `WebSocket` object (using the `wss://` protocol prefix). On the other hand, the `WebSocket` object does not itself prompt the certificate selection dialogue, and the connection will fail if there is no existing association between certificate and server in the client browser (created by a page load or the `XmlHttpRequest` object). During the application design, one must assure that a client authenticated TLS connection is established (by the `XmlHttpRequest` object or an ordinary page loading operation) before the first WebSocket TLS connection so that the necessary association is created.

D. Interoperability and performance observations

The presented client code was tested on several platforms and on several browsers and their interoperability properties were observed. The client candidates were:

- Google Chrome on ChromeOS, Linux, Android and MacOS
- Mozilla Firefox on MacOS and Linux
- Apple Safari on MacOS

The results were encouraging: Firefox required an extra CORS header (`Access-Control-Allow-Credentials`) in the HTTP response to allow client-authenticated TLS connections. Otherwise, Chrome and Firefox both executed the application without differences. Safari was not able to run the application for several reasons, the main one being an immature implementation of WCA lacking support for the chosen cryptographic algorithms.

V. Conclusion and Remaining Research

This paper has investigated the necessary mechanisms for the provision of attested integrity for cloud security. The attests provide trust in the correctness of the client platform and client application code. It has been shown that remote attestation and device-bound private keys are necessary elements, and that Google's ChromeOS provides the most complete solution for platform trust. Together with the CORS protocol and TLS communication protection, it is feasible (with a few identified reservations) to obtain trust in the client-side application software as well.

The demonstration application offers a chat forum of signed messages based on these mechanisms. The exchanged messages use the JSON syntax with digital signatures as defined by RFC 7515 [14]. The demonstrator has identified two major shortcomings in the WCA definition and library availability:

1) There is no way to import keys from the browser's key store into WCA, and the application had to import keys from less protected channels (HTTPS connections or the local file system)
2) There is no support for SOAP-based security objects, like XML-DSIG or XML-ENC, and derived objects like WSS, SAML, etc. on the client side.

Finally, the ability to trust the application code for correctness alleviates the well known *what you see is what you sign*

```
public class CrossSiteGuard implements Filter {
    PublicKey caPubKey = ... // loaded from internal resource
    final static String csName = "https://cs.ffi.no:8443";
    final static String chromeOSindicator = "OU=ChromeOS";
    public void doFilter(ServletRequest request, ServletResponse response, FilterChain chain)
        throws IOException, ServletException {
        if (request instanceof HttpServletRequest) {
            HttpServletRequest req = (HttpServletRequest)request;
            HttpServletResponse resp = (HttpServletResponse)response;
            String method = req.getMethod();
            X509Certificate[] clientCert =
            (X509Certificate[])req.getAttribute("javax.servlet.request.X509Certificate");
            if (clientCert == null) resp.sendError(401,"Client␣authentication␣is␣required");
            String clientDN = clientCert[0].getSubjectX500Principal().getName();
            try { clientCert[0].verify(caPubKey); // Throws exception if not ok
            } catch (Exception ce) { throw new ServletException("Illegal␣certificate␣issuer"); }
            if (clientDN.contains(chromeOSindicator)) request.setAttribute("no.ffi.anf.trust", "high");
            else request.setAttribute("no.ffi.anf.trust", "low");
            if (method.equals("OPTIONS")) {
                resp.addHeader("Access-Control-Allow-Headers", "Content-type");
                resp.addHeader("Access-Control-Allow-Origin", csName);
                resp.addHeader("Access-Control-Allow-Credentials", "true"); // For Firefox
            } else if (method.equals("POST")) {
                resp.addHeader("Access-Control-Allow-Origin", csName);
                resp.addHeader("Access-Control-Allow-Credentials", "true");
            } else if (method.equals("GET")) {
                resp.addHeader("Access-Control-Allow-Origin", csName);
                resp.addHeader("Access-Control-Allow-Credentials", "true");
            }
        }
        chain.doFilter(request, response);
    }
...
```

Fig. 3. Java source code for integrity attestation control through a Servlet filter

(WYSIWYS) problem, well explained in [15]. The WYSIWYS problem concerns the user's ability to ensure that the signed object really contains the data that the user intends to sign, and that the private key is not leaked during the process. Although unintended modification of the object, as well as a leaked key, can happen due to vulnerabilities in the original software, the presence of malware that affects the signature operation is a more plausible cause. It is likely that the WYSIWYS problem becomes less acute if one can ensure that the client software (which generates the signature) is integrity protected, inspected and approved by the owners of the related service. The same advantage can apply to clients who read sensor data, as long as the connection between the sensor and the computer is protected: The sensor readings can be trusted not to have been modified by malware or rogue client software.

REFERENCES

[1] N. A. Schear *et al.*, "Secure and resilient cloud computing for the department of defense," *Lincoln Laboratory Journal*, vol. 22, no. 1, pp. 123–135, 2016, https://www.ll.mit.edu/publications/journal/pdf/vol22_no1/22_1_10_Schear.pdf [Online: accessed Oct 2020].

[2] U.S. Department of Defense, "DoD Moves Data to the Cloud to Lower Costs, Improve Security," https://www.defense.gov/News/Article/Article/604023, [Online: accessed Oct 2020].

[3] World Wide Web Consortium (W3C), "Web cryptography api," http://www.w3.org/TR/WebCryptoAPI/, [Online: accessed Oct 2020].

[4] A. Fongen and F. Mancini, "The integration of trusted platform modules into a tactical identity management system," in *IEEE MILCOM*, San Diego, USA, 2013, pp. 1808–1813.

[5] Trusted Computing Group, "TPM Main Specification," http://www.trustedcomputinggroup.org/resources/tpm_main_specification, [Online: accessed Oct 2020].

[6] Google, "Verified Boot," http://www.chromium.org/chromium-os/chromiumos-design-docs/verified-boot, [Online: accessed Oct 2020].

[7] ARM, "ARM Security Technology - Building a Secure System using TrustZone® Technology," 2009, white Paper.

[8] World Wide Web Consortium (W3C), "Same origin policy," https://www.w3.org/Security/wiki/Same_Origin_Policy, [Online: accessed Oct 2020].

[9] I. Yusof and A. S. K. Pathan, "Mitigating cross-site scripting attacks with a content security policy," *IEEE Computer*, vol. 49, pp. 56–63, 2016.

[10] World Wide Web Consortium (W3C), "Cross-Origin Resource Sharing," https://www.w3.org/wiki/cors/, [Online; accessed Oct 2020].

[11] A. Cunningham, "Chrome os management console brings improvements for businesses," http://arstechnica.com/information-technology/2012/06/chrome-os-management-console-brings-improvements-for-businesses/, [Online: accessed Oct 2020].

[12] Y. Sheffer, R. Holz, and P. Saint-Andre, "Summarizing Known Attacks on Transport Layer Security (TLS) and Datagram TLS (DTLS)," IETF RFC 7457, Oct. 2015.

[13] Oracle corp., "JSR 356, Java API for WebSocket," http://www.oracle.com/technetwork/articles/java/jsr356-1937161.html, [Online: accessed Oct 2020].

[14] N. Sakimura, M. Jones, and J. Bradley, "JSON Web Signature (JWS)," IETF RFC 7515, Dec. 2015.

[15] P. Landrock and T. P. Pedersen, "Wysiwys? - what you see is what you sign?" *Inf. Sec. Techn. Report*, vol. 3, no. 2, pp. 55–61, 1998, http://dx.doi.org/10.1016/S0167-4048(98)80005-8 [Online: accessed Oct 2020].

Integration of Network Services in Tactical Coalition SDN Networks

Anders Fongen and Mass Soldal Lund
Norwegian Defence University College, Cyber Defence Academy (FHS/CIS)
Lillehammer, Norway
Email: anders@fongen.no

Abstract—**In order for Software Defined Network (SDN) technology to work in a military network, several identified problems need to be solved. This paper reports from experimental efforts to extend the application of SDN to a multi-domain, coalition, mobile network with wireless links and with end systems belonging to several Communities Of Interest (COI). The paper also demonstrates how SDN technology allows different network services to be integrated with a single class of Network Elements (NE). Considerations related to authentication, COI separation and intrusion prevention is given special attention during the discussions.**

Keywords*—*authentication; intrusion prevention; software defined networks; tactical networks; trust management

I. Introduction

Software Defined Networking (SDN) [1] offers an unprecedented flexibility in network configuration and operation. An important potential is how a spectrum of specialized Network Elements (NE), often called *middleboxes*, may be replaced with a single class of Network Elements called *switches*. The configuration and run-time operation of the NE is controlled by a single piece of programming logic running in a separate computer called the *SDN controller* (SDNC).

The SDN paradigm grew out of data center operations where links are abundant, have high capacity and low error rates. In a mobile and temporary military network used for military operations (named *tactical networks*), however, the links are often radio based. Radio links are few, costly, vulnerable, and with high error and packet loss rates. Consequently, the use of SDN in a tactical environment must consider the scarcity, latency and error rates of links in the system design [2].

SDN reduces the *complexity* of configuration, improves the *cooperation and integration* of network functions, extends the flexibility and dynamicity of traffic policing, and increases the link efficiency. The configuration of an SDN network involves fewer routine operations, but requires more software insight and programming skills.

The task at hand is to investigate the potential advantages offered by SDN in a tactical coalition network. The current problems related to this class of networks are identified as:

- They are based on Internet Protocol (IP) version 4 protocols, adding address planning, subnetting and frequent configuration changes even in small network enclaves.
- Virtual Local Area Network (VLAN) configuration in switches are weakly related to the IP layer, yet must be coordinated with the subnetting structure.
- Intrusion detection and protection is most often done in a single point, e.g., in the network backbone connection point. A compromised end system may have unrestricted access to services and end systems on the same network.
- Coalition partners wish to keep their traffic separate, but still need to coordinate their IP address plans, since separation takes place in link layer (VLAN) while sharing IP routes.
- Traffic policing becomes complicated since it requires coordinated use of IP Type Of Service (TOS) field (DiffServ) values across management domain borders.
- Authentication of end systems is based on MAC addresses, if used at all. Authentication on user level is done by application level services, e.g., MS Active Directory. No credential based scheme for authentication of *end systems* is in use.

The efforts presented in this paper address these listed problems and suggest an SDN-based configuration (based solely on SDNC software) which is purely a link-layer network. The network layer may be independently organized and the address plan does not need to be coordinated between Communities Of Interest (COIs). Any network layer protocol can be used (most likely to be IPv4 or IPv6).

The design has been prototyped in a virtualized environment and evaluated for functional correctness, performance and efficacy. Problems related to scalability are also being addressed.

The remainder of the paper is organized as follows: In Section II, a requirement analysis for a tactical SDN network will be discussed. The technology chosen for the experiment is presented in Section III and the actual network configuration is shown in Section IV. The new network functions added during this part of the study are discussed in Section V. The evaluation of the network functions is presented in Section VI, followed by a presentation of related research in Section VII. The paper concludes with a summary in Section VIII, where also topics on future research are presented.

II. Design analysis

Strong coupling between the link layer and the network layer complicates their configuration. Where MAC-learning switches are being used, the connection between the two address structures is solved by the Address Resolution Protocol

(ARP) protocol. Where VLAN separation is used, the separation will normally reflect the IP subnet separation. During splitting or joining of subnets the VLAN configurations must be configured accordingly.

Many of these problems may be solved by configuring the network purely based on link layer mechanisms, over which any network layer structure can be built. Scalability problems related to multicast distribution can be alleviated through COI separation, besides that a tactical network enclave is not expected to grow to a large scale. Functions related to load balancing and traffic policing are not easily offered in link layer network, but may be provided through SDN flow mechanisms.

A. Broadcast free operation

A link layer structure may not contain cycles, since the forwarding of broadcast frames will cause endless loops. The *spanning tree protocol* (STP) may prune a cyclic structure into a spanning tree, leaving the redundant links available only for fail-over purposes, not for load balancing. The scarcity and capacity of radio based links in a tactical network renders this limitation to be unacceptable.

It is possible, however, to command SDN switches to forward multicast frames along the links of a spanning tree with root in the originating switch, rather than to every output port in the switch. For this to be possible the SDNC need a topology map of the link structure in the network, something that has been accomplished with a link discovery protocol.

Also, the broadcast operation during the MAC-learning process of a link layer switch can be avoided through the same topology map, through which the next hop in the path towards any other switch is known. The association between the MAC address of an end system and its connected switch port is known by the SDNC from the first frame transmitted by the end system.

Frames need an extra header to convey information about the originating switch (in multicast frames) or the destination switch (in unicast frames), in addition to COI membership information. Header extensions like MPLS and 802.1Q are both candidates, possibly a combination of both. The choice will be made based on the ability of OpenFlow to set, mask and test these data elements.

B. Whitelisted flows

An obvious application of SDN flow processing is to protect end systems. Switches can block or allow traffic based on a blacklist or a whitelist made of flow rules. A whitelist is the more aggressive protection, where an end system (client or server) is allowed to transmit/receive frames only if they are related to known protocols, identified by transport level port numbers. Restrictions on IP addresses may also be applied, e.g., to specific subnets. Every end system can have different whitelists since they match individual ports or MAC addresses. Flows rejected by the whitelist may be discarded, passed on to an Intrusion Detection System (IDS) or a Honeypot system. The efficacy of this mechanism has been investigated and will be reported later in the paper.

C. Authentication of end systems

End systems should be authenticated, in particular end systems which are temporarily connected through public access networks. This mechanism must provide a link layer tunnel over a network layer connection, and *bind the authenticated connection to the link layer tunnel*. The authenticated identity of the end system should be communicated to the SDNC which will install flows enforcing the permissions granted to this end system, e.g., in the form of a flow whitelist.

On end system platforms with sufficient separation of user spaces and storage areas, user credentials can be applied to the authentication process, so that the trust relation shifts from the end *system* to one end *user*.

III. TECHNOLOGY PLATFORM

In this section, the choice of technology components will be described. The components are all software, including operating system, hypervisor and system-level components.

The study of a medium sized networks with more than 10 nodes is best conducted in a virtualized environment. The hypervisor of choice is Oracle's VirtualBox, which is free, easily configured, and offers the right degree of scalability. The limit of four ports per VM was the most limiting factor during the experiments.

For the Network Elements, complete instances of Linux were chosen. The reason for this choice is that the experimental network is used for testing several services and protocols auxiliary to the OpenFlow protocol, and a general computing platform offers the necessary flexibility and software availability, contrary to Mininet [3]. The Linux instances do not need a GUI and were installed with a text-only console interface for the sake of saving memory.

The chosen OpenFlow switch (the NE) implementation is OpenVswitch [4], which is easily installed, relatively easy to configure, and offers the necessary inspection and logging mechanisms for testing and debugging purposes.

As the network controller (SDNC), the Ryu framework was used [5]. Ryu is very popular as an experimental platform with a relatively low abstraction level: OpenFlow statements are generally not automatically generated, but individually constructed through Python programming code. For the experimentation at hand, Ryu performs well and with good stability, although the API and the required design patterns takes some time to learn.

For all the chosen technology components, an important convenience point is the community support offered. Most problems are easily solved through these support resources.

IV. EXPERIMENTAL NETWORK

The network used in the experiment is shown in Figure 1. The network consists of a number of green switching nodes (NEs), a number of yellow and brown end systems and a number of server nodes for serving OpenVPN, Dynamic Host Configuration Protocol (DHCP), Domain Name Services (DNS), Hypertext Transfer Protocol (HTTP), Server Message Block (SMB), Network Address Translation (NAT), etc. End systems are separated in two COIs indicated by their

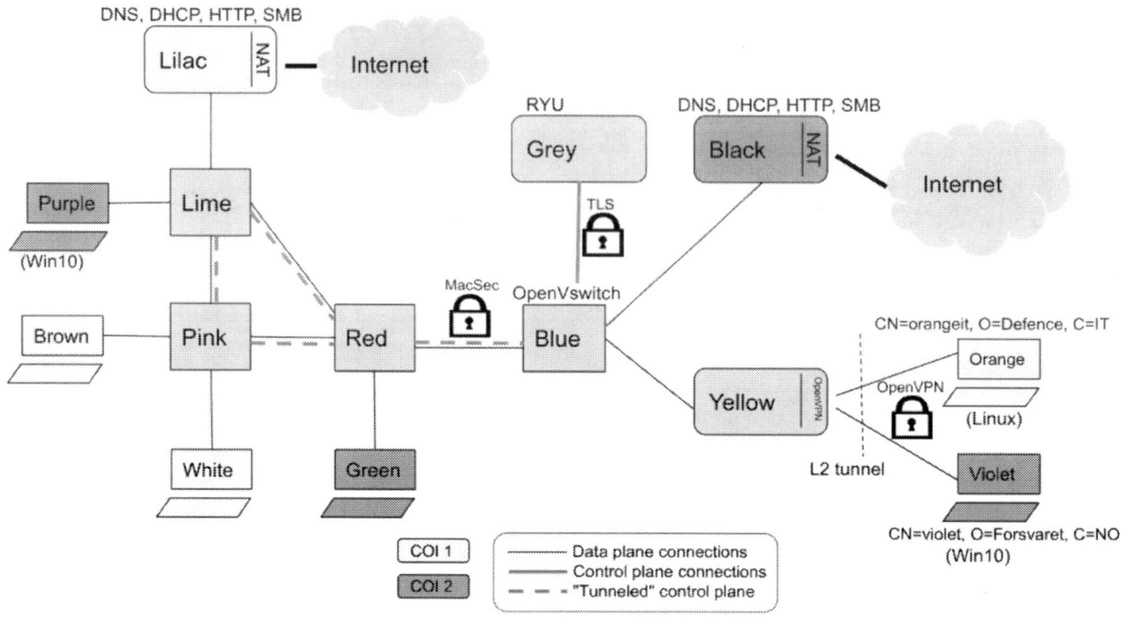

Figure 1: Current SDN laboratory configuration

brown/yellow color. The nodes are arbitrarily given names after colors, which should not be confused with the coloring codes of the diagram.

The links between the NEs Lime/Pink/Red are redundant and consequently form a loop. The redundant links are essential for the study of fail-over mechanisms and load balancing services [6]. The experimental network was used for investigating security mechanisms in an SDN based environment [7], for which reason the presence of OpenVPN, MACsec and Transport Layer Security (TLS) is indicated in the figure.

A. *Existing network functions*

From previous iterations of the SDN laboratory experiment, security functions and control plane redundancy has been investigated [6] [7]. These earlier efforts have shown:

- The links between NEs can be protected from a range of attacks using MACsec encryption. OpenFlow does not easily assist in the key management though, so static keys were installed during the NE configuration.
- NEs connect to the SDNC using TLS authentication and protection, using public key certificates and private keys for bidirectional authentication. Since the network uses in-band control plane a robust cryptographic separation between control plane and data plane was found to be mandatory. Certificate information is not made available to the Ryu application (nor the OpenVswitch code, for that matter) so the authentication control is restricted to the checking for certificate validity without revocation control.
- End systems connecting temporarily through an access network are authenticated by a Virtual Private Network (VPN) service before allowed access to the data plane. A Virtual Extensible LAN (VXLAN) tunnel through an IP Security (IPSec) connection was used in [7], but later replaced with a better solution based on OpenVPN.
- The control plane is constructed as an overlay network on top of the data plane, for more efficient use of the links available. The control plane was also constructed to automatically find alternative paths through the data plane if links were broken and NEs were isolated from the SDNC [6].

V. New Network Functions

Two new network functions have since been introduced and are subject to presentation in this paper: *COI separation* and *traffic whitelisting*.

A. *COI separation*

Coalition members do not trust each other completely, so their network traffic need to be robustly separated. Similar to VLAN functionality, both unicast and multicast frames should

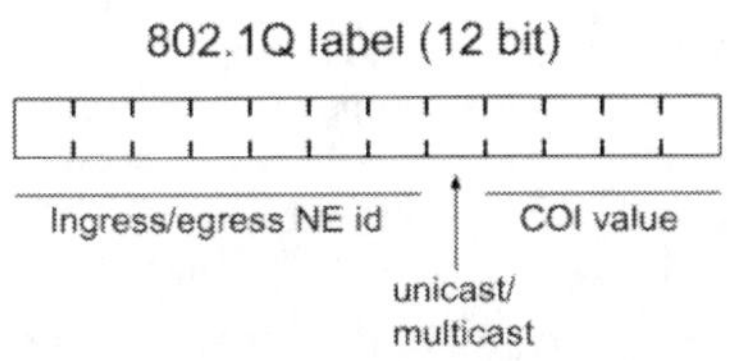

Figure 2: Encoding of NE id and COI value in 802.1Q label

only reach destinations which belong to the same *Community Of Interest* (COI) as the sender. Contrary to the well-known Ethernet switch, the presented solution does not need any direct configuration of NEs, the configuration is controlled by the SDNC software. The COI value of a frame is contained in the frame header, as described in Section V-B.

The assignment of a COI value to an end system can be based on its MAC address or its VPN authentication certificate. The latter alternative requires that the end system connects through a VPN server in a public access point and provides credentials in the form of a public key certificate. The VPN server will pass the certificate identifier to the SDNC which will decide the COI value accordingly. In both cases, the COI value of an end system is represented as a flow rule in the connected NE, the end system has no information about this value and is not able to modify it.

OpenVPN was chosen for the VPN service. OpenVPN offers a link layer tunnel as a core service, which also binds the MAC address of the tunnel adapter on the end system to the authenticated network layer connection. The end system will not be able to modify the MAC address in order to circumvent the access control. An IPSec connection can also contain a link layer tunnel (using, e.g., VXLAN), but no method to bind this tunnel to the authenticated IPSec connection was found.

For scalability reasons, multicast distribution may affect only the subset of NEs necessary to reach all end systems with the same COI value as the sender. The present implementation has a simpler implementation and distributes multicast frames to every NE.

B. Choice of link header extension

The link layer frame needs extra header information carrying its COI affiliation and the identifier of the egress (for unicast frames) or ingress (for multicast frames) NE. Since these information elements are independently processed, they need to be stored in one maskable element or two separate elements. MPLS, 802.1Q, MPLS-over-802.1Q or Q-in-Q are candidate structures for this purpose.

The chosen structure was to use one 802.1Q header for both elements. The 802.1Q label has 12 bits, which are divided into 7 bits NE designation, 1 bit for multi/unicast distinction, and 4 bits for COI value, as shown in Figure 2. The low number of bits limits the scale of the SDN network, but is sufficient for the experiment at hand.

Other type of candidate link headers were considered: The MPLS header contains more bits and could accommodate more COIs, but the MPLS header is not maskable in OpenFlow and therefore not useful for use with forwarding information (Cf. Section II-A). A combination of an outer MPLS header for forwarding information and and inner 802.1Q header for COI separation is not supported by OpenFlow. Two 802.1Q headers (called Q-in-Q or 802.1ad) is now supported by OpenVswitch, and may be considered for use in the future.

The COI relation of an end system is expressed as a numeric value 0-15 as 4 bits in the 802.1Q VLAN label of the Ethernet frame. The VLAN label value is added to the frame in the ingress NE after the whitelist control has been passed. In the egress NE, the COI value is again checked with the COI value of the MAC address associated with each port before passing the frame to the receiving end systems.

C. Traffic whitelisting

An SDN NE lends itself well to simple filtering of traffic based on flow matching, for reasons of end system protection. A client system need to connect to a set of server ports, possibly a small set of known IP addresses, in addition to services like DNS, DHCP and ARP. It should never receive a TCP segment with the flag ACK=0, since that indicates an inbound connection attempt. For a service provider end system, the opposite is the case, one would not see an outbound TCP segment with ACK=0, except to a small number of subordinate services. Through the chosen table structure (described in Section V-D) it is possible to pass both outbound and inbound frames through a set of flow rules which will submit the approved frames to the next flow table or output port, otherwise pass the frames on to an intrusion detection system (IDS) or to a Honeypot system, or to discard the frame. For the experimental evaluation, a realistic set of whitelist entries were made: ARP, DHCP (UDP/67,UDP/68), DNS (UDP/53, TCP/53), HTTP (TCP/80, TCP/443), SMB2 (TCP/445) and LLMNR (UDP/5355), which allows the client end-system to operate on the majority of web and file sharing services.

This simple arrangement does not inspect the application layer payload, and it does not aspire to replace an Intrusion Detection System (IDS). The main advantage is that the whitelist control takes place in every port connected to an end system, so it will also contribute to the internal protection in the LAN, whereas an IDS is usually seen as a single instance inspecting the traffic across a WAN connection point. Besides, an IDS do not *protect* systems, it only *detects* attacks.

The whitelist does not replace a firewall. A firewall will effectively protect an inside network (LAN) from attacks coming from outside (WAN), and stop any connection attempts to computers on the LAN, while allowing any outbound activity from end systems on the LAN. This is not the purpose of the whitelist, which will also block connection attempts to/from non-approved ports or to non-approved IP addresses.

Since a whitelist also blocks outgoing traffic and connections from server end systems, it also stops malware payloads (resulting from the exploitation of a vulnerability) from connecting back to an attacker, thus allowing for a security-in-depth arrangement.

The efficacy of the whitelist has been evaluated and will be reported in Section VI-B.

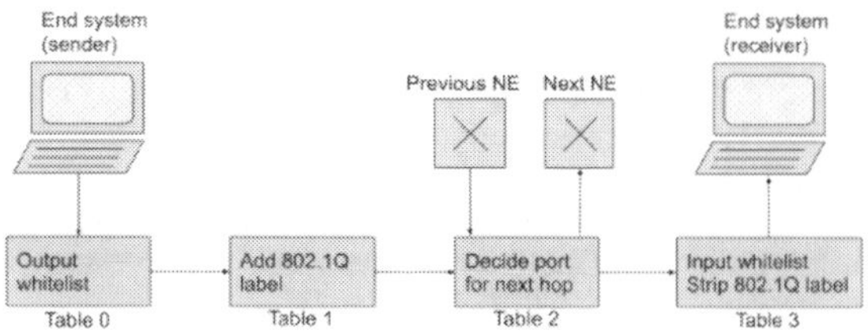

Figure 3: SDN flow table table structure in the NEs

D. Flow table structure

The flow arrangement in the NEs has been divided into several tables as shown on Figure 3, and will be presented in this section. Flows related to link and topology discovery, and path discovery in in-band control plane has been left out for reasons of clarity.

Table 0 Contains outgoing whitelist which will inspect frames from end systems connected to this NE. Frames with an 802.1Q label (added by a previous NE in the path) will be submitted directly to Table 2.

Table 1 Will assign an 802.1Q label with ID of the egress switch (ID of ingress switch in case of multicast frame) and COI value. Will then submit the frame to Table 2.

Table 2 Will determine next hop for the frames based on the 802.1Q label value, and forward accordingly. If the frame should be distributed locally, then the frame wil be submitted to Table 3.

Table 3 Strip off the 802.1Q label and apply the COI control and incoming whitelist control. If the frame passes both controls it is forwarded to the port connected to the receiving end system.

It should be pointed out that the whitelist arrangement breaks the desired isolation of the link layer since it introduces flows specific to network and transport protocols. On the other hand, the whitelist is structurally independent from the rest of the control program, and can be removed or modified at will without affecting other functionality. For the present experimentation only IPv4 packets will pass, but additional rules for IPv6 can be added with little efforts.

VI. Laboratory Evaluation

Besides the testing for functional correctness two series of experiments were conducted to evaluate the presented arrangements:

- The cost of the extensive set of flow rules which has to be evaluated for every forwarded frame, in terms of NE throughput.
- The efficacy of the traffic whitelist protection.

A. Cost of flow processing

The OpenFlow protocol is designed with execution by specialized hardware in mind. *Ternary Content Addressable Memory* (TCAM) is a memory structure which is able to match byte strings in parallel in one clock cycle and therefore will not be penalized by complicated matching criteria. When OpenVswitch runs in normal computing hardware, the opposite is expected to be true. This section will report on simple throughput measurements on traffic passing 1, 2 or 3 NEs between the communicating end systems. Throughput between end systems separated by a VPN tunnel was also measured. The MACsec protection of the Blue-Red link was disabled on one run to measure its cost. References to nodes with color names are according to the colors used in Figure 1.

In order to establish a baseline for performance, throughput through the localhost adapter (row 1 in Table I) was measured as well as through the VirtualBox internal network (row 2). The OpenVswitch was tested in *standalone fail-mode* (row 3) where it behaves like a MAC-learning switch as well with a single flow rule to make it behave like a MAC-learning switch (*action:NORMAL*, row 4) or an Ethernet hub (*action:FLOOD*, row 5).

The `iperf` program was used to measure TCP throughput between the nodes Black (running `iperf` in server mode and a TCP receive window of 85.3 kBytes) and Green, White and Violet respectively. The node Green was temporarily connected to Blue in order to measure a connection passing only one NE (rows 3-6). The measurement involving Violet determines the performance of the VPN tunnel.

TABLE I: THROUGHPUT EVALUATION OF OPENVSWITCH

#	Client end system	NEs	Throughput
1	Black (localhost comm)	0	23 Gbps
2	Green (directly connected)	0	1116 Mbps
3	Green (connected to Blue in standalone mode)	1	853 Mbps
4	Green (connected to Blue with action:NORMAL)	1	811 Mbps
5	Green (connected to Blue with action:FLOOD)	1	250 Mbps
6	Green (connected to Blue, WL in effect)	1	835 Mbps
7	Green (connected to Red, WL with MACsec)	2	250 Mbps
8	Green (connected to Red, WL w/o MACsec)	2	561 Mbps
9	White (connected to Pink, WL with MACsec)	3	260 Mbps
10	Violet (though VPN)	1	42 Mbps

Using the VirtualBox hypervisor, the upper limit of the network throughput was estimated in row 2 (1116 Mbps). Furthermore, the simplest configuration of OpenVswitch, operating it as a MAC-learning switch yielded a throughput of 853 and 811 Mbps, respectively (rows 3 and 4). Operating it as an Ethernet hub gave a significantly lower performance (row 5), unsurprisingly since this mode involves a larger traffic volume to be processed. Row 6 reports the performance when Blue was operating with whitelist in effect (WL), which is only marginally lower than in standalone mode.

The traffic via Red and Blue (both with WL enabled) was tested both with MACsec protection turned on and off (rows 7 and 8), and the numbers (250 and 561 Mbps) indicate the high cost of MACsec protection. The traffic over three NEs (White to Black, row 9) is statistically equal to traffic across two NEs (row 7) when MACsec is enabled, while rows 6 and 8 indicate a significant drop in performance when extending the path from one to two NEs.

The lower number for traffic across more NEs may partly be due to the fact that all activities in the virtual network compete for the same pool of computing resources, and when more NEs are in action the each process gets a smaller fraction.

For the purpose of design evaluation these results are encouraging, since a more comprehensive set of flow rules does not seem to impose a significant performance penalty, by comparing rows 3 and 6.

B. *Efficacy of whitelist protection*

The whitelist is a simple protection mechanism with its scope limited to the stateless inspection of link-, network- and transport header elements. The chosen design is to associate a filter with a MAC address, so that several end systems may share the same switch port if needed (although the whitelist protection will not apply to traffic between these end nodes), and to list the approved UDP and TCP ports for this MAC address. The flow rules also inspect the ACK-flag in the TCP header to ensure that TCP connections are opened in the allowed direction.

By employing whitelist protection, vulnerabilities in end systems may only be exploited through approved ports, and payloads deployed through a successful exploit will meet the same restrictions. The list of approved ports is expected to reflect the services in actual use, so the ports are likely to be occupied by running services and not available for allocation by payload scripts. Delivered payloads which do not communicate are not restricted by the whitelist protection.

IP addresses may also be subject to restrictions, although this has not been demonstrated yet. Such restrictions can avoid fake DNS and DHCP services to be accepted by end systems.

Exploits that exclusively use approved ports are not expected to be stopped by the whitelist protection. SQL injection and other attacks on poorly written web service software, EternalBlue, Heartbleed, etc. are examples of this category. General cyber hygiene for OS platform and applications should therefore still be in place in end systems.

C. *Evaluation of whitelist protection*

A number of known vulnerabilities were examined in the SDN laboratory which is shown in Figure 1. The Blue NE was configured as a MAC-learning switch and a full SDN switch with whitelist protection, respectively, while the same set of exploits where run. The focus of interest was to find exploits that could pass through the whitelist protection. Only exploits successful through the MAC-learning switch were tested on the whitelist protected NE.

Kali Linux [8] running in a virtual machine was connected to a port on Blue and given whitelist protection as a client, i.e., was only allowed to make *outbound* TCP connections on the approved ports. Also, virtual machines running Windows7, WindowsXP and Metasploitable Linux [9] were connected to other ports on Blue and were given whitelist protection as servers, where only *inbound* TCP connections are allowed.

For the evaluation we used Metasploit [9] installed on the Kali Linux virtual machine. Metasploit is a penetration testing framework shipped with a database of scripted exploits for known vulnerabilities, and various payloads to be combined with the exploits. The Windows7, WindowsXP and Metasploitable virtual machines acted as targets. Metasploitable is a deliberately vulnerable Linux server, while the Windows7 and WindowXP virtual machines were unpatched installations with Windows Firewall disabled. All three targets thus had known vulnerabilities.

From the design we expect all exploits which use destination ports other than the allowed ports (53,80,443,445) to be stopped by the whitelist protection. Exploits that depend on outbound connections from the attackee are not expected to succeed either.

These exploits were tested (names refer to their designation in Metasploit):

Unreal_ircd_3281_backdoor utilizes the IRC service port which is blocked by the whitelist. The attack is therefore not able to deploy a payload, and the attack is unsuccessful, even though Metasploitable is vulnerable to this exploit.

Ms08_067_netapi utilizes the SMB service port which is not blocked by the whitelist. A payload may be deployed to WindowsXP, but the *shell_reverse_tcp* is not allowed to make outbound TCP connections since this virtual machine is protected by a server-side whitelist. On the other hand, the *shell_bind_tcp* payload communicates over an incoming TCP connections which was bound to port 443, which is open in the whitelist. The attack was therefore successful.

Samba_symlink_traversal utilizes the SMB service port on a Linux computer and a poorly configured Samba service. The attack creates a symbolic link from a writeable share and opens every world-readable file for read access to an SMB client. Since the SMB service port is open in the whitelist, this exploit is successful.

Ms17_010_eternalblue utilizes the SMB port and exploits a bug in the server code in Windows7. It successfully deploys a payload. The chosen payload was *meterpreter_bind_tcp* which was instructed to bind to port 443 and wait for incoming connections. The exploit was successful.

Beside the Metasploit scripts, SQL injection and command injection were demonstrated on a web application on Metasploitable Linux (Mutillidae) deliberately coded for demonstration of the OWASP top ten web application vulnerabilities [10]. As long as these vulnerabilities are exploited through the normal service port, protection based on whitelists will have little effect.

The exploits shown above were carefully chosen for the demonstration of the limitation of whitelist protection mechanisms. Many possible exploits were not tested since they would obviously not succeed. It should also be noted that unpatched WindowsXP, Windows7 and Metasploitable Linux have obvious security flaws and would never be put in service in real life. And even a well maintained OS platform cannot protect a poorly programmed application service.

Some of the exploits succeeded only because there were whitelisted ports unoccupied by running services, in these cases TCP port 443. The whitelist should closely reflect the running services on the individual end system.

VII. Related Research

The SDN architecture lends itself well to a range of techniques for intrusion detection and -prevention (IDS/IPS). The techniques differs on matters like:

- Does it offer prevention in addition to detection?
- Is the detection signature based or anomaly based?
- How much traffic does it create in the control plane?
- To what extent does it involve centralized computational resources?

In [11], Jankowski and Amanowicz demonstrate a IDS mostly targeted on attacks on the SDN controller and NEs, and are employing a range of machine learning techniques to detect anomalies. They base their evaluation on the KDD99Cup reference dataset for intrusions, which is commonly regarded to be obsolete [12]. Machine learning does not take place in NEs, so the design involves the SDNC to a large extent in the communication with centralized computational resources.

Intrusion prevention using SDN would involve dynamic updates of flow statements as a result of a positive intrusion detection. False positives (something anomaly based IDS is known for) will unnecessarily block suspected flows of traffic and obstruct legitimate use of the network. There are no known examples of such arrangement in the academic litterature, only a GitHub project which demonstrates this design [13].

The OpenFlow matching function is limited to the inspection of link- network- and transport headers, although an OpenFlow switch can also report traffic volumes associated with match statements as well as volumes across ports. Intrusion detection can base its decisions on matching function alone, in combination with traffic volume counters, or through inspection by the SDNC of the entire network frame. These approaches represent different observation horizons and different traffic load on the control plane links.

Several studies on anomaly based detection are known, they often limit their sensing to the reading of traffic volume counters and some even apply machine-learning algorithms for this purpose. For a survey of these reports, see [14].

Other approaches have been to raise suspicion on the basis of traffic counter values or the matching function, and to take in suspected flows in its entirety to the SDNC for deeper and stateful inspection of the payloads [11] [15] [16].

Signature based IDS is not seen as an SDN application, probably because the detection rules are way too complicated for the SDN matching functions, and bringing all network frames to the SDNC for stateful inspection would create a performance bottleneck in the control plane links.

Blocking of traffic flows as the result from anomaly detection always runs the risk of blocking legitimate traffic. A whitelisting approach, on the other hand, becomes a part of a service contract, where the end system and the network service supplier agrees on which services are available. E.g., in the particular configuration, e-mail has to be delivered through a web interface, not through IMAP or POP protocols. The whitelist serves as a predictable part of the application service and security planning, and has been shown to thwart a wide range of cyber attacks.

VIII. Conclusion

The presented paper has addressed new network functions in a tactical coalition network and demonstrated how new functions may be integrated into existing Network Elements without requiring new hardware components. The two new network functions, COI separation and whitelist protection, were demonstrated and evaluated for computational requirements and protection efficacy. The protection based on whitelists applies to every end systems in each connection point and becomes a valuable supplement to centralized security functions like intrusion detection and firewalls.

Remaining research topics on tactical SDN include the design and study of distributed SDN controllers. Wireless links are less reliable than wired links, and an in-band control plane arrangement will need to accommodate the event of lost connection between NEs and the SDNC. For this reason, a distributed SDNC design for tactical coalition SDN will be a subject for future research.

References

[1] E. Haleplidis *et al.*, "Software-Defined Networking (SDN): Layers and Architecture Terminology," RFC 7426, Jan. 2015, last accessed Oct 2020. [Online]. Available: https://rfc-editor.org/rfc/rfc7426.txt

[2] J. Spencer and T. J. Willink, "SDN in coalition tactical networks," in *2016 IEEE Military Communications Conference, MILCOM 2016, Baltimore, MD, USA, November 1-3, 2016*, 2016, pp. 1053–1058.

[3] "Mininet," http://mininet.org, Online, Accessed Oct 2020.

[4] "Open vSwitch," http://openvswitch.org, Online, Accessed Oct 2020.

[5] "Ryu SDN Framework," https://ryu-sdn.org/, Online, Accessed Oct 2020.

[6] A. Fongen, "Dynamic path discovery for in-band control plane communication in a tactical sdn network," in *EMERGING 2019, The Eleventh International Conference on Emerging Networks and Systems Intelligence*, Porto, Portugal, 2019, pp. 9–15.

[7] A. Fongen and G. Køien, "Trust management in tactical coalition software defined networks," in *2018 International Conference on Military Communications and Information Systems, ICMCIS 2018*. Institute of Electrical and Electronics Engineers Inc., 5 2018, pp. 1–8.

[8] "Kali Linux," http://kali.org, Online, Accessed Oct 2020.

[9] "Metasploit," http://metasploit.help.rapid7.com/docs/metasploitable-2, Online, Accessed Oct 2020.

[10] "Open Web Application Security Project," http://owasp.org/www-project-top-ten, Online, Accessed Oct 2020.

[11] D. Jankowski and M. Amanowicz, "Intrusion detection in software defined networks with self-organized maps," *Journal of Telecommunications and Information Technology*, vol. nr 4, pp. 3–9, 2015.

[12] A. Özgür and H. Erdem, "A review of kdd99 dataset usage in intrusion detection and machine learning between 2010 and 2015," https://peerj.com/preprints/1954v1/, 01 2016, Not Peer Reviewed. Online, Accessed Oct 2020.

[13] "SDN-Intrusion-Prevention-System-Honeypot," https://github.com/pratiklotia/SDN-Intrusion-Prevention-System-Honeypot, Online, Accessed Oct 2020.

[14] N. Sultana, N. Chilamkurti, W. Peng, and R. Alhadad, "Survey on SDN based network intrusion detection system using machine learning approaches," *Peer-to-Peer Networking and Applications*, pp. 1–9, 01 2018.

[15] Y. Hande, A. Muddana, and S. Darade, "Software-defined network-based intrusion detection system," in *Innovations in Electronics and Communication Engineering*, H. S. Saini, R. K. Singh, and K. S. Reddy, Eds. Singapore: Springer Singapore, 2018, pp. 535–543.

[16] T. A. Tang, L. Mhamdi, D. McLernon, S. A. R. Zaidi, and M. Ghogho, "Deep learning approach for network intrusion detection in software defined networking," in *2016 International Conference on Wireless Networks and Mobile Communications (WINCOM)*, Oct 2016, pp. 258–263.

Detection Algorithm for Non-recursive Zip Bombs

1st MaoYang Chen
University of Electronic Science and Technology of China
ChengDu, China
maplejack@qq.com

2nd MingYu Fan
University of Electronic Science and Technology of China
ChengDu, China
ff98@163.com

***Abstract*—Traditional compression bombs often work by recursive decompression, so the usual defensive way is by single decompression. However, a new type of compression bombs has recently appeared, which can take effect with a single decompression. We show the two structures of this type of compression bombs and provide the basic idea of detecting such bombs. At the same time, we point out the details in need of attention in the detection process as well. Moreover, we propose a detection algorithm for this type of bombs and we analyze the accuracy and detection efficiency of this algorithm.**

***Index Terms*—Software safety; File viruses; Compression bombs.**

I. Introduction

Compression bombs are the compressed files that have a very high compression ratio and can generate a huge amount of invalid data after decompression. They can be used to cause many serious problems, such as buffer overflows, memory leaks. Some bombs even come with Trojan horse programs [4]. Sometimes, compression bombs are also used as email bombs which will lead to denial of service [3].

The zip bomb is a typical type of compression bombs. Zip bombs can be divided into two types: recursive zip bombs and non-recursive zip bombs [1].

The recursive zip bombs also fall into two types. The first type is the compression bombs, represented by the most famous zip bomb, 42.zip [7]. The original size of 42.zip is 0.6MB before decompression, but after six layers of recursive decompression, it will expand to 4.5PB. The second type is zip quines, whose feature is that once they are decompressed recursively, they will copy themselves infinitely. A typical example of zip quines is the bomb mentioned in Zip Files All The Way Down [2]. These two types of zip bombs have an obvious disadvantage: as long as they are not recursively decompressed, they will not take effect.

To overcome the obvious disadvantage, David Fifield proposes the non-recursive zip bomb [1]. This type of zip bombs uses a special structure "overlap" so that they can still work when being single decompressed. However, there is only a little decompression software currently providing detection services for non-recursive zip bombs. To the best of our knowledge, only Mark Adler has written a patch for unzip [9]. In Table 1, we test whether mainstream compression software can prevent the non-recursive zip bombs. For anti-virus software, when Kaspersky, 360 total security and Windows Defender scan these bombs, they all decompress the bombs. However, only Kaspersky can detect and defuse the bomb. Meanwhile,

TABLE I
Software Detection Result

Software	bandizip	unzip(unpatched)	360zip	tar	winrar	7-zip
bomb status	work	work	work	work	work	work

these software cannot prevent such bombs from taking effect when the existing non-recursive bombs are decompressed. So, lots of work should been done to defend against non-recursive zip bombs and it makes sense to detect this type of bombs before decompression.

This paper introduces the working principle of the non-recursive zip bombs and the detection of this type of bombs without any decompression software's help. Unlike the anti-virus programs mentioned, our detection method does not need to decompress the zip bomb.

The rest of this paper is organized as follows. The features of such bombs are outlined in Section 2. Section 3 introduces how to detect these bombs. Section 4 presents the details of the detection algorithm. Finally, we summarize our work in Section 5.

II. Non-recursive zip bomb

Before detecting zip bombs, we need to know the structures of info-zip (standard zip file) and non-recursive zip bombs.

A. The structure of info-zip

As in Figure 1, an info-zip is composed of several local file entries, a central directory and an end of central directory record [6]. Each file in an info-zip has one local file entry and one file header in the central directory. A local file entry consists of a local file header and the corresponding file data. The local file header records the metadata of the file and the file data is actually the compressed data of the origin file. The central directory is a series of file headers, which records

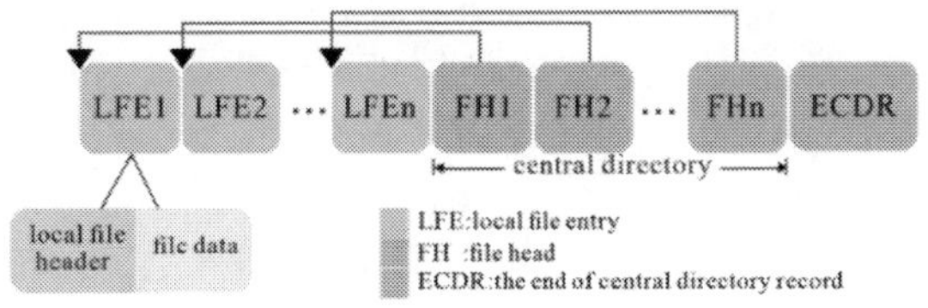

Fig. 1. The structure of info-zip

not only the metadata of the file but also the position of the corresponding local file header.

B. The structure of non-recursive zip bomb

The non-recursive zip bombs use a special structure to make the files overlap. Such a bomb consists of many local file headers, one file data, a central directory and an end of central directory record, as in Figure 2 [1]. The bomb resets the length

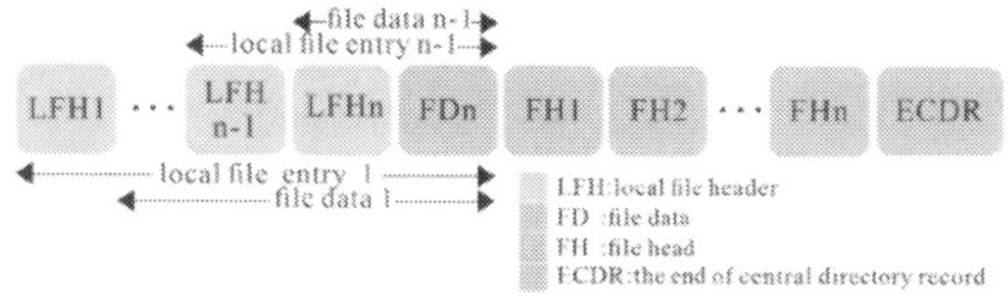

Fig. 2. The structure 1 of the non-recursive zip bombs

of each local file entry so that all local file entries overlap. Supposing there is a bomb containing n files, its i-th local file entry will consist of the i-th local file header, the i+1-th file header, ..., the n-th file header and file data n. In other words, the i+1-th local file header, ..., the n-th local file header and file data n constitute the file data of the i-th local file entry, as in Figure 2. Due to the special structure of overlapping files, the type of bombs has the characteristics of high compression ratio and it works directly after a single decompression. After

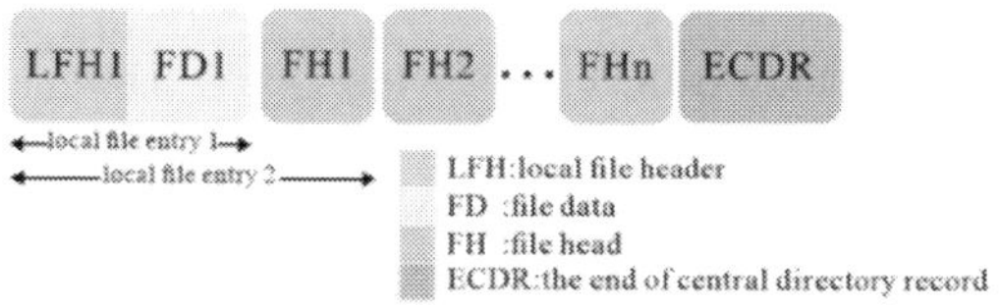

Fig. 3. The structure 2 of the non-recursive zip bombs

analyzing about 1000 non-recursive zip bombs, we find that there are some non-recursive zip bombs which have a different structure. As in Figure 3, the bombs have only one local file header and all the file headers point to this local file header. Of course, such bombs with this structure also have overlap. For example, the first local file entry consists of local file header 1 and file data 1. The second consists of local file header 1, file data 1 and file header 1. In other words, the 2nd local file entry's file data is file data 1 plus file header 1. The overlap is the whole local file entry 1. Such a type of bombs have a higher compression ratio.

III. How to detect the non-recursive bomb

This section introduces the basic idea of the detection and some questions that need attention.

A. The basic idea

According to the previous description, overlap is the most important sign of the non-recursive zip bombs. Therefore, we

TABLE II
File Header Structure

Offset	Bytes	Description
0	4	Signature(0x02014b50)
...	...	...
42	4	The position of the local file header
46	m	File name
46+m	n	Extra Field

TABLE III
Local File Header Structure

Offset	Bytes	Description
0	4	Signature(0x04034b50)
...	...	...
18	4	File data size
...	...	...
26	2	File name length
28	2	Extra field length
30	n	File name
30+n	m	Extra Field

need to check whether the detected zip bomb is a non-recursive zip bomb by detecting the overlap among the local file entries.

The first thing to do is to get the position of each local file entries. The file header can help us. In Table 2, the offset 42 in the file header records "The position of the local file header". This is the position we need.

Second, the length of each local file entry should be known. We cannot directly get this value. For the local file entry consists of the local file header and the file data, we just need to find out the length of the two parts. The length of the local file header is 30 bytes' fixed length plus the file name length and extra field length. In Table 3, the two lengths are both recorded in the local file header. The file data size is also recorded in the local file header (in some documents, the file data length is called compressed size). Then we can calculate the length of a local file entry.

Now, since we get the position of the local file header and the length of the local file entry, the last thing to do is to determine whether the overlap exists. For a pair of adjacent local file entries, if the end of the previous local file entry covers the start of the next one, then there is an overlap and the start position of a local file entry is just the position of its local file header. We can easily calculate the position of the end of the previous local file entry and compare it with the start of next one.

B. Some questions that need attention

First of all, we should open the zip file in hex because our idea requires the usage of the zip file structure in hex. Referring to Table 2, we can find out these file headers by their signature (0x02014b50). Here, we need to consider the problem of small-endian and big-endian. For the small-endian, the signature used to search the file headers is actually "0x504b0102" instead of "0x02014b50".

There is an important question: what should we do if some data segments have values exactly equal to 0x504b0102 but are not a real file header signature. Although the probability of this situation is very small, it should not be ignored. Referring to Figure 4, we happen to encounter such a situation. The data segment from 0x14ac to 0x14f5 is two local file headers in a non-recursive bomb and "file header signature" exists in the segment: the first is from 0x14c3 to 0x14c6 and the second is from 0x14e8 to 0x14eb. So to solve the above problem, we do such a thing: after finding out a file header by "0x02014b50", according to the file header's offset 42, we get and check the position of the local file header(refer to Table 2). If the first four bytes of the position are not "0x04034b50" or the position exceeds the size of the entire zip file, this file header must be fake and can be ignored. Another question to note is the search

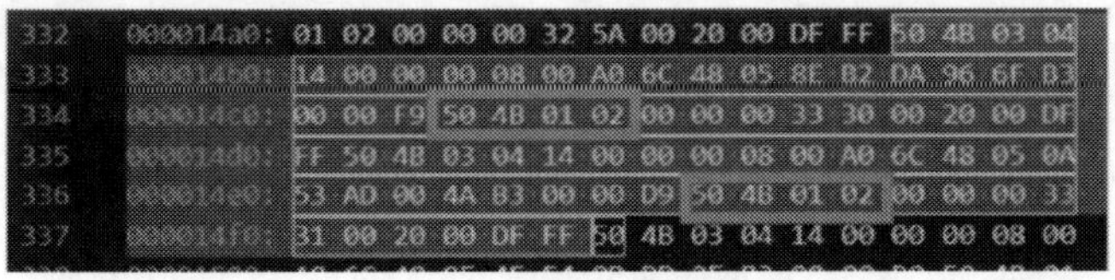

Fig. 4. Fake file header

method. The most important information is the positions of each file header because according to them, we can find the information we need. Since the file headers are concentrated at the end of the zip file, we choose to search the zip file from its end to its beginning for file headers. Obviously, we only need to search from the end of the file till we find the first file header, instead of searching the whole zip file. Thus, the key point is to know how to confirm whether a file header is the first one. We can use a trick: the position of the first local file header is always at the beginning of the zip file. In other words, if the file header is the first one, its offset 42 which records the position of the corresponding local file header is 0. So, when the offset 42 of a file header is 0, we just stop the search. But this trick does not work on the non-recursive zip bombs with the second structure because the offset 42 of each file header is always 0, as in Figure 3. Therefore, when finding out a file header whose offset 42 is 0, we should check whether there is another real file header before it. If such a file header appears, there must be overlapping files in the detected zip file.

The last question is whether it is necessary to detect all adjacent file headers in the zip file. For the non-recursive zip bombs that currently have two structures, it seems that we only need to check the last two files headers to identify whether they are non-recursive zip bombs. But we consider that it is necessary to check all the adjacent files headers, because if only the last two files headers are detected, the bomb maker can easily bypass our detection by a certain amount of forgery.

IV. ALGORITHM

This section describes the details of the algorithm, show the accuracy and the efficiency of the algorithm.

A. Algorithm Description

Previously, we explain the basic idea of detection and some questions that need attention and then let's organize the idea. First, we need to search reversely to get the first pair of adjacent file headers. We define this process as a function named "GetAdjacentFileHeader" which requires a position pointer and returns a list. This list contains the positions of the first pair of adjacent file headers which are reversely searched from this position pointer. At the same time, the function will change the position pointer's value: if such a pair of file headers can be found, supposing the file header at the front is called FH1 and the file header at the back is called FH2, at the end of the function, this pointer is set to point to the end of FH1. If not, the value is set to -1 as the sign of the search's end and the list returned is empty.

Algorithm 1: The Algorithm for Detecting the Non-recursive Zip Bomb

Input: a zip file to be detected: *File*
Output: the flag indicating whether the file is a non-recursive zip bomb: *Flag*
Function `GetAdjacentFileHeader` (*pointer*);
Function `CheckOverlap` (*list*);
Initialize *Flag* to False;
Initialize *CurPos* to point to the zip file's end;
Preprocessing the content of *File*;
Initialize *List* to Null;
while *CurPos is not -1* **do**
  List = `GetAdjacentFileHeader`(*CurPos*);
  Flag = `CheckOverlap`(*List*);
  if *Flag* **then**
    Break;
end

Fig. 5. The detection algorithm

Secondly, after we get a pair of adjacent file headers, we should check if their corresponding local file entries overlap. We define this process as a function called "CheckOverlap". This function needs a list which consists of the positions of two file headers and returns a Boolean value indicating whether there is overlap. Specifically, for the two file headers included in the list, we suppose the one at the front is called FH1 and the one at the back is called FH2. This function will get the start position of their corresponding local file entries LF1, LF2. Then it will calculate and get the end position of LF1. If the end position of LF1 exceeds the start position of LF2, this function will return True because LF1 and LF2 are overlapping. If not, it will return False.

Finally, for the whole zip file, we should traverse all adjacent file headers unless file overlaps have already been detected. To achieve it, we initialize a flag called Flag and a position pointer CurPos. Flag is set to False initially, which is used as the output of the entire algorithm to indicate whether the detected zip file is a non-recursive zip bomb. CurPos is initially set to the end of the zip file. It is passed to the function GetAdjacentFileHeader as the starting point for reverse search and when its value is -1, the search will stop and the algorithm returns Flag. We summarize the steps in Figure 5.

B. Algorithm Accuracy

To check the accuracy of the algorithm, we prepare two sets of samples. One is full of info-zip and the other is full of the non-recursive zip bombs.

TABLE IV
THE DETECTION RESULTS

File Type	Yes	No	Error
Info-zip	0	1424	0
Zip bombs	2000	0	0

For the first set involving info-zip, we prepare 1424 info-zip containing different files with different sizes. These compressed files include plain text files and the files that have their own logical structures like *.doc*. For this second set of bombs, we use the generation tool which is offered by the bomb designer [8] to make 2000 different bombs. This set contains both types of non-recursive zip bombs. The detecting results are listed in Table 4. This algorithm has extremely high detection accuracy.

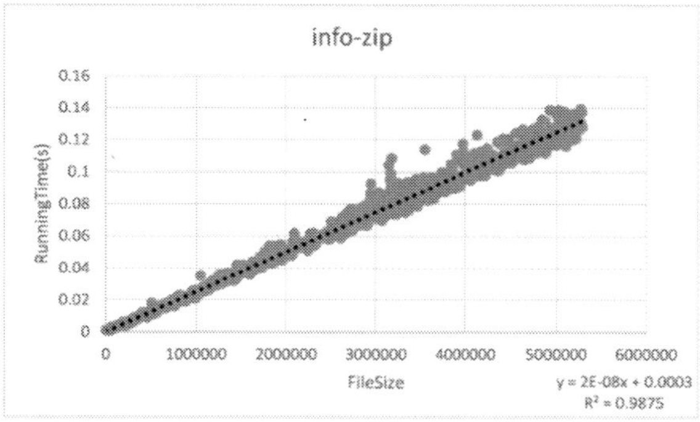

Fig. 6. The relationship between the detection time and the size of info-zip

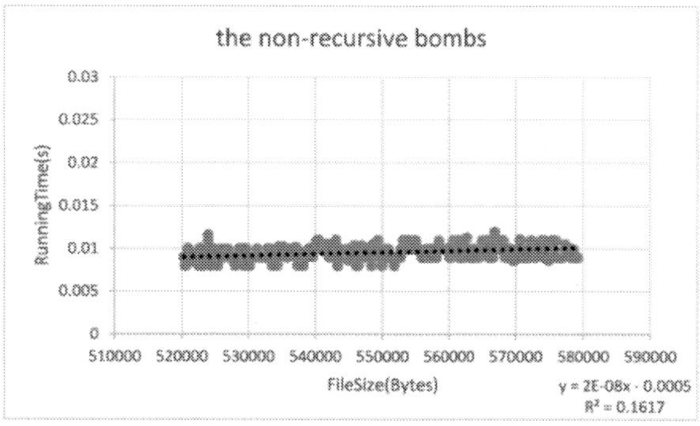

Fig. 7. The relationship between the detection time and the size of the non-recursive zip bombs

C. Algorithm Efficiency

For info-zip, this algorithm will inevitably search the entire file to confirm that all local file entries do not overlap and for non-recursive zip bombs, no matter which of the two structures the bomb has, this algorithm can determine that this is a bomb immediately after detecting the last two file headers. Therefore, for info-zip, the detection time grows linearly as the zip file size increases, as in Figure 6. For non-recursive zip bombs, the figure appears as a horizontal line which demonstrates that there is almost no connection between the detection time and the size of the zip file, as in Figure 7.

V. CONCLUSION

In this paper, we introduce the structures of the non-recursive zip bomb and design an algorithm for detecting such a zip bomb. At the same time, we list some details that should be noticed in the detection and the algorithm efficiency about non-recursive zip bombs and info-zip is given.

Most decompression software can use this algorithm as a reference to make corresponding patches. Since this algorithm does not rely on decompression software, for security software, it can be used to quickly detect whether a zip file in the emails or removable media storage devices, such as USB or disks is a non-recursive zip bomb.

In today's world of big data, more and more compressed files are transmitted on the Internet or uploaded to cloud servers. Because of the lack of detection methods for non-recursive zip bombs, it is likely that bombs will be uploaded to cloud servers or downloaded to personal computers. Once such bombs are decompressed, there will be serious consequences. Therefore, this bomb detection algorithm we propose is very useful.

In real life situations, an attacker may not use a standard structure bomb. The attacker can make a non-recursive bomb whose structure is different from the previously mentioned structures. However, as long as the bombs use overlapping structures, they will be detected by our algorithm.

We do not take zip64 and encrypted zip files into consideration, so this algorithm may not have such good compatibility with these zip files. There are some structural differences between these two types of zip files and info-zip. For example, Zip64 has some extra unique structures (such as Zip64 end of central directory locator); encrypted zip files have some additional structures to store encrypted information. These are two directions worth analyzing in the algorithm improvement in the future.

ACKNOWLEDGMENTS

We thank Yang Xiong, JiPeng Wang, DeGang Chen, WenQi Liu, JiaYu Liu, XingYu Liao for their assistance and David Fifield for his guidance on the use of non-recursive zip bomb generating tool.

References

[1] D. Fifield, "A Better Zip Bomb," WOOT @ USENIX Security Symposium, August 2019.

[2] R. Cox, "Zip Files All the Way Down," unpublished.

[3] W. T. Mambodza, R. T. Shoniwa, V. Shenbagaraman , "Cybercrime in Credit Card Systems,", International Journal of Science and Research (IJSR), 2014.

[4] H. Sowmya, "A Study on Zip Bomb." unpublished.

[5] "Python3.7," https://docs.python.org/3.7/, May 2020.

[6] P. Inc, "Appnote.txt - .Zip File Format Specification," https://pkware.cachefly.net/webdocs/APPNOTE/APPNOTE-6.2.0.txt, May 2020.

[7] "42.zip," https://www.unforgettable.dk/, March 2020.

[8] D. Fifield, "Zipbomb-20190822.zip," https://www.bamsoftware.com/hacks/zipbomb/zipbomb-20190822.zip, March 2020.

[9] M. Adle, "Fork of Infozip Unzip 6.0 For New Zip Bomb Detection Patch," https://github.com/madler/unzip/commit/47b3ceae397d21bf822bc2ac73052a4b1daf8e1c, March 2020.

Information Extraction from Darknet Market Advertisements and Forums

Clemens Heistracher
AIT Austrian Institute of Technology
Giefinggasse 4, Vienna, Austria
clemens.heistracher@ait.ac.at

Sven Schlarb
AIT Austrian Institute of Technology
Giefinggasse 4, Vienna, Austria
sven.schlarb@ait.ac.at

Faisal Ghaffar
IBM Technology Campus
Dublin, Ireland
faisalgh@ie.ibm.com

Abstract—**Over the past decade, the Darknet has created unprecedented opportunities for trafficking in illicit goods, such as weapons and drugs, and it has provided new ways to offer crime as a service. Along with the possibilities of concealing financial transactions with the help of crypto currencies, the Darknet offers sellers the possibility to operate in covert. This article presents research and development outcomes of the COPKIT project which are relevant to the SECURWARE 2020 conference topics of data mining and knowledge discovery from a security perspective. It gives an overview about the methods, technologies and approaches chosen in the COPKIT project for building information extraction components with a focus on Darknet Markets. It explains the methods used to gain structured information in form of named entities, the relations between them, and events from unstructured text data contained in Darknet Market web pages.**

Keywords–natural language processing; Information extraction; named entity recognition; relationship extraction, event detection.

I. INTRODUCTION

In the last ten years, the trade in illegal goods, such as weapons and drugs, has increased significantly in the Darknet. Financial transactions can be obscured by means of cryptocurrencies and buyers and sellers have the possibility to act covered. The Dark Net Market (DNM) landscape is continuously evolving. During the last years, many of the markets which had attracted much attention, such as SilkRoad, Alphabay, Hansa, or Wall Street Market – just to name a few examples – had been seized by the police. However, some of the markets are reopened elsewhere and new markets are continuously being opened. In such a rapidly evolving ecosystem, efficient tools are required which allow acquiring and analyzing data quickly. In this context, the European project COPKIT [1] aims at analysing, mitigating and preventing the use of new information and communication technologies by organised crime and terrorist groups.

The purpose of this paper is to give an overview about the methods and technologies based on state-of-the-art NLP technology used in the COPKIT project to extract structured information from DNM Forums. An evaluation of the performance of selected frameworks has been presented in [2], for example.

The guiding research questions in this context are the following:

- What are the domain-specific challenges for information extraction in the application domain of DNM Advertisements and Forums?
- What examples can be given for applying state-of-the art NLP technology in the domain of automated information extraction from DNM advertisements and Forums?

The NLP tasks considered for implementation were Named Entity Recognition, Relationship Extraction and Event Detection. For each of these tasks, several state of the art technologies and frameworks were considered for implementation with the purpose to determine the general applicability for information extraction in the domain DNM advertisements and Forums.

The paper is structured as follows: section II will outline related work. Section III describes the challenges of information extraction from DNM advertisements and forums. Section IV provides the general setup of the information extraction process. Section V describes the technical approach. Section VI summarises the conclusions.

II. RELATED WORK

Information Extraction (IE) is is an important field of Natural Language Processing (NLP) and linguistics which plays an important role in specific NLP tasks, such as Question Answering, Machine Translation, Entity Extraction, Event Extraction, Named Entity Linking, Coreference Resolution, Relation Extraction, etc. For this reason, we will only highlight publications which have a special focus on the DNM analysis application domain.

In the law enforcement domain, the approach of using web data to extract relationships between concepts was researched and used in the EU FP7 funded project ePOOLICE [3]. The project aimed at identifying and preventing organised crime and applying NLP text mining techniques. Concept extraction methods were applied to build conceptual graphs based on indicators and their relationships [4].

Christin [5] showed in 2012 that the DNM Silk Road was mostly about selling drugs. Following this publication, many attempts have been made to classify products on DNMs. Most of the approaches were using Bag of Words (BOW) [6] or TF-IDF [7] to vectorise texts in combination with Support Vector Machines, Logistic Regression and Naive Bayes as machine learning models. Feature reduction is often performed using principle component analysis [8] and latent Dirichlet allocation [9].

More recently, Long Short-Term Memory (LSTM) [10] and word embeddings [11] have been used for the task of text classification of product descriptions in DNMs to differentiate between legal and illegal text in the Dark-net.

Regarding the NER task, the research focus lied in the Labelling & Model Building phase and the goal was to choose a basic framework for the NER model creation. An overview and comparison of popular frameworks for this kind of NLP tasks was published by [12].

An unsupervised approach to extract semantic relationships from grammatically correct English sentences has been proposed by [13]. The assumption of the authors is that relationships can be derived patterns of the deep grammatical structure of sentences and structured knowledge is deliberately not considered in order to make this approach universally applicable. However, in the form proposed and stated by the authors themselves, the method is limited to extracting entity relationships that are found within a single sentence.

First, the difference of our approach compared to the above mentioned ones is the focus on the cold-start-problem, i.e., if no labelled data is available for a new use case. Second, the COPKIT information extraction focuses on the ability of making use of labels from pre-trained models, i.e., transfer learning. Third, COPKIT is researching the integrated use of the NER, relationship extraction, and event detection NLP tasks.

III. Challenges Extracting Information From Darknet Market Advertisements

NER is one of the typical Information Extraction tasks in Natural Language processing. The goal is to identify selected information elements, so called Named Entities (NE), a term which was originally coined at the 6th Message Understanding Conference (MUC) to denote names for people, organizations, locations, and numerical expressions [14]. In the Automatic Content Extraction (ACE) Program lead by the National Institute of Standards and Technologies (NIST) additional entity types, such as organization, geo-political, facility, vehicle, weapon, were introduced. Nowadays, a plethora of specific entity types are defined across various application domains, such as Biomedicine, Chemistry, Finances, etc. Differences do not only concern the entity types, but also the way the performance of named entity recognisers is evaluated. The performance numbers reported by evaluations that relate to different corpora, such as MUC, CoNLL03, and ACE, for example, can therefore not be compared directly [15].

Regarding the classical NER element types, the task usually achieves high success ratios over 95% in terms of precision and recall on task specific evaluation data sets [15]. While the task is very successful on typical entity types, it remains challenging to adapt NER classifiers to perform accurately on new entity types in specific application domains. One of the main challenges in this regard is to optimise NER to extract the entity types of interest, such as the weapon, drugs, or digital fraud, as well as common entity types, such as locations and organizations, for example.

An example for information extraction are the so called "infoboxes" of some Wikipedia articles which are gained by extracting related attribute/value pairs from the article text. In the domain of DNM forums and marketplaces, the main challenge lies in the amount and the diversity of the structure and content that needs to be dealt with. Texts from Wikipedia articles are usually written in grammatically correct language and without spelling errors because there is a crowd-based quality control procedure. In contrast to that, a significant part

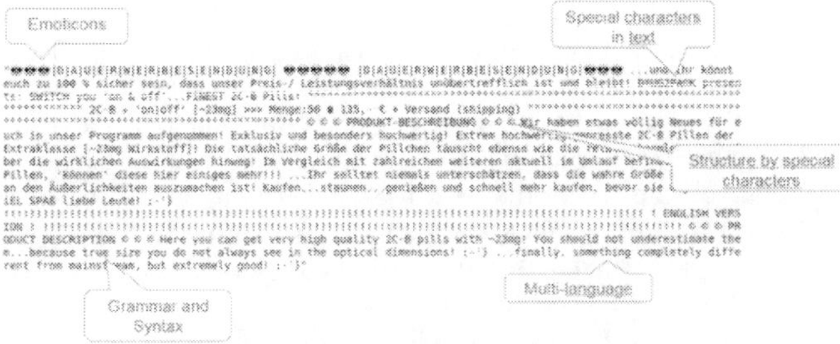

Figure 1. DNM Advertisement (German)

of the unstructured text that can be found in DNM forums and marketplaces have grammatically incorrect sentences, spelling errors, and is using slang. Published advertisement texts or postings were often created with little care or decorated with emoticons and ASCII art (see Figure 1). The assumption of a meaningful semantic and grammatical structure is therefore inadequate in many cases.

Another challenge arises because of the specific characteristics of the texts published in online markets. The most outstanding difference compared to standard corpora is that the data is not always structured in sentences and paragraphs. Figure 1 shows an example of a drug advertisement with special characters, emoji and ASCII art which are used to structure the text and to make the advertising more appealing.

On top of that, grammar and syntax are not always strictly followed. In many cases, the offers consist of bullet lists and enumerations rather than full sentences. The style of the remaining text can be compared to the type of language used in typical advertisements. Additionally, offers occur in multiple languages and the dataset contains PGP keys and lists of keywords for search engine optimization that needs to be filtered. On top of that, the true nature of products is often obfuscated using code words or vague language.

In the COPKIT project, event extraction is associated with extracting knowledge from DNM forum's online discussions. Event extraction in the domain of text-mining in general is regarded as a complex task of extracting complex relationship between various heterogeneous entities. Efficient methods of extracting event from unstructured text requires knowledge and experience from a number of domains, including computer science, linguistics, data mining, and knowledge modelling. The first and foremost challenge in event extraction from text is that there is no strict definition of event. General consensus is that event is something that happens at a particular time and place [16], a specific occurrence involving participants, or a change of state of a monitored quantity/measure. Generally, an event is represented with a "template" of who did what to whom when and where. The event detection method generally aims to fill (a subset of) this information where who, when and where are common and basic dimensions in information retrieval which can be retrieved with NER (discussed previously). However, who vs whom and what dimensions of the event require deep understanding of underlying text and its semantics.

The second challenge in event detection is the selection of appropriate approach for a given task. Event detection techniques are generally classified into two main categories; closed-domain and open-domain [17]. The closed domain events detection technique is where a set of event types are given, and task is to identify each type of event from the raw text whereas open-domain event detection refers to extracting different types of events from text without prior knowledge on the events. Techniques in closed-domain event extraction scenarios are usually cast as supervised-classification tasks that rely on keywords to extract event related text. The open-domain event detection is more challenging since it is not limited to a specific type of events and usually requires training of unsupervised models. In the COPKIT project, our approach of extracting events from DNM forum data is based on unsupervised methods and belongs to the open-domain event detection scenario.

A machine-learning based event detection pipeline extracts events from documents that already contain annotated entities. Given appropriate training data, a processing pipeline can be trained to extract different types and structures of events. A learning-based event detection module generally contains POS tagging, entity/trigger detection, and argument detection modules. All these modules are generally trained on large corpora where to perform general tasks. However, in COPKIT one of the main challenges is to train these modules on Darknet data and build the required ground-truth specific to event triggers and arguments.

IV. Information extraction process

Figure 2 illustrates the general information extraction process which is separated into the Harvesting, Scraping, and Information Extraction steps. The process starts with the Harvesting step by collecting web data from online or DNMs or forums. This process preserves the evidence of collected web data in its original form.

After the Harvesting step, the Scraping step performs the transformation of unstructured web data into structured information tables (CSV files). These tables can already contain specific information entities. For example, in a typical online market, the vendor, price or shipment details appear on specific locations of the web pages, and it is possible to directly extract them. Apart from these structured information entities, the scraping also extracts unstructured information in form of descriptive texts.

The design of the information extraction components takes the context of harvesting and scraping into account. Related to the use case of extracting information from DNM crawls, this means that the harvested data is done with a specific purpose at a specific point in time (snapshot). The scraping extracts information from semi-structured web documents which allows relating entities extracted from descriptive text paragraphs to the entities, which are given by the context from the scraping results. For example, if we know the market and user of a crawl from the scraping results, we can conclude with a certain probability that a user entity is the vendor which issued an offer in form of a DNM advertisement. Therefore, we can introduce these entities in the result relationship graph and claim relations based on the automatically extracted entities (e.g., offered products).

V. Implementation of NLP tasks

This section describes the technical approach chosen for the implementation of the NER, Relationship Extraction, and Event Detection NLP tasks.

Figure 2. Main processing steps

A. *Datasets used*

The components for named entity detection and relationship extraction provide custom models for the detection of weapons. The model is trained on a subset of the Grams crawl in Gwern's archive [18] that contains strings from a list of weapon related terms.

Additionally, a collection of Darknet forum posts, collected on September 25, 2019 from the Avengers forum, a DNM forum for discussions focusing on the purchase and testing of drugs in DNMs was used.

B. *Processing steps*

Generally, the processing of data after completing web harvesting is divided into different phases which are described in the following. In order to *create an overview* about the harvested data, a set of techniques are applied to highlight important keywords and topics that are present in the data set. As the data collected from Darknet sources contained different areas, Topic Modelling was used to get insights about the thematic distribution of a dataset.

The subsequent phase of pre-processing & filtering deals primarily with the preparation and cleaning of the data for the model creation. The overview of the topic distribution is helpful in this phase to find adequate labels for the automated classification of the data. Topic Modelling can highlight thematic clusters (e.g., weapons, drugs) and show the ranking of important keywords required to build a classifier. The results of the overview tools are used to find suitable labels for the classification and, if necessary, for filtering the dataset according to specific categories. For example, suppose a DNM's dataset contains weapons and drug advertisements and the goal is to create a model which is able to distinguish weapons and drugs in advertisements (note that strings, such as "AK 47" can refer to both, a weapon or a drug). After classifying the text contents, advertisements about weapons and drugs can be extracted to build a classifier for this specific purpose.

In the labelling & model building phase, the preparation of the data for creating machine learning models takes place. For the creation of supervised machine learning models this includes the creation of Ground Truth data where human annotators label the data according to defined features which are then utilised to learn a model optimised to find similar patterns in previously unseen data.

For the initial release, the relationship extraction was implemented using a rule-based approach for extracting relationships based on results from SpaCy's Part of Speech tagging and dependency tree parsing [19]. It is assumed that the rule-based approach will provide a higher precision and lower recall in identifying relationships in comparison to a model-based extraction. The disadvantage is that the rules are highly dependent on the use case, i.e., switching from a DNM offering weapons and drugs to a forum that is about crime-as-a-service requires manual effort in adapting and customizing the rules. The intention is therefore to add model based relationship recognition as an experimental feature to the relationship recognition of the final release.

Another specific information extraction task is the "event detection", which is related to the COPKIT project use-case of knowledge discovery from DNMs and aims to process forum discussions between DNM members. Forum posts test are processed and converted into vector representations. For the model creation, an unsupervised clustering approach is adopted due to unavailability of labels in the dataset. Clusters represent posts with a definite number of topics and topics are assigned manually after inspecting posts in each cluster. Events are then considered a post which does not belong to any cluster. In the final release, a hybrid approach will combine linguistic features of each post with features learnt through machine-learning based methods.

C. Named Entity Recognition

NER is one of the classical NLP tasks with a wide range of applications that is of relevance in fields such as information retrieval, question answering, text summarization, and machine translation [20].

Neural networks have proven to be successful in natural language processing and to generalise better to new datasets [21], and they are now also increasingly being applied in the domain-specific language used in organised crime and terrorism textual sources. An intrinsic difficulty in the domain of fighting organised crime and terrorism where textual sources are likely to be not well written (informal, linguistically incorrect, ...). On top of that, best of class technologies based on automatic learning still rely on human/expert feedback to accurately learn models. The absence of efficient tools supporting the elicitation of this ground true limit the application of these technologies.

In the context of DNM advertisements, these entities can be names of objects that are relevant in criminal investigations, such as weapons or drugs, or entities which are related to digital identities or shipment details provided as part of an offer, for example.

In a supervised machine learning approach, a labeled training set is used to create a model for automatically extracting entities. Recently, the use of word embeddings has become one of the most significant advancements in natural language processing (NLP). Word embeddings are usually trained on large text corpora and convey knowledge about the general structure of the language by providing comparable vectors for words and expressions.

The text corpus is the starting point for the supervised training of a named entity recogniser and highly depends on the texts of the corresponding application domain and use cases. Specific vocabulary for labelling named entities is used, such as "weapon", "calibre", "price" in the weapon advertisements domain, and "exploit kit", "hacking", "keylogger", "malware" in the crime-as-a-service domain, for example. For this reason, the data is first collected from a variety of web data sources which are specific to the law enforcement domain.

The first version of the COPKIT NER service integrates several state-of-the-art named entity recognisers, such as the Natural Language Toolkit (NLTK) and SpaCy, each of them with standard models [22] [23]. Apart from these standard models, domain specific models for the COPKIT project which are focused on text data acquired through crawling DNMs offering weapons and drugs were added.

D. Relationship Extraction

Relationship Extraction is one of the classical NLP tasks, which aims at extracting semantic relationships from unstructured or semi-structured text documents. Extracted relationships usually occur between two or more entities of a certain type (e.g., Person, Organisation, Location).

It aims at finding relationships that exist between the entities, which in the DNM application domain could be "vendor X is selling a Glock 17", for example, or the properties of an entity, such as "calibre" of a weapon or "price" of a product. Information regarding the entity relationships can be either present in the analyzed text itself or available from the context of the text. In the COPKIT project, individual text paragraphs can be advertisements published in online markets, for example. The complete set of web data from this market represents the context that can be taken into consideration when suggesting relevant relationships between named entities.

The Relationship Extraction Component developed in COPKIT takes a the text of a DNM advertisement as input and it produces a named entity graph. The component depends on the entities recognised by the NER module. With the rule-based approach, the results depend on an adequate set of rules which can be applied in the specific application domain. The examples provided offer the extraction of entity relations and properties which are present in weapon advertisements of DNMs and would not be applicable to other application domains.

In the current state, the relationship extraction component takes only texts from individual offerings as input and produces the named entity graph without taking the context into consideration. Entities which are given from the harvesting context, such as a concrete "vendor" or "market" are therefore variables which can be replaced if the vendor is given as input from the web scraping or if it is detected as an entity in the text (functionality planned for the final release).

It must be noted that the result of the relationship extraction must be revised in order to gain validated knowledge from the automatically extracted information. This is a labour-intensive process. However, to cope with the challenge of a steadily growing anonymous marketplace ecosystem [24] methods are needed that can deal with large amounts of existing data without requiring human intervention.

E. Event detection

This component is focused on the detection of events in the context of DNMs, and, more specifically, their associated Forums. A forum generally is a platform for DNM members to have discussions on various topics and a thread in the forum is a sequence of messages posted by members on a particular topic. In this regard, each thread on the forum has a title, an initial post and one or more posts responding to initial post. Discussions on forums are generally lengthy and are highly unstructured which means understanding of these discussions and

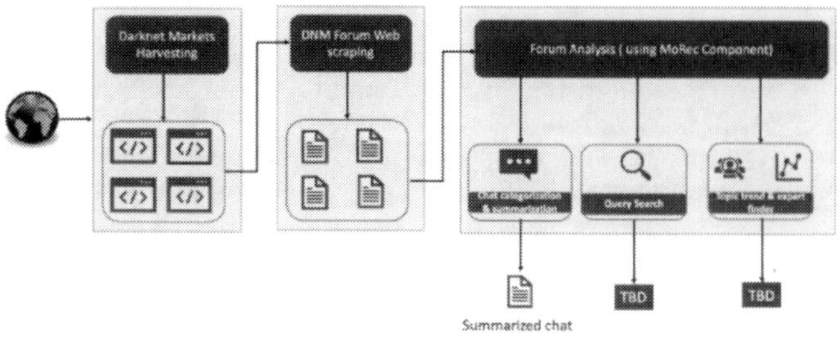

Figure 3. MoRec component flow diagram

extracting intelligence from them is a challenge for LEAs in the context of organised crime. Therefore, the MoRec (Moment recogniser) component enables LEA analyst to understand the forum discussions in the knowledge discovery phase. The component provides functionality for the analysis of forums at two levels; (i) thread level, (ii) individual post level. The component parses forum posts and clusters them into following themes.

- Business – these are forum posts of business nature where author of the post is selling or buying products that are advertised on DNM (Agora in our case). These type of posts also include exchange of information related to products.
- Community support – Posts in this category include content for community and social support. For example, posts welcoming new users and providing best practices can fall under this category.
- Risk Management – this type of forum posts represent content related to manage risks by users. For example, product reviews related posts can influence the buying decision and these posts can support in controlling the risk of buying from fraudulent vendors.

The current release contains a custom BERT (Bidirectional Encoder Representations from Transformers) [25] model fine-tuned on DNM forums dataset. The model is trained for classification task, more specifically for categorizing the forum posts into categories of dialogue acts. The sentence level word embeddings are extracted from BERT and used in the clustering of posts. The clustering part aims to cluster posts in groups based on their content similarity. We used Word2Vec [26] and BERT embeddings for sentence-based vector representation for posts. For clustering, an unsupervised clustering approach Density-based Spatial Clustering of Applications with noise (DBSCAN) [27] is adopted due to unavailability of labels in the dataset. The DBSCAN algorithm groups posts into clusters based on their similarity with each other. We used Cosine similarity as the measure of similarity between forum posts. Clusters represent posts with a definite number of topics and topics are assigned manually after inspecting posts in each cluster. Events are then considered a post which does not belong to any cluster. In the final release, the intention is to adopt a hybrid approach combining linguistic features of each post with features learnt through machine-learning based methods. The service interface is mainly for making technical integration into a system environment easy.

This component has three phases as shown in Figure 3 which will be explained in the following.

1) Phase 1: Raw Data Extraction: This component first extracts text from HTML pages of DNM forum. In particular following data elements are extracted:

- Forum topic (title)
- Initial post text (This is the text that initiates a thread of discussion. For example, a question is asked by a member of the DNM)
- Text from all the reply posts
- Meta-data associated with posts. This includes post-author, author rating, published date and time, sequence within the thread, etc.

2) Phase 2: Pre-processing and Intelligence extraction: In this phase, extracted text data is cleaned and transformed into the format which machine learning models can understand. Over the course of COPKIT project, analysis of DNM forums for the following tasks is in scope:

1) Categorise posts into categories of crimes such as hacking, carding, trafficking, etc.
2) Search for text with context related to a query
3) Identify the trend of a topic over time
4) Finally, highlight the important moments during the discussions to help LEAs in intelligence elicitation.

3) Phase 3: Integration: At this phase, trained machine learning models are made available as a service to be used by other components. The features of this component will be available as REST services and user-guide will be provided for easy adoption of those services.

VI. Conclusions

In the current release, the model creation process of the the information extraction components is implemented as a fixed order of steps that starts with the pre-processing and filtering of datasets to prepare the training data required for model building. The entity recognition and relationship extraction models are the result of this process and are integrated into the demonstrators.

For the final release, an extended pipeline will be available which allows continuous model creation and adaption based on human annotators are reviewing labels predicted by the models. It is therefore required that the model creation process supports continuous model adaption regarding the automatic recognition of named entities as well as the extraction of relationships between them.

The baseline of NER was established by providing custom NER models that were trained on DNM datasets related to drugs and weapons (a note regarding the baseline dataset can be found in [2]). Research in this field lead to choosing SpaCy as the framework for implementing the named entity recognition for the final release. The next step is therefore to built upon the model training pipeline.

Concerning the relationship extraction, the module was implemented as a rule-based and pattern matching approach using shallow linguistic features. The plan for the final release is to use a dataset with annotated relationships between selected entities to build an automatic relationship classifier. The service for named entity recognition takes individual text paragraphs (e.g., from DNM advertisements) as input and produces a graph for the input text without taking the context (DNM crawl) into consideration. However, the service is designed to load a set of result tables from web scraping to support the injection of context information (e.g., market name, recognised vendor names, shipment location, etc.). For the final release it is planned to produce a merged graph for a set of harvested files which can be imported into a results graph database.

The DNM forum discussions provide invaluable information for LEAs to enhance the comprehension of users interest and the onset of new events. Forum discussions can contribute to situation awareness as well as to understand trending topics over the DNM. However, the comprehension of unstructured text in discussions is a challenge for LEAs. The first release of event extraction component includes a unsupervised technique to cluster forum posts into various topics and then summarizing each topic for the LEAs. It labels each post with cluster it belongs to and builds a baseline labelling method for new upcoming posts. Future release of event extraction aims to develop a hybrid approach combining lexical and machine learning based features into an online clustering method to discover events of interest over a period of time.

ACKNOWLEDGMENT

This article is based on research undertaken in the context of the EU-funded COPKIT project, which has received funding from the European Union's Horizon 2020 research and innovation program under grant agreement No 786687.

REFERENCES

[1] "Copkit project website," https://www.copkit.eu (accessed: 2020-11-10).

[2] C. Heistracher and S. Schlarb, "Machine learning techniques for the classification of product descriptions from darknet marketplaces," in Proceedings of the 11th International Conference on Applied Informatics, 2020.

[3] R. Pastor and J. M. Blanco, "The epoolice project: Environmental scanning against organised crime," European Law Enforcement Research Bulletin, no. 16, Aug. 2017, pp. 27–45. [Online]. Available: https://bulletin.cepol.europa.eu/index.php/bulletin/article/view/240

[4] B. Brewster, S. Polovina, G. Rankin, and S. Andrews, "Using conceptual knowledge representation, text analytics and open-source data to combat organized crime, graph-based representation and reasoning," in Proceedings of the 21st International Conference on Conceptual Structures, N. Hernandez, R. Jäschke, and M. Croitoru, Eds. Springer, July 2014, pp. 104–117.

[5] N. Christin, "Traveling the silk road: A measurement analysis of a large anonymous online marketplace," in Proceedings of the 22nd international conference on World Wide Web, 2013, pp. 213–224.

[6] L. Armona and D. Stackman, "Learning darknet markets," Federal Reserve Bank of New York mimeo, 2014.

[7] M. W. Al Nabki, E. Fidalgo, E. Alegre, and I. de Paz, "Classifying illegal activities on tor network based on web textual contents," in Proceedings of the 15th Conference of the European Chapter of the Association for Computational Linguistics: Volume 1, Long Papers, 2017, pp. 35–43.

[8] M. Graczyk and K. Kinningham, "Automatic product categorization for anonymous marketplaces," Tech. Rep., 2015.

[9] H. Adamsson, "Classification of illegal advertisement : Working with imbalanced class distributions using machine learning," Master's thesis, Uppsala University, Department of Information Technology.

[10] J. Li, Q. Xu, N. Shah, and T. K. Mackey, "A machine learning approach for the detection and characterization of illicit drug dealers on instagram: model evaluation study," Journal of medical Internet research, vol. 21, no. 6, 2019, p. e13803.

[11] L. Choshen, D. Eldad, D. Hershcovich, E. Sulem, and O. Abend, "The language of legal and illegal activity on the darknet," in Proceedings of the 57th Annual Meeting of the Association for Computational Linguistics, 2019, pp. 4271–4279.

[12] A. A. et al., "Pytext: A seamless path from NLP research to production," CoRR, vol. abs/1812.08729, 2018. [Online]. Available: http://arxiv.org/abs/1812.08729

[13] A. Akbik, D. Blythe, and R. Vollgraf, "Contextual string embeddings for sequence labeling," in COLING 2018, 27th International Conference on Computational Linguistics, 2018, pp. 1638–1649.

[14] R. Grishman and B. Sundheim, "Message understanding conference-6: A brief history," in Proceedings of the 16th Conference on Computational Linguistics - Volume 1, ser. COLING '96. Stroudsburg, PA, USA: Association for Computational Linguistics, 1996, pp. 466–471. [Online]. Available: https://doi.org/10.3115/992628.992709

[15] M. Marrero, J. Urbano, S. Sánchez-Cuadrado, J. Morato, and J. M. Gómez-Berbís, "Named Entity Recognition: Fallacies, Challenges and Opportunities," Computer Standards & Interfaces, vol. 35, no. 5, 2013, pp. 482–489.

[16] J. Allan, R. Papka, and V. Lavrenko, "On-line new event detection and tracking," in Proceedings of the 21st annual international ACM SIGIR conference on Research and development in information retrieval, 1998, pp. 37–45.

[17] F. Atefeh. and W. Khreich, "A survey of techniques for event detection in twitter. computational intelligence," Computational Intelligence, no. 1, 31 2015, pp. 132–164.

[18] Gwern, "Open dataset, darknet archive, collection of advertisements collected on various market," 2015. [Online]. Available: https://www.gwern.net/DNM-archives (accessed: 2020-06-25)

[19] M. Honnibal and M. Johnson, "An improved non-monotonic transition system for dependency parsing," in Proceedings of the 2015 Conference on Empirical Methods in Natural Language Processing. Lisbon, Portugal: Association for Computational Linguistics, September 2015, pp. 1373–1378. [Online]. Available: https://aclweb.org/anthology/D/D15/D15-1162

[20] J. Li, A. Sun, J. Han, and C. Li, "A survey on deep learning for named entity recognition," CoRR, vol. abs/1812.09449, 2018. [Online]. Available: http://arxiv.org/abs/1812.09449

[21] Y. Goldberg, "A primer on neural network models for natural language processing," CoRR, vol. abs/1510.00726, 2015. [Online]. Available: http://arxiv.org/abs/1510.00726

[22] C. Walker, S. Strassel, J. Medero, and K. Maeda, "Ace 2005 multilingual training corpus," https://catalog.ldc.upenn.edu/LDC2006T06 (accessed: 2020-11-10).

[23] R. W. et al., "Ontonotes release 5.0," https://catalog.ldc.upenn.edu/LDC2013T19 (accessed: 2020-11-10).

[24] K. Soska and N. Christin, "Measuring the longitudinal evolution of the online anonymous marketplace ecosystem," in 24th USENIX Security Symposium (USENIX Security 15). Washington, D.C.: USENIX Association, Aug. 2015, pp. 33–48. [Online]. Available: https://www.usenix.org/conference/usenixsecurity15/technical-sessions/presentation/soska

[25] J. Devlin, M.-W. Chang, K. Lee, and K. Toutanova, "BERT: Pre-training of deep bidirectional transformers for language understanding," in Proceedings of the 2019 Conference of the North American Chapter of the Association for Computational Linguistics: Human Language Technologies, Jun. 2019.

[26] T. Mikolov, I. Sutskever, K. Chen, G. Corrado, and J. Dean, "Distributed representations of words and phrases and their compositionality," 2013.

[27] M. Ester, H.-P. Kriegel, J. Sander, and X. Xu, "A density-based algorithm for discovering clusters in large spatial databases with noise," in Proceedings of the Second International Conference on Knowledge Discovery and Data Mining, ser. KDD'96. AAAI Press, 1996, p. 226–231.

WAF Signature Generation with Real-Time Information on the Web

1st Masahito Kumazaki
Graduate School of Informatics
Nagoya University
Nagoya, Japan
Email: kumazaki@net.itc.nagoya-u.ac.jp

2nd Yukiko Yamaguchi
Information Technology Center
Nagoya University
Nagoya, Japan
Email: yamaguchi@itc.nagoya-u.ac.jp

3rd Hajime Shimada
Information Technology Center
Nagoya University
Nagoya, Japan
Email: shimada@itc.nagoya-u.ac.jp

4th Hirokazu Hasegawa
Information Security Office
Nagoya University
Nagoya, Japan
Email: hasegawa@icts.nagoya-u.ac.jp

***Abstract*—Zero-day attacks and attacks based on publicly disclosed vulnerability information are one of the major threats in network security. To cope with such attacks, it is important to collect related information and deal with vulnerabilities as soon as possible. Therefore, we propose a system that collects vulnerability information related to Web applications from real-time information on the Web and generates Web Application Firewall (WAF) signatures. In this paper, at first, we collected vulnerability information containing the specified keyword from the National Vulnerability Database (NVD) data feed and generated WAF signatures automatically. Then, we confirmed the possibility of WAF signature generation from one tweet. Finally, we extracted tweets that may contain vulnerability information and labeled them according to the filtering algorithm. From these results, we could prove the efficiency of the proposed system.**

Keywords–Web Application Firewall(WAF); Zero-day Attack; Vulnerability Information; Real-time Information.

I. INTRODUCTION

Web applications are recognized as an important part of the social infrastructure and we use various Web applications every day. On the other hand, cyberattacks are increasing year by year and are widely recognized as an obstacle to social infrastructure. There are many cases of serious damage such as classified information leak by unauthorized access and attacks using vulnerabilities [1] [2].

Among cyberattacks, attacks that used published vulnerabilities are especially increasing [3] [4]. As an actual case, the number of detected attacks for Apache Struts 2 has increased immediately after the announcement of its vulnerability [5], and some of them resulted in personal information leakage due to lack of necessary countermeasures such as timely system update [6] [7]. Another major information security issue, zero-day attacks that occur before both a release of vulnerability information and a provision of patches [18]. For example, Google Chrome suffered such a zero-day attack in 2019 [9].

Generally recommended countermeasure against such cyberattacks is to apply fixed patches distributed by the vendor on time. However, there is an unprotected period against cyberattacks until the patch has released if the attack is a zero-day attack.

In this paper, we propose a Web Application Firewall (WAF) signature generation system using real-time information on the Internet to mitigate zero-day attack problems. Real-time information sources like twitter are used for a variety of purposes [10] [11]. They may contain the latest vulnerabilities and emergency plans, which are useful to mitigate the problem before formal vulnerability information and patches are released. Therefore, in this study, we propose a system that automatically collects vulnerability information to construct new WAF signatures to mitigate the problems until the release of formal countermeasures. Although there are previous studies on the automatic generation of signatures for Intrusion Detection System (IDS) [12] [13] [14], we use WAF in this study because it targets web applications. To acquire the latest vulnerability information from the Web, the system collects vulnerability information from real-time data feeds such as a Social Networking Service and websites for discussions on security technologies. After performing data cleansing on the collected data, the system checks for associated vulnerable Web applications and generates WAF signatures for them as a virtual patch.

In this paper, we extracted the vulnerability information including the specified keyword from the vulnerability information provided by the National Vulnerability Database (NVD) [15], and automatically generated the signature of WAF, as a proof of the concept. Then, we collected vulnerability information from Twitter, which is one of the well-known real-time information sources, and attempted to generate WAF signatures from tweets. Finally, we extracted and filtered tweets using a manual approach. From the results, we could prove the efficiency of the proposed system.

In the following, in section II, we describe the background of this study, such as exisiting countermeasures. In section III, we describe our proposed system and architectures which implement this system. In section IV, we describe the experiments using the inplemented system. In section VI, we discuss additional real-time information sources. Finally, we summarize this paper in section VI.

II. BACKGROUND

Existing countermeasures against zero-day attacks include defense-in-depth solutions that combine multiple security appliances such as firewalls, IDS/Intrusion Prevention System (IPS) based allow/deny list, and so on. However, these countermeasures may result in an unprotected period against attacks if the countermeasure is based on static rules. To mitigate the damage caused by the zero-day attacks, we propose a WAF signature generation system using real-time information on the Web. The proposed system generates a WAF signature for blocking access to the vulnerable Web application when the system finds vulnerability information of the Web application from real-time information on the Internet. As a result, the unprotected time against attacks is shortened and the damage may be mitigated.

A. Web Application Firewall (WAF)

Web applications are becoming more complicated year by year so that it is getting harder to detect vulnerabilities from Web application implementations. Therefore, WAF is used as a security measure to protect Web applications from ingress traffic and mitigate attacks that exploit vulnerabilities [16]. The WAF could be installed at multiple locations, such as a host type installed on a Web server, a network type installed on a communication path to the Web server, and a cloud type using WAF services on a cloud provided by the cloud service provider. By setting rules to prevent attacks aiming at typical Web application vulnerabilities, we can protect the Web server from attacks that used the typical vulnerability. Some WAFs allow you to set your own rules for specific attacks so that it is possible to prevent the zero-day attacks by applying custom signatures. The WAF uses the following basic functions to prevent external attacks and notify the administrator.

Analyzing
: Analyze Hypertext Transfer Protocol (HTTP) communication based on the detection pattern defined as to allow/deny list.

Processing
: Performs pass-through processing, error processing, replacement processing, blocking processing, and so on. Judgement is based on the result of the analysis function.

Logging
: Record WAF activity. An audit log records the unauthorized HTTP communication detected and its processing method. An operation log records WAF operation information and error information.

B. ModSecurity

ModSecurity is an open-source host type WAF software provided by Trustwave. ModSecurity has the following functions.

- Recording and auditing whole HTTP traffic
- Real-time monitoring of HTTP traffic
- Flexible enough rule engine to act as an external patch for Web applications
- Can be embedded as a module of Web server software Apache, IIS, and Nginx

Also, the Open Web Application Security Project (OWASP) [17] provides the Core Rule Set (CRS) that includes signatures for typical cyberattacks for ModSecurity. In this study, we use ModSecurity as WAF for our proposed system in later experiments, considering the flexibility of the rule engine and the versatility of the module.

III. PROPOSED SYSTEM

We assume that The organization utilizing proposed system is running WAF and the administrator can customize the rule of this WAF.

The proposed system consists of four modules:

(1) Collection module
(2) Cleansing module
(3) Signature generation module
(4) Notification generation module.

TABLE I. REAL-TIME INFORMATION SOURCES

	API	Identification	Timestamp
Twitter [18]	✓	✓	✓
Stack Overflow [19]	✓	✓	✓
Reddit [20]	✓	✓	✓
teratail [21]	×	✓	✓
Security StackExchange [22]	✓	✓	✓

Figure 1 shows the architecture of the proposed system and its data flow.

First, the collection module collects vulnerability information from real-time information sources such as social networks (Fig. 1 (1)). After that, the proposed system performs data cleansing on the collected data (Fig. 1 (2)). Finally, the proposed system generates WAF signatures and set them (Fig. 1 (3)). At the same time, the proposed system generates a notification file for the administrator (Fig. 1 (4)).

In this system, it is assumed that the administrator registers the names of the Web applications and its version information into the system beforehand. Based on the registered information, the system extracts vulnerability information from the Internet.

A. Collection module

The proposed system generates WAF signatures from real-time information shown in Table I. Subsequent processes will need IDs and timestamps to identify the articles and the date of publication. As shown in Table 1, these sources are equipped with IDs and timestamps. The collection module collects vulnerability information from these sources and saves their ID, timestamp, and body.

B. Cleansing module

The proposed system performs data cleansing on collected data to remove duplicate information and get the necessary information. The cleansing module extracts the following attributes from text and Web page. The system uses the following attributes for generating WAF signatures.

- Application name
- Vulnerability type
- Version information
- Vulnerability identification information such as a Common Vulnerabilities and Exposures (CVE)-ID

C. Signature generation module

If the Web application name which is used in operating Web application system is included in attributes from the cleansing module, the system generates a WAF signature to block HTTP requests to that Web application and apply it into the WAF. In addition, the signature generation module notifies the notification generation module regarding the signature generated.

D. Notification generation module

The proposed system generates a notification to the administrator. This notification includes information such as the name of the vulnerable web application and its version. We expect that when the vulnerability is resolved, for example by applying a patch, the administrator will use this notification to remove the signature.

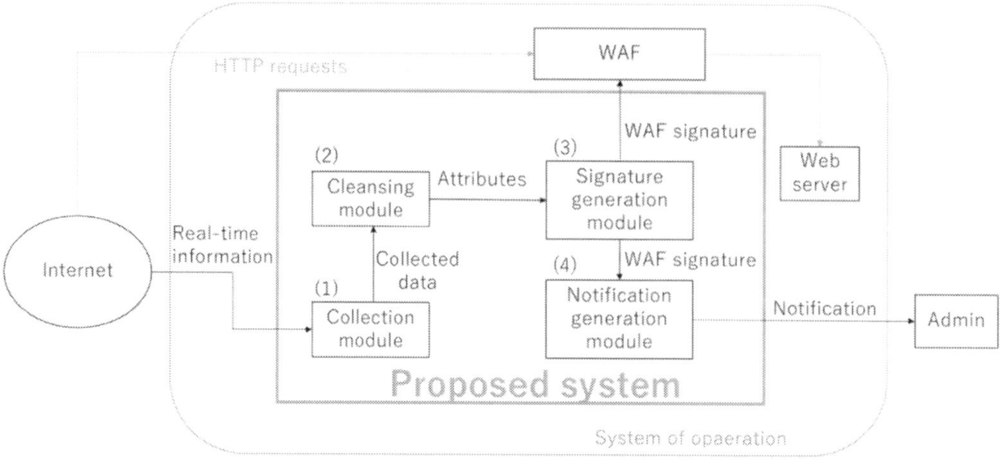

Figure 1. System architecture and data flow.

IV. Experiments

In this study, we conducted the following evaluation experiments. As a Web application to collect vulnerability information, we used WordPress as a keyword for extracting vulnerability information due to its known history of many vulnerabilities.

A. *Experiment 1: WAF signature generation using CVE information*

As a proof of concept, we implemented the proposed system shown in Figure 1 with Python 3.6.8 and AWK scripts and examined the automatic generation of WAF signatures using NVD data feeds instead of real-time information.

1) Processing Method: In the collection module (Fig.1(1)), we obtained NVD data feed on a daily basis. This data feed contains CVEs. In the cleansing module (Fig.1 (2)), we checked whether the keyword was included in the Common Platform Enimeration (CPE) name for each vulnerability information of the data feed. After that, following data has been extracted.

1) CVE-ID
2) CPE name
   CPE name is a name that identifies the platforms [23].

   ```
   cpe:2.3:[Part]:[Vendor]:[Product]:[Version]
   :[Update]:[Edition]:[SW_Edition]:[Target_SW]
   :[Target_HW]:[Language]:[Other]
   ```

   In this experiment, we used [Part] and [Product] from the CPE name. [Part] represents a product type with one character, where 'a' is an application, 'o' is an operating system, and 'h' is hardware. [Product] is the product name.
3) Version information

We extracted these data and stored them into JavaScript Object Notation (JSON) format.

In signature generation module (Fig.1 (3)), we generated a signature for ModSecurity from extracted information to prevent access to the Web application. With reference to `ModSecurity_41_xss_attacks.conf` and `ModSecurity_41_sqlinjection_attacks.conf` from ModSecurity's CRS, we added following signatures to ModSecurity.

- **VARIABLES:** REQUEST_COOKIES | !REQUEST_COOKIES:/__utm/ | REQUEST_COOKIES_NAMES | ARGS_NAMES | ARGS | XML:/
- **OPERATOR:** Regular expression using Web application names
- **ACTIONS:** phase:2,block,msg:'*application name* injection.',severity:'2',id:'15000+line number'

In addition, we generated text files to notify the signature generation in notification generation module (Fig.1 (4)).

2) Result: We performed this daily process for 10 days from 21st December, 2019 to 30th December, 2019.

Since the results for all days during the collection period was same, a single day result is depicted as a sample in Figure 2.

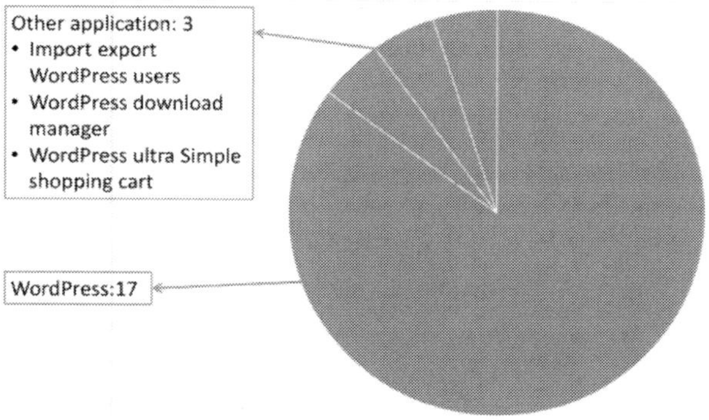

Figure 2. Extracted information in Experiment 1

The result of automatically generated WAF signatures is shown in Figure 3. The signature for WordPress was generated from 17 cases of WordPress vulnerability information and other signatures were generated from 1 case corresponding to each application.

```
SecRule REQUEST_COOKIES|!REQUEST:/__utm/|
    REQUEST_COOKIES_NAMES|ARGS_NAMES|ARGS|XML:/* "
    import_export_wordpress_users" "phase:2,block,msg:'
    WordPress injection.'severity:'2',id:'15001'"
SecRule REQUEST_COOKIES|!REQUEST:/__utm/|
    REQUEST_COOKIES_NAMES|ARGS_NAMES|ARGS|XML:/* "
    wordpress" "phase:2,block,msg:'WordPress injection.'
    severity:'2',id:'15002'"
SecRule REQUEST_COOKIES|!REQUEST:/__utm/|
    REQUEST_COOKIES_NAMES|ARGS_NAMES|ARGS|XML:/* "
    wordpress_download_manager" "phase:2,block,msg:'
    WordPress injection.'severity:'2',id:'15003'"
SecRule REQUEST_COOKIES|!REQUEST:/__utm/|
    REQUEST_COOKIES_NAMES|ARGS_NAMES|ARGS|XML:/* "
    wordpress_ultra_simple_paypal_shopping_cart" "phase:2,
    block,msg:'WordPress injection.'severity:'2',id
    :'15004'"
```

Figure 3. Generated WAF signature in Experiment 1

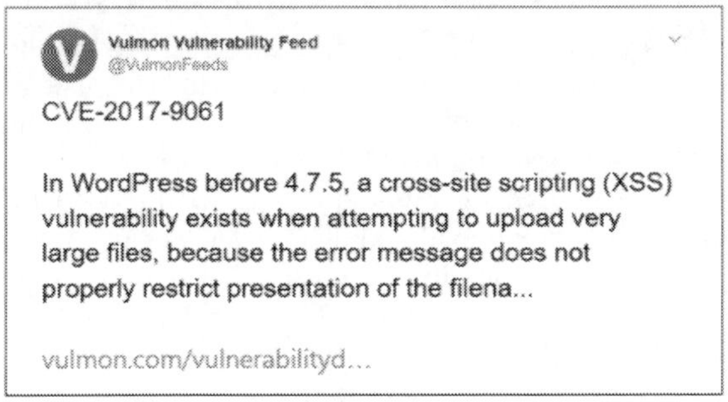

Figure 4. The tweet used in Experiment 2

TABLE II. EXTRACTED ATTRIBUTES OF THE TWEETS

key	Type	Description
id	Int64	tweet_id as an integer.
created_at	String	The time when the tweet was created.
username	String	User name who posted the tweet.
text	String	The tweet contents in UTF-8 format.
urls	List	Uniform Resource Locators (URLs) in the tweet[1].

3) Consideration: From the generated signatures it could be seen that in addition to the signature for actual WordPress application, other applications that include " wordpress " in their name have been blocked. These redundant rules give an additional burden to the WAF. To overcome this limitation, we need to improve the signature generation rule and tune it.

B. Experiment 2: Generation of WAF signatures using twitter feed

To confirm the possibility of WAF signature generation from real-time vulnerability information, we collected tweets from twitter feeds, chose one tweet, and generated a WAF signature from it. We collected tweets using the search Application Programming Interface (API) by setting query parameters to "wordpress" and chose the tweet shown in Figure 4. The proposed system uses information listed in Table II from tweets, so we extracted the following information.

- **id:** 1200259525707796482
- **created_at:** 2019-11-29 03:45:45
- **username:** Vulmon Vulnerability Feed
- **text:** CVE-2017-9061\n\nIn WordPress before 4.7.5, a cross-site scripting (XSS) vulnerability exists when attempting to upload very large files, because the error message does not properly restrict presentation of the filena...\n\nhttps://t.co/anaw5-QSAoa"
- **urls:** [http://vulmon.com/vulnerabilitydetails?qid=CVE-2017-9061]

```
SecRule REQUEST_COOKIES|!REQUEST:/__utm/|
    REQUEST_COOKIES_NAMES|ARGS_NAMES|ARGS|XML:/* "
    wordpress" "phase:2,brock,msg:'WordPress XSS.'severity
    :'2',id:'15001'"
```

Figure 5. Generated WAF signature in Experiment 2

1) Method and Result: As a result of a visual check of the Web application and vulnerability information contained in the tweet, we got the following attributes from the text.

- **Application name:** WordPress
- **Vulnerability type:** XSS
- **Version information:** 4.7.5 and earlier
- **CVE-ID:** CVE-2017-9061

We also checked the Web page indicated by the URL, but we couldn't get any more attributes. Similar to experiment 1, we generated the ModSecurity signature from these attributes. The generated signature is shown in Figure 5.

2) Consideration: From the experiment, it was confirmed that WAF signatures could be generated from collected tweets. However, a method to select a relevant tweet is needed. We expect to be able to extract information such as Web application name, its version, and type of vulnerability through the pattern matching approach.

C. Experiment 3: Filtering and extracting tweets through pattern matching approach

Based on the results of Experiment 2, we extracted and filtered vulnerability information from the tweets. Through twitter API We collected tweets every day for the following period. After eliminating the duplicates of the collected tweets, we further processed 1,116 tweets.

- **Collection period:** From 4th December, 2019 to 8th January, 2020
- **Search query:** "WordPress AND Vulnerability", "WordPress AND XSS", and "WordPress AND injection"

To check the results of the filter, we manually assigned the following labels to the tweets based on the relevance to the WordPress vulnerability.

0: WordPress vulnerability information
1: Other information

As a result of the manual labeling, 76 tweets regarding WordPress vulnerabilities have been identified. The remaining 1,040 tweets were mistakenly extracted since its URL referred to the Webpage created using WordPress, for example.

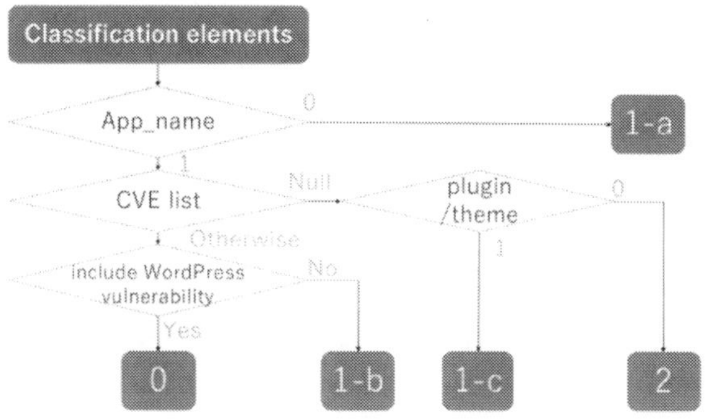

Figure 6. Flowchart of estimated label setting

TABLE III. FILTERING RESULTS

		estimated label					
		0	1-a	1-b	1-c	2	total
correct label	0	13	0	6	0	57	76
	1	1	94	292	191	462	1,040
	total	14	94	298	191	519	1,116

TABLE IV. NUMBER OF SEARCH HITS

	2018-20148	2019-17669	2019-20041
Stack Overflow	10(-)	6(-)	10(-)
Reddit	2(-)	15(-)	11(-)
teratail	6(-)	6(-)	3(-)
Security StackExchange	2(-)	0(-)	2(-)

(): Number of search hits related CVEs

1) Method: At first, we collected the attributes shown in Table II, from the tweet and then filtered them on its text context by pattern matching using regular expressions to the tweet's text and web page body which is indicated by URL. The following attributes are extracted from the tweet and stored in JSON format.

- **ID:** tweet-id
- **App_name:** If the string includes "wordpress" this element is 1, otherwise 0.
- **CVE:** Extract the string "CVE-\d{4}-\d+" and store it as a list.
- **plugin / theme:** If the string includes "plugin" or "theme" this parameter is 1, otherwise 0.

From these attributes and a list of CVEs corresponding to the target application, we automatically assigned an estimated label to tweets according to the flowchart shown in Figure 6. Each label indicates the following categorization result.

0: WordPress vulnerability information
1: Other information
  1-a: Not included the string "wordpress"
  1-b: Expected as a WordPress plugin or theme
  1-c: No WordPress vulnerability in CVE list
2: Unfiltered by this method

2) Result: We implemented the filter in Python as per the flowchart shown in Figure 6 and ran it on the collected 1,116 tweets. The result is shown in Table III. This method filtered 597 tweets and 98.5% of them were filtered correctly. On the other hand, 519 were unfiltered. By using the pattern matching approach, the number of objects of analysis could be reduced by half.

Out of 7 tweets that have been failed to be correctly filtered, 6 tweets were supposed to be labeled as 0 whereas it was mistakenly labeled as 1-b. they were weekly summaries of vulnerability information for WordPress and related modules. They contained information about WordPress and its plugins at the same time. Therefore, the filter misjudged them as information about WordPress plugins.

3) Consideration: The information required for the proposed system is vulnerability information that is up-to-date or has not been officially announced, which is included in the tweets labeled as 2 in this experiment. Therefore, there needs to be a way to extract the required information from these tweets.

V. CONSIDERATION OF ADDITIONAL SOURCES

Currently, the real-time information source is only Twitter and it could be prone to be disinformation. Therefore, we discussed the possibility of using other information sources which are shown in Table I.

To analyze whether those information sources are moderate sources or not, we explored discussions about following three WordPress vulnerabilities in those communities. These vulnerabilities are registered in the NVD and have a high Common Vulnerability Scoring System (CVSS) score.

- CVE-2018-20148 Published: 14th December, 2018
- CVE-2019-17669 Published: 17th October, 2019
- CVE-2019-20041 Published: 27th December, 2019

Since we cannot collect information from teratail via API, we searched the above vulnerabilities by Google search with queries "WordPress" and "vulnerability". The duration of the search was set to one month before and after the vulnerability announcement. The results are shown in Table IV. The numbers in parentheses are the number of search hits. The result shows that we could not obtain information about these vulnerabilities from these communities in a timely manner.

Since the results shown in Table IV are not suitable for a comparison of each knowledge community, we tried additional exploration. We compared the number of search hits per site using the Custom Search API provided by Google to see the number of discussions about vulnerabilities in each knowledge community. We set the query "vulnerability" for all sites, and the period is from 1st January, 2017 to 31st December, 2019. Since Reddit has a lot of topics that are not security-related, we only explored two subreddits, "security" and "cybersecurity".

The results are shown in Table V. Among the knowledge communities explored in this study, Stack Overflow and Security StackExchange are the most active in discussions about the

TABLE V. NUMBER OF SEARCH HITS IN EACH KNOWLEDGE COMMUNITY

knowledge community\Year	2017	2018	2019	total
Stack Overflow	2,166	2,072	1,837	6,075
Reddit[cybersecurity]	31	172	266	469
Reddit[security]	16	60	151	227
teratail	241	196	172	609
Security StackExchange	1,166	1,072	768	4,006

vulnerability so that they can be used as a good information source.

VI. CONCLUSION

In this study, we proposed the WAF signature generation system using real-time information on the Internet and conducted three types of experiments as initial studies. From a filtering experiment for 1,116 Tweet data, we were able to narrow down the required data to half of the total data. We also discovered the following challenges in those three experiments.

- How to clearly distinguish vulnerability information of other Web applications which may have a similar name as Web application name
- How to select the necessary information effectively from vulnerability information

In addition, the following challenges may occur when implementing the whole proposed system.

- How to determine the disinformation
- What to do with vulnerability information for which version information could not be extracted
- Block legitimate Web applications which include the name of the target application in their names
- React other than blocking based on the type of vulnerability
- Generalize of the system to other than WordPress

In order to solve these problems, we will consider and verify the following approaches.

- Defining reliability based on the account which posted information to the information sources
- Creating additional signatures to block the target only

REFERENCES

[1] Significant Cyber Incidents — Center for Strategic and International Studies https://www.csis.org/programs/technology-policy-program/significant-cyber-incidents [retrieved: July, 2020]

[2] The 15 biggest data breaches of the 21st century | CSO Online https://www.csoonline.com/article/2130877/the-biggest-data-breaches-of-the-21st-century.html [retrieved: August, 2020]

[3] 10 Major Security Threats 2019 — Information-Technology Promotion Agency (IPA), Japan https://www.ipa.go.jp/files/000076989.pdf [retrieved: July, 2020]

[4] Think Fast: Time Between Disclosure, Patch Release and Vulnerability Exploitation — Intelligence for Vulnerability Management, Part Two | FireEye Inc https://www.fireeye.com/blog/threat-research/2020/04/time-between-disclosure-patch-release-and-vulnerability-exploitation.html [retrieved: August, 2020]

[5] Attacks Heating Up Against Apache Struts 2 Vulnerability | Threatpost https://threatpost.com/attacks-heating-up-against-apache-struts-2-vulnerability/124183/ [retrieved: July, 2020]

[6] US House of Representatives Committee on Oversight and Government Reform, "The Equifax Data Breach", Majority Staff Report 115th Congress, 2018. https://republicans-oversight.house.gov/wp-content/uploads/2018/12/Equifax-Report.pdf [retrieved: July, 2020]

[7] GMO Payment Gateway, "Apology and Report for Leak of Personal InformationDueto Unauthorized Access", 2017. https://www.gmo-pg.com/en/corp/newsroom/pdf/170310_gmo_pg_en.pdf [retrieved: July, 2020]

[8] Committee on National Security Systems, "Committee on National Security Systems(CNSS) Glossary", CNSSI No. 4009, 2015

[9] Chrome Releases: Stable Channel Update for Desktop https://chromereleases.googleblog.com/2019/03/stable-channel-update-for-desktop.html [retrieved: July, 2020]

[10] T. Sakaki, O. Makoto, and M. Yutaka, "Earthquake shakes Twitter users: real-time event detection by social sensors.", In Proceedings of the 19th international conference on World wide web, p. 851-860, 2010

[11] O. Oh, M. Agrawal, and H. R. Rao, "Information control and terrorism:Tracking the mumbai terrorist attack through twitter.", Information-Systems Frontiers, vol. 13, no. 1, pp. 33–43, 2011

[12] S. More, M. Matthews, A. Joshi, and T. Finin, "A Knowledge-Based Approach To Intrusion Detection Modeling.", In Proceedings of 2012 IEEE Symposium on Security and Privacy Workshops, pp. 75-81, May 2012.

[13] C. Kreibich and J. Crowcroft, "Honeycomb: Creating Intrusion Detection Signatures Using Honeypots.", SIGCOMM Computer Communication Review., Vol. 34, No. 1, pp. 51-56, January 2004.

[14] S. Singh, C. Estan, G. Varghese, and S. Savage, "Automated Worm Fingerprinting.", In Proceedings of the 6th Symposium on Operating Systems Design and Implementation, pp.4-4, December 2004.

[15] NVD - Home https://nvd.nist.gov/ [retrived: October, 2020]

[16] K. Lawrence and L. Luo, "Interactive management of web application firewall rules.", U.S.Patent, No. 9,473,457, 2016

[17] OWASP Foundation | Open Source Foundation for Application Security https://owasp.org/ [retrived: October, 2020]

[18] Twitter https://twitter.com [retrived: October, 2020]

[19] Stack Overflow - Where Developers Learn, Share, & Build Careers https://stackoverflow.com [retrived: October, 2020]

[20] reddit: the front page of the internet https://www.teratail.com [retrived: October, 2020]

[21] teratail teratail.com [retrived: October, 2020]

[22] Information Security Stack Exchange https://security.stackexchange.com/ [retrived: October, 2020]

[23] B. Cheikes, D. Waltermire, and K. Scarfone, "Common platform enumeration: naming specification version 2.3", NIST Interagency Report 7695, pp.11-13, 2011.

Securing Smart Homes using Intrusion Detection Systems

Christoph Haar

Hochschule für Telekommunikation
Gustav-Freytag-Straße 43-45
Leipzig, Germany
Email: haar@hft-leipzig.de

Erik Buchmann

Hochschule für Telekommunikation
Gustav-Freytag-Straße 43-45
Leipzig, Germany
Email: buchmann@hft-leipzig.de

***Abstract*—Botnets, such as Mirai or Reaper show that many Smart Home devices are low-hanging fruits for attackers. Nevertheless, it is an ongoing trend to replace everyday devices, such as TV, fridges or doorbells by smart successors. Thus, securing Smart Homes operated by private users remains an open issue. In this paper, we explore options to integrate an Intrusion Detection System (IDS) in a Smart Home installation. Smart Home devices use well-established technology. From a technical perspective, existing IDS approaches can be applied. We focus on non-technical challenges. This includes a system design that allows for a pre-configuration. It also calls for processes which allow users to invoke a security expert in the case of an attack that cannot be handled by simple means. We demonstrate our approach with a prototypical implementation.**

***Index Terms*—IT Security; Smart Home Security; Intrusion Detection Systems**

I. Introduction

The number of Smart Home devices is increasing day by day. Almost any recent TV is "'smart"'. It possesses computational resources, an operating system, various applications, and an Internet connection via WLAN. Countless everyday devices from lightbulbs [1] to gardening equipment [2] have smart successors that use the Internet to provide new modes of use. Typically, Smart Homes are operated by private users without IT-Security expertise. For such users it is not obvious that the new TV needs frequent security updates, while its non-smart predecessor could be used years without care. It is also not obvious that security measures like a simple firewall on the Internet router or an anti-virus software on some devices cannot protect the Smart Home sufficiently. Botnets, such as Mirai [3] or Reaper [4] show that Smart Home devices are in the focus of adversaries already.

A well-established approach to ward off such risks is to use an Intrusion Detection System (IDS) [5] [6]. An IDS detects attempts to break into a network segment and allows the user to take appropriate countermeasures. From a technical perspective, existing IDS consider network protocols, services, operating systems, software libraries, etc. that are used by Smart Home devices. However, due to some non-technical aspects it is challenging to apply IDS to Smart Homes:

It is not feasible for a private user without security expertise to configure an IDS. It is neither feasible for this user to distinguish between a false alarm and an attack, and to identify appropriate countermeasures. Furthermore, it must be explainable to the private user in which way an IDS secures a Smart Home installation, which devices are secured, and who is responsible to what extent if an attack goes unnoticed. It is also problematic to integrate an IDS into a Smart Home as a security appliance, which is constantly configured, monitored and maintained by an external security expert. First, this approach is prohibitively expensive for private users. Second, the security expert would have full access to the monitored network segment, which violates the privacy of the user.

In this paper, we focus on two research questions:

1) How can an IDS be integrated into a Smart Home operated by private users without IT-Security expertise?
2) Which IDS approaches can be adapted for that purpose?

We systematically explore how network segmentation, system architecture, security process and specification of product features for an IDS must be adapted to secure Smart Home installations. By means of an experiment, we demonstrate that both anomaly-detecting IDS and signature-detecting IDS are applicable, but the latter ones generate fewer false alarms.

Paper structure: In Section II, we review related work. In Section III, we provide a problem statement. We will answer the first research question in section IV and the second research question in Section V. Section VI concludes.

II. Related Work

In this section, we briefly describe Smart Homes, existing IDS approaches and components, and the IT-Security Process.

A. Smart Homes

The term "Smart Home" refers to the use of information and communication technology for domestic use [7]. This ranges from (a) home automation over (b) controlling domestic appliances to (c) smart devices with extended modes. An example for (a) is the use of smart gardening equipment [2] that waters the plants depending on the weather and moves the lawn automatically. An example for (b) is a smart light bulb [1], which simulates an indoor sunset and synchronizes with a movie shown in TV. Finally, an example for (c) is a smart speaker [8]. By using a cloud service to realize voice control, a smart speaker plays music, reads emails and news, manages appointments etc. The sum of all smart devices is a Smart Home installation. Since a Smart Home connects devices in private spaces to the Internet, it is problematic both from a privacy and security perspective [9].

B. Intrusion Detection Systems

IDS strive to detect attacks [10] to the devices in the network. Such attacks might come from the outside, e.g., over the Internet. Insiders are also possible sources of attacks, e.g., employees. Typical attacks include *Scanning Attacks* like Portscans or network scans [11]. Scanning attacks help an attacker to identify potential vulnerabilities in a system. *Denial of Service Attacks* flood a network or a device with data packets. Since such packets consume computational resources, the availability of the attacked system is at stake [12]. Service-specific attacks, such as a *Telnet Attack* aim for vulnerable services [13]. Recently, many Smart Home devices allowed unencrypted access with a hard-coded administrator password, which can be exploited with a Telnet Attack.

Host-based IDS detect attacks directly at the monitored devices [14]. To implement a host-based IDS, it must be possible to install software on the devices that should be secured. In contrast, *Network-based IDS* are stand-alone systems that monitor entire network segments [10]. For this purpose, in each segment a network appliance, such as a router, bridge or firewall must sent a copy of all data packets to the IDS. This allows to secure all devices in a network segment without having to install software on each device.

C. IDS Components

Each IDS realizes a number of components. A *Knowledge Base* contains all information necessary to distinguish an attack from normal network traffic. Information about the current state of the IDS is provided by a *Configuration Component*. A *Sensor* fetches data packets gathered at an *Information Source*, i.e., a monitored device or an appliance in a certain network segment. The *Detector-ID Engine* compares the data from the Sensor with the information from the Knowledge Base to identify attacks. If an attack is detected, a *Response Component* raises an alarm and initiates an automated or an human involved action [15].

Two alternatives exist to implement the Detector-ID Engine. A *signature-detecting IDS* applies a preconfigured set of pattern and rules (the signature) to the data packets in order to identify attacks. These signatures can be defined by the IDS operator according to match a company-wide IT-Security policy. It is also possible to import signatures from well-researched attacks from external repositories [16].

Anomaly-detecting IDS use machine learning and artificial intelligence to learn what is normal data traffic [17]. A voting algorithm decides if new data packets differ so much from normal data traffic that an alarm is generated.

Typically, an IDS comes with a basic pre-configuration that considers the characteristics of the implemented components. However, this pre-configuration is only meant to speed up the configuration process for the security expert, and to demonstrate the use of configuration parameters. Using an IDS out of the box does not result in a reasonable network-security advantage. Thus, existing IDS approaches must be part of an IT-Security Process, which is executed by security experts [18], [19], [20].

D. IT-Security Process

The IT-Security Process follows a plan-do-check-act cycle [21]. In the *Plan* phase, the management defines a general IT-Security policy. Furthermore the needed controls and procedures are identified. In the *Do* phase the identified controls and procedures are implemented. During the *Check* phase all the implemented controls and procedures are evaluated. In this phase security incidents are identified as well. The *Act* phase includes a constant improvement of the implemented measures based on the identified security incidents. These improvements are leading back to Plan, in which the policy can be improved [22]. Depending on the company structure, different persons are involved in this process. However, every person needs expertise in IT-Security.

The phases of the generic IT-Security Process are adapted to the needs of an IDS, as follows: In the *Plan* phase, the IDS is configured to distinguish attacks from normal network traffic. In the *Do* phase, those information are implemented in an IDS instance. In the *Check* phase, the IDS detects attacks. Finally, in the *Act* phase the performance of the IDS is reviewed to adapt the Knowledge Base for attacks that went unnoticed.

III. Problem Statement

We strive to integrate an IDS in Smart Home installations connected to the Internet. To this end, we distinguish two roles:

A ***security expert*** possesses the IT-Security expertise needed to develop an IT-Security policy, to configure an IDS respectively, to operate the IDS and understand its alarms, and to react with appropriate measures to alarms.

A ***private user*** lacks this kind of expertise. Such a private user can follow manuals written without technical vocabulary. It is difficult for a private user to find out if an IDS alarm comes from an attack or a misconfigured network appliance.

Our objective is to use an IDS to increase the security of a Smart Home installation in the possession of a private user.

Observations show that Smart Home devices use protocols, libraries and technologies which have been developed for years [23]. From a technical point of view it is feasible to configure an IDS [24] for Smart Homes. However, IDS approaches have been developed to secure complex corporate networks. Existing IDS put an emphasis on the integration into security management processes, which allow experts to implement a comprehensive security strategy. It is not in the focus of such IDS to provide intuitive explanations.

In order to integrate an IDS into a Smart Home, we specifically consider non-technical aspects of an IDS. Our starting point is a set of three requirements that arise from security challenges for Smart Home devices:

Expertise: The user does not need to possess in-depth expertise of technical internals, such as network protocols and IT-Security [25]. This requirement is valid for any Smart Home device tailored for private users.

Separation: Smart Home devices have dedicated use cases that can be separated from others. In many cases, Smart Home devices have traditional, non-smart predecessors. Such predecessors have built expectations and experiences regarding modes use and handling [26] [25].

Understandability: The interaction between a user and a Smart Home device should be as understandable as possible [27], [28]. This is challenging, as private users cannot expected to comprehend technical vocabulary.

IV. An IDS approach for Smart Homes

To systematically approach an IDS that secures Smart Homes, we investigate the four levels *Network Segmentation*, *System Architecture*, *IT-Security Process* and *Contract Liabilities*. Our levels have been compiled from proposals to secure Smart Home networks [6], [25], from well-known IT-Security concepts [18]–[21], and from challenges discussed in the IDS context [15], [16], [24]. In the following, we briefly explain each level, and we apply the requirements from Section III.

A. *Level* Network Segmentation

The concern of this level is to separate the Smart Home devices under observation of the IDS from all other devices that might be part of the network of the user.

Existing IDS approaches are configurable for corporate networks. Such networks feature multiple segments which transport data from different applications. Each segment comes with specific security requirements. Within each network segment, a network appliance, such as a router or a firewall sends copies of the data stream to an IDS, e.g., via a Security Incident and Event Management System. Alternatively, IDS software components can be installed on each device in a network segment (cf. Section II-C). However, typical Smart Home installations use a simpler configuration, as shown in Figure 1. In the figure, arrows describe data transmissions and rounded rectangles depict network segments.

From Requirement **Separation** follows that it must be clear which devices are under observation. We propose to span a separate Smart Home network containing all Smart Home devices, as illustrated in Figure 2. All devices in the Smart Home network have similar properties and security requirements. That is, the Smart Home devices have a single purpose, observe the user context, handle person-related data and possibly communicate over the Internet. For this reason, it makes sense to operate all Smart Home devices in a separate network. Furthermore, in case of an attack, conventional devices such as PCs or laptops remain unaffected.

Requirement **Expertise** rules out host-based IDS that require a technically demanding installation and configuration. Figure 1 shows that the best place for an IDS in a Smart Home installation is the router. The router controls the network boundaries and handles data transfers between the Smart Home devices. Figure 2 illustrates this approach.

Regarding **Understandability**, an isolated network for Smart Home devices allows to explain to the private user which devices are under observation and where security alarms are located. Because all devices in the Smart Home network have similar security properties, it is not necessary to let the private user generate a complex IDS configuration. Instead, the IDS can be preconfigured for typical Smart Homes.

B. *Level* System Architecture

This level considers the system architecture of the IDS. Figure 3 depicts a typical IDS installation (cf. Section II-B). Components are depicted as gray rectangles, black lines illustrate information flows and ovals represent roles. The dashed lines are responsibilities. All components that need supervision or configuration are assigned to the security expert. This is particularly problematic for the Response Component. It delivers alarms which can be explained only when knowing the signatures that have been configured. We tackle this issue by modifying the information flows, changing responsibilities and introducing a new component, as shown in Figure 4.

Separation calls for a clear distinction between different tasks. We distinguish between a *preconfiguration stage* and an *operational stage*. The components assigned to the preconfiguration stage are in the responsibility of the IDS manufacturer. In particular, the manufacturer possesses security experts, which specify the general IT-Security policy and signatures for the Knowledge Base. The components assigned to the operational stage are in the responsibility of the private user.

Expertise means that the private user cannot be expected to take actions depending on expert knowledge. With our approach, the components in the operational stage are automated so that no expert knowledge is necessary.

However, the Response Component cannot be fully automated. The response to an alarm depends on the Smart Home devices installed, the kind of alarm and the IDS (pre)configuration, which violates **Understandability**. To solve this issue, we introduce a Reporting Component. This component allows to invoke a security expert with all information needed to find out if it was a false alarm, and to devise an adequate response if not. In particular, the Reporting Component automatically generates a report, based on the system state from the Configuration Component and the alarms from the Response Component.

Observe that the Reporting Component forwards reports to a security expert only if instructed by the user. Thus, the security expert cannot permanently observe the Smart Home network. Because Smart Homes typically cover private areas of the user's life, this is important.

C. *Level* IT-Security Process

The level IT-Security Process ensures that there is an appropriate response on IDS alarms, and the IDS will be adapted to changing properties of the network if necessary.

Corporate networks are frequently adapted to new demands, and adversaries might develop new attacks. An IDS increases the network security only if it is constantly monitored and improved. To this end, an IDS is part of the company's IT-Security Process, as shown in Figure 5. In the figure, rectangles denote process steps and black lines the information flow. Ovals depict roles and dashed lines responsibilities.

With our approach, only Smart Home devices are part of the Smart Home network monitored by the IDS. Such Smart Home devices rarely change its functionality. The security

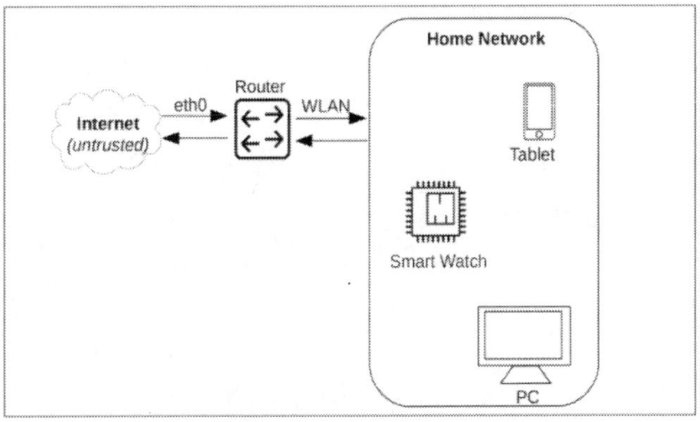

Fig. 1. Typical Smart Home Architecture

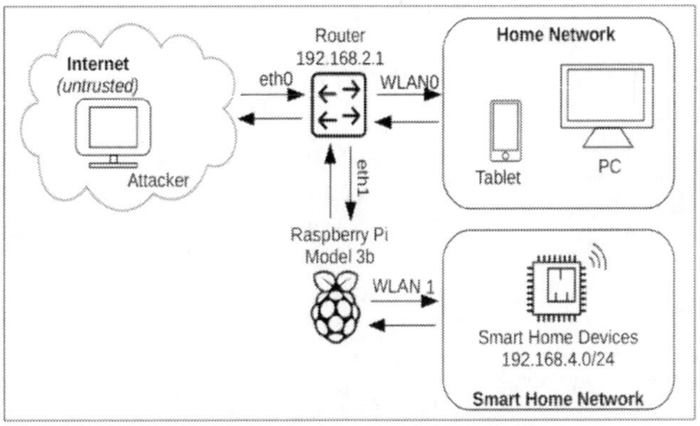

Fig. 2. Experimental Smart Home Architecture

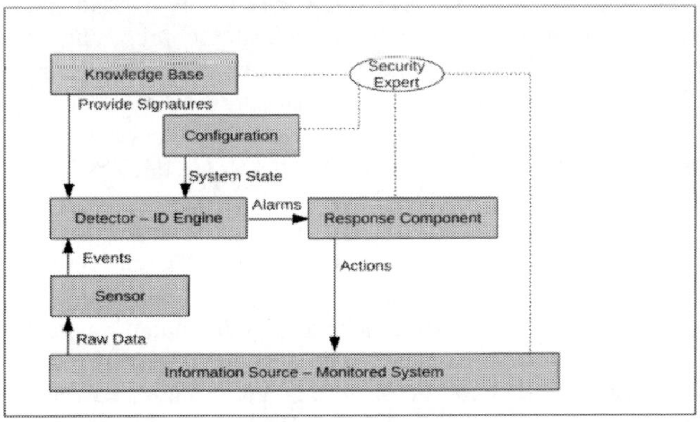

Fig. 3. Existing IDS

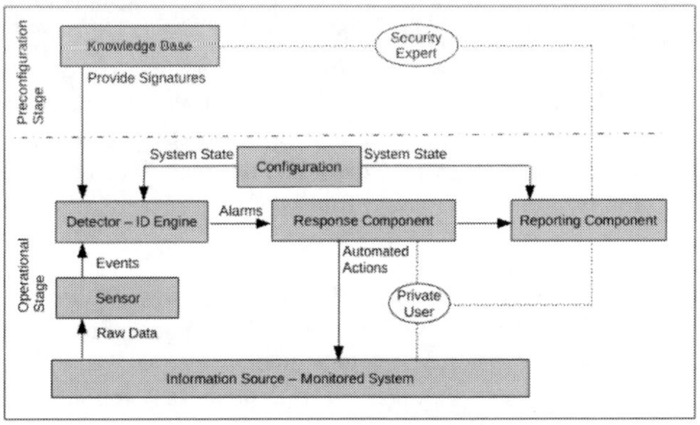

Fig. 4. Smart Home IDS

requirements of the Smart Home network stem from the Smart Home concept and do not change over time. Thus, the IT-Security Process can be streamlined for Smart Homes.

Separation requires to separate the IT-Security Process into phases that have a distinct purpose. We distinguish between four phases *Preconfiguration*, *Installation*, *Detection* and *Countermeasures*, as shown in Figure 6.

The Pre-configuration phase is related to the pre-configuration stage from Section IV-B. Regarding **Expertise**, a private user cannot be expected to devise an IDS configuration. With our approach, the security expert defines an IDS configuration tailored for a network segment with the security properties of a Smart Home network.

The other phases are taking place at the operational stage, i.e., make use of IDS components that have been automated. In the Installation phase, the private user must only connect the IDS to the Internet router and the Smart Home devices to the IDS. After that the IDS starts monitoring the Smart Home network. In the Detection phase, the IDS automatically identifies potential attacks and raises the alarms if necessary.

In the Countermeasures phase, the IDS suggests actions to the private user to ward off attacks. If the IDS detects an attack that has been preconfigured in the Knowledge Base, it suggests reasonable measures, e.g., re-starting or disconnecting the Smart Home device. If there is no countermeasure that is explainable to the private user, **Understandability** means that the private user must invoke an external security expert. In this case, the Reporting Component helps the user to provide the security expert with all information necessary to devise reasonable measures, and to update the Knowledge Base.

D. *Level* Contract Liabilities

This level considers in which product features a Smart Home IDS manufacturer can assure to a private user.

Traditional IDS are sold as a "‘construction kit"’, which needs to be configured by the customer's security expert to be effective. If such an IDS does not ward off an attack, it is in the responsibility of the security expert. The expert has compared the abilities of the IDS with the demand of the company network and generated the configuration of the IDS. However, such an approach is not suitable for private users.

From **Separation** follows that a Smart Home IDS must be able to define a distinct service. With our approach, the manufacturer can define this service in the pre-configuration phase. It includes all devices in the Smart Home network that are connected to the IDS.

Expertise requires to specify the abilities of the IDS without referring to certain transmission protocols or attack names. However, many Smart Home devices have a similar architecture and use similar communication protocols [29]. Thus, it

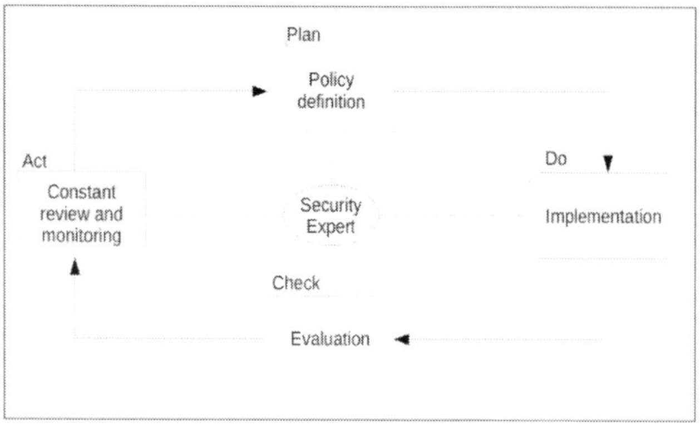

Fig. 5. IT-Security Process

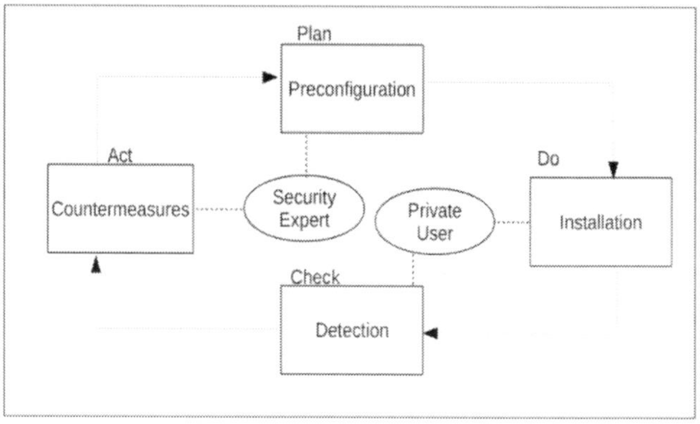

Fig. 6. Adapted IT-Security Process

might be feasible to promise a certain level of protection for certain product groups or manufacturers.

Requirement **Understandability** means that it must be clearly communicated to the private user that an IDS does not offer a complete protection against any kinds of attack to the Smart Home devices. Otherwise, the manufacturer would be held responsible in case of an attack.

E. Discussion

We have shown how an IDS can be used to secure a Smart Home operated by private users, on four distinct levels. However, this might result in new challenges. One issue is that the IDS is operated in a potentially insecure environment. For example, a private user might turn off the IDS by mistake, or misconfigure the Internet connection so that the Reporting Component cannot send information to the security expert.

Another potential issue is the check phase of the IT-Security Process, which we have automated. If mistakes in the pre-configuration result in successful attacks, such attacks might not be apparent during the check phase. Thus, the IDS will not be updated for this kind of attack.

V. SIGNATURE- OR ANOMALY-BASED DETECTION

In this section, we want to confirm that current IDS can be used as described in Section IV. We also want to find out if signature-based or anomaly-based IDS are better suited.

A. Experimental Setup

We have conducted experiments with the system architecture illustrated in Figure 2. The IDS was installed on a Raspberry Pi 3B that operates as a Wi-Fi Bridge between the Smart Home network (WLAN1) and the Internet router (eth1). The Raspberry Pi 3B is sufficient to evaluate network packets in real-time. We have tested two different IDS:

Suricata realizes a signature-based detection. Reviews [30] show that Suricata is widely used, implements state-of-the-art detection algorithms and makes use of multi-core processors. Suricata starts with approx. 27.000 preconfigured signatures, and it allows to update the signatures from a repository.

Kitsune is an anomaly-detecting IDS which implements a number of neuronal networks to detect attacks [31]. To this end, Kitsune constructs a feature vector from each data packet, which is transferred to the set of neural networks. The output of the networks is forwarded to a voting mechanism. Kitsune is installed with neuronal networks and a voting mechanism that are pre-trained and preconfigured for services and network protocols that are also used by Smart Home devices.

Both IDS approaches provide the features needed according to Section IV: Both approaches are network-based IDS, which can be installed on a bridge between Internet and Smart Home network. Suricata and Kitsune use a modular architecture, which allows to implement the components shown in Figure 4. Finally, both IDS can be preconfigured and updated remotely by a security expert, which is needed by our security process.

Our Smart Home network contains four different devices:

- The *Amazon Dash-Button* connects to the Smart Home network when the button is pressed. Then it fetches the current time from an NTP server over the Internet, opens a HTTPS connection to the Amazon cloud and places an order for a specific product. After that, it disconnects from the network until the button is pressed again.
- The *Amazon Echo Dot* (2nd generation) is a smart speaker with a voice assistant. As soon as the speaker recognizes a wake-up word, it sends voice samples to the Amazon cloud for natural language processing. The response data that is sent to the smart speaker depends on the voice command. A wide number of activities from playing music to controlling other Smart Home devices is supported.
- The *Temperature Sensor* communicates via MQTT protocol [32] with a server that logs temperature readings. To this end, the Temperature Sensor resolves an IP address for a preconfigured domain from an DNS, and connects to this IP at port 1883.
- The *IP-Camera* is always connected to a server with the IP address 35.177.224.169. This server is used to establish connections between a client and the IP-Camera. Thus, the private user can connect to the IP-Camera from different networks.

TABLE I. STAGE 1: NORMAL USE

Device	Intervall	Duration	Interactions
Amazon Dash	10 minutes	1 sec.	6
Amazon Echo	10 minutes	5 minutes	6
IP-Camera	10 minutes	2 minutes	5
Temperature	10 seconds	-	60

B. Experimental Procedure

Our experiment takes place in three stages. In each stage, the Raspberry Pi records all data packets using tcpdump.

In the *first stage*, all four Smart Home devices were used for 60 minutes. Table I shows in which time intervals and for how long each device was used. For example, the first line means that the Dash Button was pressed every 10 minutes for one second. The Temperature Sensor sends the temperature automatically every 10 seconds. In this stage, we have recorded 112.602 packets. All packets refer to normal operations.

In the *second stage*, we have used nmap to perform a Portscan from the Internet to the Smart Home network. With a Portscan, a network appliance will be searched for ports that are open to the Smart Home network. A Portscan is a threat, because it identifies characteristics of a device. This includes the services it offers to the network, and the applications or software libraries listening to open ports. Our Portscan starts after 48 minutes of normal activity. In total, we have recorded 237.609 packets, and 131.137 of them belong to the attack.

In the *third stage*, we have executed a Telnet Attack from the Internet to the Smart Home network. Telnet is a plaintext protocol to access devices offering unencrypted services. For example, the Mirai Botnet used a Telnet Attack to infect Smart Home devices with a hard-coded admin password. To mimic a Telnet attack that was successful, we have extended the firmware of the Temperature Sensor with a simple Telnet server. Again, the attack starts after 48 minutes. We have recorded 114.501 packets, 1.107 of them belong to the attack.

After the execution of the stages, Suricata and Kitsune process the records. Thus, both IDS analyze the same data.

C. Experimental Results

In this section, we evaluate if the IDS approaches are (a) sufficiently accurate to increase the security of a Smart Home installation and (b) applicable for a private user. Regarding (a), we map the detection results to a confusion matrix. Such a matrix shows in each column the number of packets the IDS has classified as malicious or benign. Each row shows which packets were indeed malicious or benign. With an ideal IDS, only the upper left and lower right fields in the matrix contain numbers > 0.

1) Normal Operations: As Table II shows, Suricata identified all packets correctly as begin. In contrast, Kitsune has misclassified 43 packets as malicious.

2) Portscan Attack: Table III contains the classification of the packets from the Portscan. A Portscan might have a benign reason. For example, a network operator might want to confirm that all network services are well. On the other hand, a Portscan can be the first step of an attacker who wants to identify vulnerable services. Suricata has identified 48 packets from the Portscan as malicious, but 131.089 others as benign. During our experiments, we have learned that Sucicata does not consider a Portscan as an attack. Thus, depending on the point of view, either 48 or 131.089 packets were misclassified.

In contrast, Kitsune has classified 129.987 packets from the Portscan as malicious. Sending packets to all ports on all Smart Home devices differs from normal network operations. Kitsune recognizes this behavior as an anomaly and raises an alarm.

TABLE II. NORMAL OPERATION

		Suricata		Kitsune	
		Malicious	Benign	Malicious	Benign
Reality	Malicious	0	0	0	0
	Benign	0	112.602	43	112.559

TABLE III. PORTSCAN

		Suricata		Kitsune	
		Malicious	Benign	Malicious	Benign
Reality	Malicious	48	131.089	129.987	1.150
	Benign	0	106.472	178	106.294

3) Telnet Attack: No device must allow unencrypted login over the Internet. Thus, a Telnet access is an attack. As Table IV shows, Suricata has correctly identified all benign and malicious packets. To our surprise, Kitsune was unable to identify malicious packets. We think that this is because the unencrypted TCP packets sent by the Temperature Sensor with low data rate resemble the Telnet packets from our attack. Furthermore, Kitsune has classified 2.848 benign packets as malicious. In this case, we observed that Kitsune was confused by the user switching the radio station played by the Echo Dot. This caused an anomaly in the data transfers, but must be considered a false alarm.

TABLE IV. TELNET ATTACK

		Suricata		Kitsune	
		Malicious	Benign	Malicious	Benign
Reality	Malicious	1.117	0	0	1.117
	Benign	0	113.384	2.848	110.536

D. Discussion

Our observations indicate that signature-detecting IDS find attacks more reliably than anomaly-detecting ones. However, the preconfigured set of signatures stems from well-researched attacks from the past. Novel attacks might pose a challenge for signature-detecting approaches, until the signatures are updated. Furthermore, a Smart Home installation might contain specific or rare Smart Home devices that are not considered in the preconfigured set of signatures. This is particularly problematic, as our role "‘private user"’ cannot be assumed to successfully define IDS signatures, but needs an expert. Our experiments have also shown that anomaly-detecting IDS might generate many false positives. This is because some of our Smart Home devices change their communication behavior from time to time. For example, the Echo Dot might switch from reading the weather report to playing music.

Furthermore, the learning phase of an anomaly-detecting IDS in a Smart Home is not monitored by an expert. If the Smart Home network is already compromised when the IDS is put into operation, this state is considered as normal. Thus, there exist situations in which anomaly-detecting IDS cannot increase the network security. We conclude that signature-based IDS are better-suited to secure Smart Homes at the moment. However, the pre-configuration needs special attention.

Note that IDS are able to detect more complex attacks than Portscans or Telnet attacks, even before such attacks were successful. Nevertheless, it is a challenge already to present the private user with an understandable solution for simple attacks, which can be implemented without expert knowledge. In the case of an unsuccessful attack, generic solutions such as "Please check with the manufacturer how to proceed in case of a security incident" cannot be applied. For this reason, we assume that for complex attack attempts, involving an expert via Reporting becomes even more important.

VI. Conclusion

To secure a Smart Home installation is challenging. Typically, private users do not possess the IT-Security expertise needed to implement adequate security measures. Furthermore, almost all Smart Home devices hide security-related details from the user and do not allow to inspect its software.

In this paper, we have developed a concept to implement an Intrusion Detection System into a Smart Home installation without violating the user's privacy, and without requiring the user to possess in-depth expertise. We have analyzed in which way the network segmentation, system architecture, IT-Security Process and the contractual liabilities of an IDS must be adapted for that purpose. We have tested our concept with a series of experiments on four different Smart Home devices. Our experiments have indicated that at this moment, signature-detecting IDS, such as Suricata are suitable to secure Smart Home installations. In contrast, anomaly-detecting IDS like Kitsune are problematic. The anomaly detection algorithms tend to misclassify changing user behavior as an attack, but the user lacks the expertise needed to rule out false alarms.

As a part of our future work we will consider specific situations which occur when new Smart Home devices are added to the network segment or the devices change their behavior after a functional update.

References

[1] TI Media Limited, "philips smart light," https://www.trustedreviews.com/best/best-smart-lighting-3600693, accessed: 2020-08-14.

[2] CBS Interactive Inc., "c-net smart gardening," https://www.cnet.com/news/smart-garden-buying-guide/, accessed: 2019-06-06.

[3] IBM, "Security intelligence," https://securityintelligence.com/news/latest-mirai-malware-variant-contains-18-exploits-focuses-on-embedded-iot-devices/, accessed: 2020-08-19.

[4] PR Newswire Association LLC, "New reaper iot botnet leaves 378 million iot devices potentially vulnerable to hacking," https://www.prnewswire.com/news-releases/new-reaper-iot-botnet-leaves-378-million-iot-devices-potentially-vulnerable-to-hacking-300542019.html, accessed: 2020-08-19.

[5] M. Gajewski, J. M. Batalla, G. Mastorakis, and C. X. Mavromoustakis, "A distributed ids architecture model for smart home systems," *Cluster Computing*, pp. 1–11, 2017.

[6] E. Anthi, L. Williams, M. Słowińska, G. Theodorakopoulos, and P. Burnap, "A supervised intrusion detection system for smart home iot devices," *IEEE Internet of Things Journal*, pp. 9042–9053, 2019.

[7] B. L. R. Stojkoska and K. V. Trivodaliev, "A review of internet of things for smart home: Challenges and solutions," *Journal of Cleaner Production*, vol. 140, pp. 1454–1464, 2017.

[8] Wareable Ltd., "Amazon Echo voice control," https://www.the-ambient.com/guides/best-amazon-alexa-commands-280, accessed: 2019-02-25.

[9] C. Wilson, T. Hargreaves, and R. Hauxwell-Baldwin, "Benefits and risks of smart home technologies," *Energy Policy*, vol. 103, pp. 72–83, 2017.

[10] S. Kumar, "Survey of current network intrusion detection techniques," *Washington Univ. in St. Louis*, pp. 1–18, 2007.

[11] G. A. Marin, "Network security basics," *IEEE security & privacy*, vol. 3, no. 6, pp. 68–72, 2005.

[12] G. Carl, G. Kesidis, R. R. Brooks, and S. Rai, "Denial-of-service attack-detection techniques," *IEEE Internet computing*, vol. 10, no. 1, pp. 82–89, 2006.

[13] B. Harris and R. Hunt, "Tcp/ip security threats and attack methods," *Computer communications*, vol. 22, no. 10, pp. 885–897, 1999.

[14] H.-J. Liao, C.-H. R. Lin, Y.-C. Lin, and K.-Y. Tung, "Intrusion detection system: A comprehensive review," *Journal of Network and Computer Applications*, vol. 36, no. 1, pp. 16–24, 2013.

[15] A. Lazarevic, K. Vipin, and S. Jaideep, "Intrusion detection: A survey," in *Managing Cyber Threats. Massive Computing*. Springer, 2005, pp. 19–78.

[16] A. K. Saxena, S. Sinha, and P. Shukla, "General study of intrusion detection system and survey of agent based intrusion detection system," in *2017 International Conference on Computing, Communication and Automation (ICCCA)*. IEEE, 2017.

[17] P. Garcia-Teodoro, J. Diaz-Verdejo, G. Maciá-Fernández, and E. Vázquez, "Anomaly-based network intrusion detection: Techniques, systems and challenges," *computers & security*, 2009.

[18] G. Disterer, "Iso/iec 27000, 27001 and 27002 for information security management," 2013.

[19] Federal Office for Information Security, "BSI-Standard 200-2, IT-Grundschutz-Methodology," *https://www.bsi.bund.de*, 2017.

[20] O. of Government Commerce, *Introduction to ITIL*. Van Haren Publishing, 2005.

[21] J. Eloff and M. Eloff, "Information security architecture," *Computer Fraud & Security*, 2005.

[22] Federal Office for Information Security, "BSI-Standard 200-1, Information Security Management Systems (ISMS)," *https://www.bsi.bund.de*, 2018.

[23] S. S. I. Samuel, "A review of connectivity challenges in iot-smart home," in *2016 3rd MEC International conference on big data and smart city (ICBDSC)*. IEEE, 2016, pp. 1–4.

[24] R. A. Kemmerer and G. Vigna, "Intrusion detection: a brief history and overview," *Computer*, vol. 35, no. 4, pp. supl27–supl30, 2002.

[25] W. Ali, G. Dustgeer, M. Awais, and M. A. Shah, "Iot based smart home: Security challenges, security requirements and solutions," in *2017 23rd International Conference on Automation and Computing (ICAC)*. IEEE, 2017, pp. 1–6.

[26] N. Gupta, V. Naik, and S. Sengupta, "A firewall for internet of things," in *2017 9th International Conference on Communication Systems and Networks*. IEEE, 2017, pp. 411–412.

[27] B. Zhang, P.-L. P. Rau, and G. Salvendy, "Design and evaluation of smart home user interface: effects of age, tasks and intelligence level," *Behaviour & Information Technology*, vol. 28, no. 3, pp. 239–249, 2009.

[28] C. Beckel, H. Serfas, E. Zeeb, G. Moritz, F. Golatowski, and D. Timmermann, "Requirements for smart home applications and realization with ws4d-pipesbox." IEEE, 2011, pp. 1–8.

[29] S. Zamfir, T. Balan, I. Iliescu, and F. Sandu, "A security analysis on standard iot protocols," in *2016 International Conference on Applied and Theoretical Electricity (ICATE)*. IEEE, 2016.

[30] SolarWinds Worldwide, "7 Best Intrusion Detection Software and Latest IDS Systems," https://www.dnsstuff.com/network-intrusion-detection-software, accessed: 2020-06-18.

[31] Y. Mirsky, T. Doitshman, Y. Elovici, and A. Shabtai, "Kitsune: an ensemble of autoencoders for online network intrusion detection," *arXiv preprint arXiv:1802.09089*, 2018.

[32] wolfSSL Inc., "wolfMQTT Client Library," https://www.wolfssl.com/products/wolfmqtt, accessed: 2020-8-14.

Automatic Mapping of Vulnerability Information to Adversary Techniques

Otgonpurev Mendsaikhan
Graduate School of Informatics
Nagoya University
Nagoya, Japan
Email: ogo@net.itc.nagoya-u.ac.jp

Hirokazu Hasegawa
Information Security Office
Nagoya University

Yukiko Yamaguchi
and Hajime Shimada
Information Technology Center
Nagoya University

Abstract—**Along with the growth in the usage of software in almost every aspect of human life, the risks associated with software security vulnerabilities also increase. The number of average daily published software vulnerabilities exceeds the human ability to cope with it, hence various threat models to generalize the threat landscape has been developed. The most popular threat model MITRE ATT&CK proved to be a very useful tool for the security analyst to perform cyber threat intelligence, red and blue teaming, and so on. However, for his daily operation, the security analyst has to prioritize his defense by manually mapping the daily published software security vulnerabilities to the adversarial techniques listed in MITRE ATT&CK. In this paper, we propose a method to automatically map the software security vulnerability using a multi-label classification approach. We took the vector representation of the vulnerability description and classified it with various multi-label classification methods to evaluate in different measures and found out the LabelPowerset method with Multilayer Perceptron as base classifier performs best in our experiment.**

Keywords–Multi-label classification; MITRE ATT&CK; Security Vulnerability;

I. Introduction

The digital age has presented various opportunities to society along with different challenges. One of the biggest challenges comes with the risk of cyber-attack, data breach and loss of intellectual property, and so on. Software security vulnerability is one of the biggest factors behind these challenges. According to the US National Vulnerability Database (NVD), the total number of reported vulnerability as of June 2020 is 146,000 [1] and this number is increasing year by year. In 2019 alone 20,362 vulnerabilities are reported on NVD which is a 17.6% increase from 2018 (17,308) and 44.5% increase from 2017 (14,086) and the trend is likely to be upwards [2].

Given this large number of reported vulnerabilities, tracking individual vulnerabilities is nearly impossible. Hence, there have been various approaches and threat models developed to generalize the threat landscape and to ease the burden of a security analyst. One of the most commonly used approaches is a curated knowledge base called MITRE ATT&CK® that enlists adversary behaviors including their tactics and techniques based on real-world observations. It is a powerful framework commonly used as a threat model in adversary emulation, red and blue teaming, and cyber threat intelligence practices [3]. MITRE ATT&CK generalizes the adversary attack techniques and tactics based on the common weaknesses of the systems without mentioning specific product or vulnerability.

Even though the MITRE ATT&CK proved to be a useful framework, the need to identify the specific threat that individual vulnerability poses in the adversarial landscape still exists. In layperson's terms, MITRE ATT&CK is the playbook of steps that house robber would take in order to rob a house (e.g., find open access) and software security vulnerability is the weaknesses of the house security (e.g., unlocked door or broken window). For the effective defense, the house owner needs to combine this information, the most common approaches that house robbers use and weaknesses of his house, so that he can better understand the situation and prioritize his defenses.

In this paper, we propose a method to automatically map the vulnerability information to adversary techniques and tactics. Since a specific vulnerability can be used in more than one adversarial technique we believe developing a multi-label classification model that can infer the adversarial techniques to given vulnerability would be suitable. Since every vulnerability has associated textual description, we believe using the features of this text, a classic multi-label classification algorithm could produce a result that could be useful for a practical purpose. Hence, we experimented with various multi-label classification methods to evaluate the performance to automatically map the vector representations of vulnerability description to adversary techniques and tactics as prescribed in the MITRE ATT&CK framework.

Mapping individual vulnerabilities to adversarial tactics and techniques require a certain level of expertise and domain knowledge. Thus it may consume a considerable amount of time for the security analyst. To the best of our knowledge, currently, there are no published works that directly address this problem. Therefore we believe by utilizing existing tools and data, the task of mapping vulnerability information could be automated to spare the human analyst from manual labor. Hence, the goal of the paper is to seek the possibilities to automate the mapping of vulnerability descriptions to adversarial techniques by exploring the existing tools.

The specific contributions of the paper are as follows:

1) To propose an approach to automate the mapping of vulnerability description to adversarial technique.
2) Explore and experiment with various multi-label classification methods to compare the performance.

The remainder of this paper is organized as follows. Section II will review the related research and how this paper differs in its approach. In Section III, we will briefly discuss the background information to be used for this research. In Section IV, the experiment of the proposed multi-label classification and the corresponding evaluation will be discussed. Finally, we will conclude by discussing future work to extend this research in Section V.

II. Related work

There has been an attempt to use a multi-label classification approach to map cyber threat intelligence reports to adversarial techniques and tactics. Legoy et al. implemented a tool called rcATT, a system that predicts tactics and techniques related to given cyber threat reports and outputs the results using Structured Threat Information eXpression (STIX) format [4]. They focused to extract MITRE ATT&CK techniques and tactics from cyber threat reports and used simpler approaches for text representation and classification algorithms, whereas we focused to map the vulnerability description to the same framework, though using more neural and deep learning approaches.

Also, extracting general Tactics, Techniques, and Procedures (TTP) from cyber threat information is gaining some attention. Husari et al. developed a system to automate Cyber Threat Intelligence (CTI) analytics that learns attack patterns [5]. They combined Natural Language Processing (NLP) and Information Retrieval (IR) techniques to extract threat actions from threat reports based on their semantic relationships. Their focus was to extract actionable TTP from threat reports, whereas our focus is to identify the adversarial techniques that can exploit the specific vulnerability.

Apart from extracting an adversarial technique from textual documents, there have been some studies to directly map the malware behavior to the MITRE ATT&CK framework. Oosthoek et al. did the automated analysis of 951 unique families of Windows malware and mapped them onto the MITRE ATT&CK framework [6]. They generated a behavior signature of the malware in the sandbox and mapped the signature to the corresponding MITRE ATT&CK technique. Their work focused to map the malware based on its behavior to the adversarial techniques defined in MITRE ATT&CK framework whereas our focus is to map the vulnerability description that could be exploited by the adversary to the same techniques through its textual representation.

Some researchers have been working on the information provided by the MITRE ATT&CK framework to improve the adversarial predictions. Al-Shaer et al. presented their statistical machine learning analysis on Advanced Persistent Threat (APT) and software attack data reported by MITRE ATT&CK to infer and predict the techniques the adversary might use [7]. They associated adversarial techniques using hierarchical clustering with 95% confidence, providing statistically significant and explainable technique correlations. Our focus is to correlate individual vulnerability descriptions to the adversarial techniques and create a model that can be used to automatically map new vulnerability to the MITRE ATT&CK framework.

There have been also research on classifying the vulnerability information based on its textual description. Huang et al. proposed an automatic vulnerability classification model built on Term Frequency-Inverse Document Frequency (TF-IDF), Information Gain (IG), and deep neural network [8]. They validated their model with CVE descriptions of the National Vulnerability Database and compared them to the performances of SVM, Naive Bayes, and kNN algorithms. We are also attempting to classify the vulnerability information based on its textual description, but Huang et al. focused a multi-class classification that each vulnerability belongs to a specific category, whereas we attempt to classify a vulnerability into multiple adversarial techniques at the same time.

As listed above, there have been some attempts to utilize the MITRE ATT&CK framework or vulnerability classification in the academic context. However, most of the works took different directions such as [6] focused on mapping malware behavior on the adversarial technique, and [5] focused on extracting the TTPs. The only similar work [4] used some traditional methods to extract techniques from cyber threat reports, whereas we believe by using more neural and deep learning approaches, it would be possible to achieve better results.

III. Background

Since this study is on the intersection of different fields, the theoretical background knowledge is briefly explained in this section.

A. *Vulnerability Modeling*

There have been several attempts to standardize the reporting and modeling of software security vulnerabilities or weakness and threat landscape in general. In this section, we will discuss a few relevant schemes for this study.

1) Common Vulnerabilities and Exposures: Common Vulnerabilities and Exposures (CVE) is a list of entries, each containing an identification number, description, and at least one public reference for publicly known cybersecurity vulnerabilities [9]. CVE was launched in 1999 and now became the standard naming convention to address the interoperability and disparate databases and tools. CVE entries, also called CVEs, CVE IDs, and CVE numbers by the community provide common reference points so that cybersecurity products and services can speak the same language. CVE is an international cybersecurity community effort and each new CVE entry is assigned by CVE Numbering Authorities (CNAs).

The majority of the disclosed vulnerabilities are stored at the NVD for centralized vulnerability management purposes. The NVD is the U.S. government repository of standards-based vulnerability management data and is known as the de facto central database of software security vulnerabilities [10]. CVEs stored at NVD proved to be a useful resource for vulnerability management and overall cybersecurity-related research.

2) Common Attack Pattern Enumeration and Classification: Common Attack Pattern Enumeration and Classification (CAPEC) efforts provide a publicly available catalog of common attack patterns that helps users understand how adversaries exploit weaknesses in applications and other cyber-enabled capabilities [11]. CAPEC was established by the U.S Department of Homeland Security in 2007 and continuously evolved to include public participation and contributions. CAPEC defines "Attack Patterns" as descriptions of the common attributes and approaches employed by adversaries to exploit known weaknesses in cyber-enabled capabilities. Each attack pattern captures knowledge about how specific parts of an attack are designed and executed and gives guidance on ways to mitigate the attack's effectiveness.

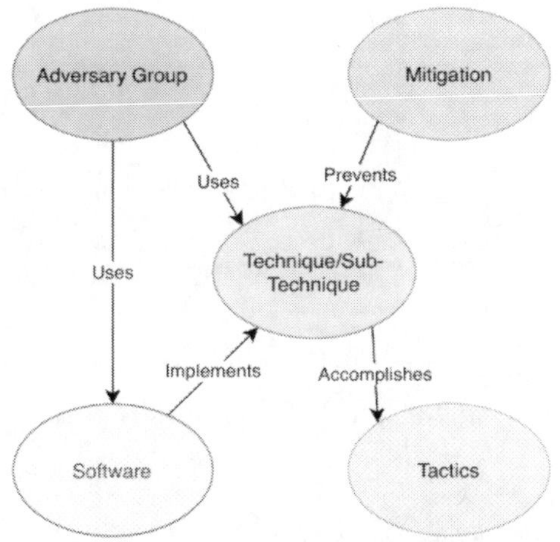

Figure 1. MITRE ATT&CK components and their relationship

CAPEC differs from MITRE ATT&CK framework in a way that it focuses on the application security and enumerates exploits against vulnerable systems, whereas the MITRE ATT&CK framework focuses on network defense and provides a contextual understanding of malicious behavior. CAPEC is mainly used for application threat modeling and developer training and education, whereas ATT&CK is used for comparing network defense capabilities and hunting new threats.

3) MITRE ATT&CK framework: Adversarial Tactics, Techniques, and Common Knowledge (ATT&CK) was created at MITRE corporation to systemically categorize adversary behavior in September 2013 [3]. It was originally designed as a project to document and categorize post-compromise adversary TTPs against Microsoft Windows systems and later added other platforms and called ATT&CK for Enterprise and publicly released in May 2015. Subsequently, complementary models such as PRE-ATT&CK, ATT&CK for Mobile, and ATT&CK for ICS has been published in 2017 and 2020. The ATT&CK framework consists of the following components:

- **Adversary group**: Known adversaries that are tracked and reported in threat intelligence reports.
- **Tactics**: Tactics represent the adversary's tactical objective: the reason for performing an action.
- **Technique/Sub-Technique**: Techniques represent "how" an adversary achieves its tactic, whereas Sub-technique further breaks down techniques into more specific descriptions of actions to reach the goal.
- **Software**: Software represents an instantiation of a technique or sub-technique at the software level.
- **Mitigation**: Mitigation represents security concepts and technologies to prevent a technique or sub-technique from being successfully executed.

The relationship between the components is visualized in Figure 1.

The MITRE ATT&CK framework is constantly enriched with techniques and sub-techniques. At the time of writing, there are 266 techniques/sub-techniques of 12 tactics in the MITRE ATT&CK Enterprise model, 174 techniques of 15 tactics in the PRE-ATT&CK model and 79 techniques of 13 tactics in ATT&CK for Mobile model.

B. Multi-label classification

Classification is the task of learning to classify the set of examples that are from a set of disjoint labels L, $|L| > 1$. If $|L| = 2$, then the learning problem is called a binary or single-label classification and if $|L| > 2$, it is a multi-class classification. In the case of multi-class classification, the example should correspond to a single class or label whereas multi-label classification the examples are associated with a set of labels $Y \subseteq L$ [12]. According to Madjarov et al. the multi-label classification methods could be of the following categories [13].

1) **Algorithm adaptation methods:** The existing machine learning algorithms that are adapted, extended, and customized for multi-label classification problem. The examples include: boosting, k-nearest neighbors, decision trees, and neural networks.
2) **Problem transformation methods:** This method transforms the multi-label classification into one or more single-label classification or regression problems. It is further divided into categories as binary relevance, label power-set, and pair-wise methods.
3) **Ensemble classification:** The ensemble methods are developed on top of existing problem transformation or algorithm adaptation methods. The examples include Random k-label sets (RAkEL) and ensembles of pruned sets (EPS) etc.

C. Evaluation measures of multi-label classification

Since the multi-label classification task is different from the traditional binary classification, the evaluation metrics to measure the performance of the method also differs. The multi-label classification measures generally fall into the following categories according to [13].

1) Example based measures
2) Label based measures
3) Ranking based measures

The evaluation measures used in this study are briefly discussed below. In the definitions, y_i denotes the set of true labels for example x_i and $h(x_i)$ denotes the set of predicted labels for the same examples. N is the number of examples and Q denotes the total number of possible class labels.

1) Subset Accuracy: Subset Accuracy, also called as Exact Match Ratio is the most strict metric, indicating the percentage of samples that have all their labels classified correctly. It can be calculated as shown in (1):

$$Accuracy(h) = \frac{1}{N} \sum_{i=1}^{N} I(h(x_i) = y_i) \tag{1}$$

where $I(true) = 1$ and $I(false) = 0$.

2) Micro averaged F1 score: Since the classification is on multiple labels the results have to be averaged out. Micro-precision and micro-recall are the measures averaged over all the example/label pair. In the definitions below TP_j, TN_j denote the number of True Positive and True Negative, FP_j,

FN_j denote the number of False Positive and False Negative examples per label λ_j when considered as binary classification.

$$Precision = \frac{\sum_{j=1}^{Q} TP_j}{\sum_{j=1}^{Q} TP_j + \sum_{j=1}^{Q} FP_j} \tag{2}$$

$$Recall = \frac{\sum_{j=1}^{Q} TP_j}{\sum_{j=1}^{Q} TP_j + \sum_{j=1}^{Q} FN_j} \tag{3}$$

Micro averaged F1 Score is the harmonic mean between micro-precision and micro-recall.

$$F1 = \frac{2 \times microPrecision \times microRecall}{microPrecision + microRecall} \tag{4}$$

3) Macro averaged F1 score: Macro-precision and macro-recall are the measures averaged across all labels and defined as shown in (5) and (6).

$$Precision = \frac{1}{Q}\sum_{j=1}^{Q} \frac{TP_j}{TP_j + FP_j} \tag{5}$$

$$Recall = \frac{1}{Q}\sum_{j=1}^{Q} \frac{TP_j}{TP_j + FN_j} \tag{6}$$

Macro-F1 is the harmonic mean between precision and recall where the average is calculated per label and then averaged across all labels. If P_j and R_j are the precision and recall for all $\lambda_j \in h(x_i)$ from $\lambda_j \in y_i$ then Macro F1 is defined as in (7):

$$F1 = \frac{1}{Q}\sum_{j=1}^{Q} \frac{2 \times P_j \times R_j}{P_j + R_j} \tag{7}$$

4) Hamming loss: Hamming loss evaluates how many times an example-label pair is misclassified i.e., fraction of labels that are incorrectly predicted.

$$HammingLoss(h) = \frac{1}{N}\sum_{i=1}^{N} \frac{1}{Q} \mid h(x_i) \Delta y_i \mid \tag{8}$$

where Δ stands for the symmetric difference between two sets. The smaller the Hamming loss better the model performance.

5) Ranking loss: Ranking loss evaluates the average fraction of label pairs that are reversely ordered for the particular example.

$$RankingLoss(h) = \frac{1}{N}\sum_{i=1}^{N} \frac{\mid D_i \mid}{\mid y_i \mid\mid \bar{y_i} \mid} \tag{9}$$

where

$D_i = \{(\lambda_m, \lambda_n) \mid f(x_i, \lambda_m) \leq f(x_i, \lambda_n), (\lambda_m, \lambda_n) \in y_i \times \bar{y_i})\}$, while $\bar{y_i})\}$ denotes the complementary set of y in L. The smaller the Ranking loss better the model performance.

IV. Experiment

Using the background information of Section III we conducted the experiment on the multi-label classification of vulnerability information.

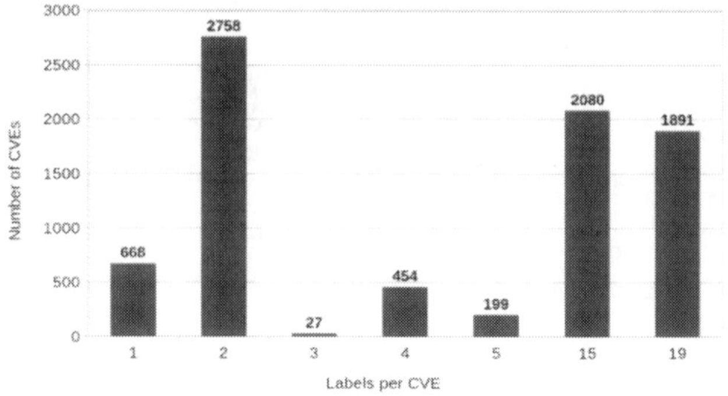

Figure 2. CVE to Label mapping of the dataset

A. Experimental Dataset

The European Union Agency for Cybersecurity (ENISA) published a report in December 2019 titled State of Vulnerabilities 2018/2019 [14]. The report aimed to provide an insight into both the opportunities and limitations of the vulnerability ecosystem. They collected in total 27,471 vulnerability information published during 1st January 2018 to 30th September 2019 from various data sources. As part of the analysis of the collected data, authors mapped the CVEs to the MITRE ATT&CK technique using the common CAPEC information found in both NVD and ATT&CK. The authors generously made available the dataset they've analyzed [15] and we utilized the CVE information mapped to MITRE ATT&CK tactics and techniques for training and testing the multi-label classification model.

The ENISA report dataset contained 8,077 CVEs that are mapped to 52 unique MITRE ATT&CK techniques or in this instance labels. The dataset cardinality (mean of the number of labels of the instances) is 9.43 and density (mean of the number of labels of the instances that belong to the dataset divided by the number of dataset labels) is 0.18. The dataset CVEs are distributed into 7 discrete buckets of technique combinations. For example, there are 668 CVEs that have a single label or technique associated with it and 1,891 CVEs that have 19 labels assigned to them. Figure 2 shows this distribution.

From the ENISA report dataset of 8,077 examples, we held out 200 examples to validate and analyze the trained model. The remaining 7,877 examples were used to train and evaluate the various multi-label classification methods.

In this study, we focused to do multi-label classification based on the textual features of the CVE descriptions. The mean length of the CVE description is 368 characters and minimum/maximum lengths are 40 and 3,655 characters long. The oldest CVE updated during the data collection period is CVE-2007-6763 and the newest is CVE-2019-9975.

B. Text representation

In order to conduct the multi-label classification, the given text needs to be converted into numerical vectors, also known as embeddings. Conventionally, vector embeddings were achieved through shallow algorithms such as Bag of Words (BoW) or Term Frequency-Inverse Document Frequency (TF-IDF). These approaches have been superseded by predictive representation models such as Word2Vec [16],

GloVe [17], and so on. Since the utilization of deep neural networks has been proven to be superior in different fields, various studies have adopted deep neural models to embed the text into vector space, such as Facebook's InferSent [18] and Universal Sentence Encoder (USE) from Google Research. Perone et al. evaluated different sentence embeddings and Universal Sentence Encoder outperformed InferSent in terms of semantic relatedness and textual similarity tasks [19]. Therefore, for the purpose of this research, Universal Sentence Encoder has been utilized to generate the vector embeddings of the text.

Since the sentence embeddings from USE produce good task performance with little task-specific training data, a Deep Averaging Network (DAN)-based USE model introduced in [20] has been used to represent the CVE descriptions in numerical vectors, so that multi-label classification methods could be applied. The model takes English sentences of variable lengths as input and produces 512 fixed-dimensional vector representations of the sentences as output [21].

C. Model selection

The CVE descriptions of the dataset have been initially converted into numerical vectors using USE. Every CVE description becomes a 512 fixed-dimensional vector that can be treated as features for the classifier. To determine the suitable model to map the vulnerability description to MITRE ATT&CK techniques we experimented with 1 Algorithm Adaptation, 3 Problem Transformation, and 1 Ensemble multi-label classification methods using the open-source library scikit-multilearn [22]. The experimented methods are listed below.

- **Multi-label k-nearest neighbors (MlkNN)** is the adaptation of the popular k-nearest neighbors (kNN) algorithm to the multi-label classification task and an example of Algorithm adaptation method. We estimated the number of neighbors k to be most optimal when $k = 3$ where $1 \leq k \leq 30$ when optimized for macro-average F1 measure.
- **LabelPowerset** is a Problem Transformation method that transforms a multi-label problem to a multi-class problem with 1 multi-class classifier trained on all unique label combinations. It maps each combination to a unique id number and performs multi-class classification using the classifier as a multi-class classifier and combination ids as classes.
- **ClassifierChain** is also a Problem Transformation method. The classifiers are linked along a chain where the i-th classifier deals with the binary relevance problem associated with its label. The feature space of each link in the chain is extended with the 0/1 label associations of all previous links.
- **BinaryRelevance** is the well known one-against-all method. It learns one classifier for each label using all the examples labeled with that label as positive and remaining as negative. And while making a prediction each binary classifier predicts whether its label is relevant for the given example or not. It is an example of the Problem Transformation method.
- **RAndom k-labELsets multi-label classifier (RAkELd)** is an Ensemble method that divides the label space into equal partitions of size k, trains a LabelPowerset classifier per partition and predicts by summing the result of all trained classifiers.

The above-mentioned methods use traditional classification algorithms for the multi-label classification task. Since the utilization of neural networks has been proven to be superior in almost every task we also experimented with more neural approaches as multi-label classification algorithms. Since the multi-label classification task of our experiment doesn't require the sequential input or memory state of the input we experimented with a simple Multilayer Perceptron (MLP) neural model to conduct the classification. Szymański et al. included a wrapper in a scikit-multilearn library that allows any Keras or PyTorch compatible backend to be used to solve multi-label problems through problem-transformation methods [23]. We utilized it to conduct the same experiment with neural methods. The following lists the neural methods we used along with their basic parameters.

- **LabelPowerset (neural)** LabelPowerset method with the Multilayer Perceptron as the base classifier. It has 2 hidden layers and the softmax function is used for activation.
- **BinaryRelevance (neural)** BinaryRelevance method with the Multilayer Perceptron as base classifier. It has 2 hidden layers and the sigmoid function is used for activation.

In the next section, we will discuss the evaluation results of these different methods.

D. Model Evaluation

Since the dataset is limited in size we evaluated the models with 10-fold cross validation method. The evaluations results as the average of 10-fold validation is listed in Table 1.

From the results listed in Table 1, we could see that LabelPowerset using the neural model as base classifier has the best results in all except one evaluation measures we selected. In terms of Hamming loss, the neural BinaryRelevance has a better score, but neural LabelPowerset is second in place and outperforms in every other measure. Hence, neural LabelPowerset model has been chosen as the best performing model.

There is no rule-of-thumb for "good" multi-label classification result and it depends upon various factors such as classification domain, dataset, and evaluation measures. However, in order to understand the efficiency of the model we compared our results with the results published in [24] in which Pakrashi et al. did a benchmarking study on various multi-label classification algorithms using eleven different datasets. When compared with their results it has revealed that the least performance in our experiment is better than the best performing results of 4 of the 11 datasets in the same measure as Macro Averaged F1 score. Hence, we concluded that the experimental results are good enough to be considered for discussion.

E. Model analysis

After training and testing the best performing model we conducted an in-depth analysis of the model using the held-out validation data. A total of 200 examples were held out from the training dataset to validate and analyze the best performing

TABLE I. EXPERIMENT RESULT.

Algorithm	*Accuracy score*	Micro Average *Precision*	Micro Average *Recall*	Micro Average *F1 Score*	Macro Average *Precision*	Macro Average *Recall*	Macro Average *F1 Score*	*Hamming loss*	*Ranking loss*
MlkNN	0.6138	0.7376	0.6211	0.6740	0.6507	0.5081	0.5576	0.1079	0.3595
LabelPowerset	0.6133	0.7186	0.5741	0.6369	0.5753	0.5412	0.5174	0.1157	0.3654
ClassifierChain	0.5036	0.5978	0.6208	0.6089	0.4209	0.4715	0.4243	0.1427	0.4298
BinaryRelevance	0.3744	0.5798	0.6576	0.6158	0.4638	0.6193	0.4907	0.1471	0.3263
RakelD	0.4237	0.6255	0.6216	0.6230	0.5021	0.5884	0.5024	0.1340	0.3411
LabelPowerset (neural)	**0.7432**	0.7532	0.7380	**0.7452**	0.6827	0.6264	**0.6396**	0.0911	**0.2448**
BinaryRelevance (neural)	0.5538	0.7789	0.7100	0.7426	0.6924	0.5957	0.6279	**0.0883**	0.2885

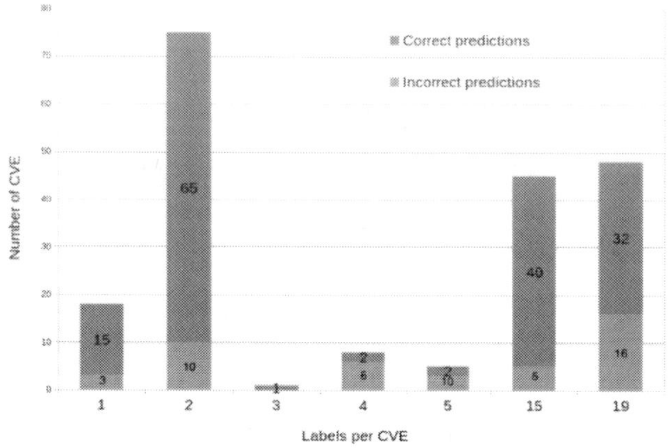

Figure 3. CVE to Label mapping of validation dataset of 200 examples

model. Neural LabelPowerset model trained and tested with 7,877 examples is used to predict the labels for the previously unseen 200 examples. Figure 3 depicts the prediction result in terms of distributions of CVEs per label. In this experiment, we considered the correct prediction only if all the expected labels are correctly predicted.

From Figure 3, it could be seen that when the number of labels to be predicted increases, the chances of incorrect prediction also increases. We believe such bias could be as a result of the skewed training data. Since the experiment dataset is small in size and limited to only 52 adversarial techniques of 266 techniques/sub-techniques of MITRE ATT&CK Enterprise model and distributed to only 7 different buckets of the number of labels (see Figure 2), the model tends to inadequately classify the examples. However, based on this analysis, we believe with a comprehensive training dataset, the multi-label classification method could be applied to the mapping of vulnerabilities to the adversarial techniques.

V. CONCLUSION

In this paper, we proposed an approach to automatically map the vulnerability information to adversary techniques in the cybersecurity context. We converted vulnerability descriptions into vector space and experimented with various multi-label classification methods to identify the most suitable method to map the vulnerability into MITRE ATT&CK adversarial techniques. We used 8,077 examples from open datasets prepared by ENISA, of which 7,877 have been used to train and test 7 multi-label classification methods in 9 evaluation measures. We also did a comprehensive analysis of the remaining 200 examples as a prediction only task using the best performing neural LabelPowerset model.

Due to the partial nature of the experimental dataset, the experimental result could not be fully tested in real-life scenarios. However, in the given dataset, the chosen methods show good performance, indicating a comprehensive dataset may yield a production-ready system that could be used to automate and prioritize the cyber defense operations.

In the future, we would like to build a comprehensive dataset by correlating CAPEC information of the vulnerability with MITRE ATT&CK techniques and create a model that can be used in production systems.

REFERENCES

[1] National Vulnerability Database, 2020 (accessed June 1, 2020). [Online]. Available: https://nvd.nist.gov/general/nvd-dashboard

[2] D. Bekerman and S. Yerushalmi, The State of Vulnerabilities in 2019, 2020 (accessed June 10, 2020). [Online]. Available: https://www.imperva.com/blog/the-state-of-vulnerabilities-in-2019/

[3] B. E. Strom, A. Applebaum, D. P. Miller, K. C. Nickels, A. G. Pennington, and C. B. Thomas, "MITRE ATT&CK®: Design and philosophy," The MITRE Corporation, Tech Report, 2020.

[4] V. Legoy, M. Caselli, C. Seifert, and A. Peter, "Automated retrieval of att&ck tactics and techniques for cyber threat reports," ArXiv, vol. abs/2004.14322, 2020.

[5] G. Husari, E. Al-Shaer, M. Ahmed, B. Chu, and X. Niu, "Ttpdrill: Automatic and accurate extraction of threat actions from unstructured text of cti sources," in Proceedings of the 33rd Annual Computer Security Applications Conference, ser. ACSAC 2017. New York, NY, USA: Association for Computing Machinery, 2017, p. 103–115. [Online]. Available: https://doi.org/10.1145/3134600.3134646

[6] K. Oosthoek and C. Doerr, SoK: ATT&CK Techniques and Trends in Windows Malware, 12 2019, pp. 406–425.

[7] R. Al-Shaer, J. M. Spring, and E. Christou, "Learning the associations of mitre att&ck adversarial techniques," 2020.

[8] G. Huang, Y. Li, Q. Wang, J. Ren, Y. Cheng, and X. Zhao, "Automatic classification method for software vulnerability based on deep neural network," IEEE Access, vol. 7, 2019, pp. 28 291–28 298.

[9] Common Vulnerabilities and Exposures, 2020 (accessed June 25, 2020). [Online]. Available: https://cve.mitre.org/

[10] National Vulnerability Database, 2020 (accessed June 22, 2020). [Online]. Available: http://nvd.nist.org

[11] About CAPEC, 2020 (accessed June 25, 2020). [Online]. Available: https://capec.mitre.org/about/index.html

[12] G. Tsoumakas and I. Katakis, "Multi-label classification: An overview," IJDWM, vol. 3, 2007, pp. 1–13.

[13] G. Madjarov, D. Kocev, D. Gjorgjevikj, and S. Deroski, "An extensive experimental comparison of methods for multi-label learning," Pattern Recogn., vol. 45, no. 9, Sep. 2012, p. 3084–3104. [Online]. Available: https://doi.org/10.1016/j.patcog.2012.03.004

[14] V. Katos, S. Rostami, P. Bellonias, N. Davies, A. Kleszcz, S. Faily, A. Spyros, A. Papanikolaou, C. Ilioudis, and K. Rantos, "State of vulnerabilities 2018/2019," European Union Agency for Cybersecurity (ENISA), Tech Report, 2019.

[15] ENISA's state of vulnerabilities 2018/2019 report, 2019 (accessed May 10, 2020). [Online]. Available: https://github.com/enisaeu/vuln-report/

[16] T. Mikolov, K. Chen, G. Corrado, and J. Dean, "Efficient estimation of word representations in vector space," in 1st International Conference on Learning Representations, 2013. [Online]. Available: http://arxiv.org/abs/1301.3781

[17] J. Pennington, R. Socher, and C. D. Manning, "Glove: Global vectors for word representation," in Empirical Methods in Natural Language Processing (EMNLP), 2014, pp. 1532–1543. [Online]. Available: http://www.aclweb.org/anthology/D14-1162

[18] InferSent, 2018 (accessed January 10, 2020). [Online]. Available: https://github.com/facebookresearch/InferSent

[19] C. S. Perone, R. Silveira, and T. S. Paula, "Evaluation of sentence embeddings in downstream and linguistic probing tasks," CoRR, vol. abs/1806.06259, 2018. [Online]. Available: http://arxiv.org/abs/1806.06259

[20] D. Cer, Y. Yang, S. Kong, N. Hua, N. Limtiaco, R. S. John, N. Constant, M. Guajardo-Cespedes, S. Yuan, C. Tar, Y. Sung, B. Strope, and R. Kurzweil, "Universal sentence encoder," CoRR, vol. abs/1803.11175, 2018. [Online]. Available: http://arxiv.org/abs/1803.11175

[21] universal-sentence-encoder, 2018 (accessed January 11, 2020). [Online]. Available: https://tfhub.dev/google/universal-sentence-encoder/2

[22] Multi-Label Classification in Python, 2018 (accessed May 15, 2020). [Online]. Available: http://scikit.ml/

[23] P. Szymański and T. Kajdanowicz, "A scikit-based Python environment for performing multi-label classification," ArXiv e-prints, Feb. 2017.

[24] A. Pakrashi, D. Greene, and B. MacNamee, "Benchmarking multi-label classification algorithms," in 24th Irish Conference on Artificial Intelligence and Cognitive Science (AICS'16), Dublin, Ireland, 20-21 September 2016. CEUR Workshop Proceedings, 2016.

Introduction to being a Privacy Detective: Investigating and Comparing Potential Privacy Violations in Mobile Apps Using Forensic Methods

Stefan Kiltz and Robert Altschaffel and Thorsten Lucke and Jana Dittmann

Otto von Guericke University Magdeburg
Magdeburg, Germany
Email: Kiltz@iti.cs.uni-magdeburg.de

Abstract—**This paper discusses means to evaluate the potential impact of data flows caused by the use of smartphone apps (*app*lications) on the privacy of the user. While the data flows are often caused by trackers, permissions set the framework on which data can flow between the smartphones and the remote party. Hence, we devise a concept to examine privacy violations caused by trackers and permissions in mobile apps and to render the results of said examination more comparable and reliable based on the characteristics of the examination methods (custody, examined forensic data streams and type of communication). We define two different examination scenarios in which this approach can be deployed and conduct practical tests in these two scenarios. For the first scenario, the concept is applied to the static evaluation of 8 exemplary mobile apps running on the Android platform using 3 different methods (*Exodus Privacy*, *Exodus Standalone* and *AppChecker*) identifying 162 permissions and 42 trackers in total. The second scenario employs these three methods in order to examine the extent to which three mobile browsers reveal information towards the respective developers. Our main contributions are the application of a model of the forensic process to the examination of the loss of potential privacy due to the use of mobile apps in order to provide comparability of the findings. In addition, a proposal for a visualization scheme capable of displaying test results from privacy examinations covering a large number of examination items is proposed.**

Keywords–Privacy Measurement; Data sovereignty.

I. INTRODUCTION

Privacy and data protection are very relevant topics from a legal and data sovereignty perspective. While the legal perspective is no part of this paper, the *Principles relating to processing of personal data* of Article 5 of the GDPR[1] provide a useful overview on the topic of privacy related data. These principles include *data minimisation*, *storage limitation* and *lawfulness, fairness and transparency* - principles often not used in app deployment, most apps contain trackers [2].

This paper aims at supporting privacy and data protection by providing the user with methods to identify data flows caused by the use of mobile apps (executed on the smartphone), which could threaten the privacy. Knowledge about these data flows is essential to obtain some degree of data sovereignty. These data flows could be used by third parties to identify customers, create profile, send targeted advertisement (including those leading to generally known negative social consequences like advertisement for alcohol or micro-targeting during political campaigns) or exclude customers from services based on their liquidity. In addition, these trackers use unnecessary resources (e.g., CPU power, bandwidth, energy) without a benefit to the user and the environment. This increased need for resources also leads to a more negative global ecological footprint.

The discussion whether certain data flows violate the right of privacy of an user relies on legal background and a review of the relevant laws. However, this paper focuses on a purely technical approach based on the technical properties we can identify. However, knowledge about the presence of these data flows is by itself a necessary requirement to achieve data sovereignty. This is of relevance when deciding whether an app is appropriate for a given use case, e.g., the use in an educational or corporate setting. In these scenarios, a teacher or IT specialist could be the data detective identifying various trackers.

This knowledge can be used to prevent privacy-related leakage. Users can prevent trackers by using various blocking mechanisms like NoScript [3] or the use of a Pi-hole [4]. However, these mechanisms all have their limitations and require installation and configuration for use. The knowledge about tracker detection techniques has other uses; developers of apps can also use the knowledge about trackers within their apps to remove such trackers, introduced by e.g., software development kits or libraries.

A necessary property to identify trackers is the destination of a given data flow. During the course of this paper, we identify two different potential destinations for data flows common in the use of mobile apps:

- Data flow to the service provider (DF_{fp})
- Data flow to a third party (DF_{tp})

The second property catches the aspect of whether the data flow is necessary in order for the app to provide the functionality. Either the app is able to provide the functionality without this data data or it is not. Hence, we can further specify the potential data flows:

- Data flow to the service provider necessary for the functionality of the app ($DF_{fp.req}$)
- Data flow to the service provider not necessary for the functionality of the app ($DF_{fp.nrq}$)
- Data flow to a third party necessary for the functionality of the app ($DF_{tp.req}$)
- Data flow to a third party not necessary for the functionality of the app ($DF_{tp.nrq}$)

A common example for those data flows unnecessary to provide the functionality intended by the user include *trackers*.

These trackers are embedded into many apps in order to gather data about the user and the use patterns of the given tools. This is often used as a foundation for the identification of users which can in turn be used for ads targeted at specific users. These trackers pose a risk to the privacy of the user. In *disconnect-tracking-protection* [5] a detailed description based on a technical review is given as to why a specific item is listed as a tracker and might be used as guideline to discern whether the data flows identified using the approach in this paper are threats to privacy.

For the sake of simplicity, we refer to any data flow not necessary to provide the functionality intended by the user as a *tracker* during the course of this paper. Various tools designed to identify these trackers are available with an overview on these provided in Section II-C. A fundamental problem is that the results provided by these tools are not comparable. This increases the difficulty of verifying the results provided by one such tool through the use of a different tool. This is due to different underlying criteria used for the identification of trackers and a varying degree of documentation provided to the examiner by these tools. This paper explores the use of a structured investigative approach as used in the field of computer forensics to achieve this comparability in finding unnecessary data flows.

However, the absence of any unnecessary data flows does not guarantee the absence of risk for the user's privacy. For example, the service provider could aggregate $DF_{fp.req}$ or $DF_{tp.req}$ over the course of various requests and compile them to form an user profile. However, the data that could be transferred is limited by the access the specific app has to the operating system. This is controlled by permissions. Hence, identifying these permissions offers additional information relevant to judge potential data protection violations.

In general, we identify two different scenarios in which the approach presented in this paper can be used:

- Examination Scenario 1 (**ES1**): one (or multiple) app(s) are examined for trackers and permissions
- Examination Scenario 2 (**ES2**): various alternative apps for a specific use case are compared with regards to potential privacy violations

Due to the complexity of this topic this paper focuses on the identification of the four formerly defined data flows during the use of mobile apps as well as the permissions used by these apps. In order to achieve this goal, this paper is structured as follows: Section II gives an overview on the domain investigated in this paper, the current tools used to identify trackers and permissions in mobile apps and the structured approach to perform an investigation as used in the field of computer forensics. Section III applies the structured approach of a forensic investigation to the identification of trackers (and data flows in general). This includes a discussion on how the tools detecting trackers and identifying permissions work in detail and how this type of examination is currently conducted showing the challenges of the specific domains in question. Section IV describes the creation of a testbed which includes the tool sets necessary to conduct such an investigation following the structured approach. It also shows how this testbed is then used to identify and categorize various data flows during the use of eight selected exemplary mobile apps in **ES1**. In addition, three exemplary selected different browser are compared as an example for **ES2** providing a more in-depth comparison on what the achieved results reveal about potential violation of the user privacy by the use of these apps. This paper closes with an overview and an outlook provided in Section V.

II. FUNDAMENTALS

This section provides some background helpful to follow the discussions laid out during the subsequent chapters. An overview on the various approaches to evaluate the privacy of websites and apps is provided. This includes the identification of various data flows. In addition, the properties specific to apps in the mobile domain affecting the identification of trackers are explored.

A. Exemplary selection of approaches to evaluate the privacy of websites and apps

Several approaches to determine the privacy and IT security of websites exist. In [6] a system to improve the privacy and IT security is described, which analyses selected privacy and IT security aspects. A special feature of the resulting analysis site *privacyscore.org* [7] is that arbitrary users can supply a single URL to be tested or a list thereof (crowd-sourced list). The system design allows revisiting those existing URL(s) and thus enables an analysis of the privacy and IT situation of said URL(s) over time and for privacyscore.org users alike.

One empirical study to systematically determine the privacy and IT security of apps for the android operating environment is described in [2]. It reveals that most apps contain trackers, that the tracking is category-sensitive and a highly trans-national phenomenon. A guideline on how Apps are tested for trackers is provided by various sources. One example includes *mobilsicher.de* [8] which provides an outline of their approach in German.

B. Mobile Apps

The topics discussed in this paper are also relevant in the domain of desktop computer systems. Indeed, some of the concepts presented in this paper can be transferred to this domain. However, for the sake of brevity, this paper focuses on the mobile domain in order to discuss some of the specific challenges of this domain when investigating potential privacy leaks. Hence, for the course of this paper, an app(*lication*) refers to any type of application that is executable on a smartphone and which is distinguishable from the operating environment (for example in that it is downloaded or updated separately).

Apps use the resources of the smartphone as provided by an underlying operating system. During the course of this paper, all apps examined and methods used are running on the Android platform [9]. This does not represent any inclination of the authors towards this platform nor should it indicate that the methods used in this paper are not applicable to different platforms. In the case of Android operating systems, the access of the apps is restricted by the use of various permissions. Permissions describe the access rights granted for a specific app. In essence, they restrict access to given information. Examples include the access to camera or the address book. Hence, these permissions are useful to discern which information could be communication within the specific data flows.

C. Methods to identify data flows

Identifying data flows forms the foundation of identifying potential privacy violations. Two principal approaches exist to identify such data flows in mobile apps. These approaches are implemented in various tools but these tools represent insulated solutions rather than a comprehensive approach providing comparable results.

a) Static Analysis: Static Analysis describes analysis performed by investigating the binary representation of an app. This binary representation can be interpreted in order to identify certain functions. Trackers for example usually employ a set of specific function calls or employ communication to certain known servers. Such patterns are referred to as signatures. As long as the signature for a given tracker is known, it can be identified. The complexity of this interpretation depends on the complexity of the programming technology used to develop the app. Some apps might use standardized development tools while others might have their binary formats obfuscated to prevent such analysis.

A tool implementing static analysis of mobile apps is *Exodus Privacy* [10]. The characteristics and the operations methods of this tool are described in III-B. The tool is then used during the case study as described in IV-B providing insight into its use and usefulness.

b) Dynamic Analysis: Dynamic Analysis investigates the runtime behaviour of an app during its execution. In the context of this paper, this mostly includes the communication behaviour of the app. Hence, the data flows are observed while they occur. A tool useful for the capturing of data flows is *Wireshark* [11].

c) Specifics of mobile apps relevant during examination: There are some factors which impact the capabilities to examine apps in the mobile domain:

- **Prop1**: *large amount of background processes*: in general, many background processes are active on a mobile system implying the presence of background noise which must be taken into account
- **Prop2**: *very low control over operating system*: mobile operating systems generally limit the user in the access to various system information
- **Prop3**: *standardization of development tools*: apps are developed using standard frameworks and languages which makes analysis easier
- **Prop4**: *reliance on system functions*: apps often use libraries and operating system calls which are protected or obfuscated against analysis
- **Prop5**: *apps contain a manifest*: this gives some information about the use of certain system permission by the app, but practical tests have shown that these are not necessarily conclusive
- **Prop6**: *various variants*: there are usually various variants of apps in the mobile domain compiled for various architectures and operating systems with a potentially different behaviour in regards to data flows
- **Prop7**: *App bundles*: sometimes these different variants are combined into an App Bundle which includes various resources necessary in order to create a device specific installation

Prop1 and **Prop2** have a negative impact on the capabilities to perform dynamic analysis in the context of mobile apps, while **Prop5** eases the complexity of of detecting permissions during static analysis. **Prop6** and **Prop7** raise the difficulty of obtaining the correct binary for analysis in the first place. Here, the use of checksums and other methods in order to identify the specific binaries is necessary.

D. The structured approach of Computer Forensics

According to [12] computer forensics is *The use of scientifically derived and proven methods toward the preservation, collection, validation, identification, analysis, interpretation, documentation and presentation of digital evidence derived from digital sources for the purpose of facilitating or furthering the reconstruction of events found to be criminal, or helping to anticipate unauthorized actions shown to be disruptive to planned operations.*

Such an approach implies the use of proven methods in a structured process in order to document various traces with the overall aim to present them in a manner which enables a person reviewing the result to form a well-founded conclusion based on these traces. When investigating potential privacy violations during the use of mobile apps the same traceability and comparability of the results is intended. Hence, methods from the field of computer forensics could potentially be used to achieve this.

In general, computer forensic investigations follow a structured process. This process is often described by forensic process models. During the course of this paper, we employ a forensic process model based on the one described in [13] (which is based on [14]) as it offers some advantages for the task at hand.

This forensic process model structures the forensic process along the lines of six *Investigation Steps*. A main advantage of this forensic process model is the inclusion of a Strategic Preparation (**SP**) which covers *measures taken by the operator of an IT-system in order to support a forensic investigation prior to an incident* [14].

The forensic traces originate from three distinct forensic *Data Streams* as described in [15]. These data streams identify the various sources of forensic evidence within the forensic process and assign general properties to these sources:

- Non-volatile Memory: *Memory inside a computing unit which maintains its content after the unit is disconnected from its respective power supply.* (denoted as DS_T in this paper)
- Volatile Memory: *Memory inside a computing unit which loses its content after the unit is disconnected from its respective power supply.* (denoted as DS_M)
- Communication: *All the data transmitted to other computing units via communication interfaces.* (denoted as DS_N)

The potential traces relevant during the forensic investigation are categorized into nine *Data Types* based on how the respective data is handled during the forensic process. The following relevant Data Types are identified in [13]:

- hardware data (**DT1**): *Data in a computing unit which is not, or only in a limited way, influenced by software.*

- raw data (**DT2**): *A sequence of bits within the data streams of a computing systems not (yet) interpreted.*
- details about data (**DT3**): *Data added to other data, stored within the annotated chunk of data or externally*
- configuration data (**DT4**): *Data which can be changed by software and which modifies the behaviour of software and hardware, excluding the communication behaviour*
- network configuration data (**DT5**): *Data that modifies system behaviour with regards to communication*
- process data (**DT6**): *data about a running software process within a computing unit*
- session data (**DT7**): *data collected by a system during a session, which consist of a number of processes with the same scope and time frame*
- application data (**DT8**): *data representing functions needed to create, edit, consume or process content relied to the key functionality of the system*
- functional data (**DT9**): *data content created, edited, consumed or processed as the key functionality of the system*

Six *Classes of Methods* describe the requirements for the use of the various forensic methods by categorizing them based on what kind of software provides said method. This corresponds to the use of specific tools (or tool chains) in order to investigate a certain type of data. Some of these classes of methods defined in [14] are relevant for this paper. These are the Operating system (**OS** - *methods provided by the operating system [...]*), Explicit means of intrusion detection (**EMID** - *methods provided by additional software [...] being executed autonomously on a routine basis and without a suspicion of an incident*), IT application (**ITA** - *methods provided by IT-Applications that are operated by the user [...]*) and Scaling of methods for evidence gathering (**SMG** - *methods to further collect evidence to be used if a suspicion is raised [...]*).

III. Structured Approach to Investigate and Compare Potential Privacy Violations in Mobile Apps

In this section, the approach for digital forensics discussed in Section II-D is applied to achieve comparability between the various methods to examine third and first party tracking employed in mobile apps.

A. System landscape analysis and its resulting forensic process as part of Strategic Preparation (SP) and its impact on comparability

The investigation step of Strategic Preparation (see Section II-D) plays a decisive role during this process in trying and testing the measures ahead of an incident and setting the system boundaries of systems which are examined and those used for examination. Hence, this step directly impacts the results and their credibility. Setting these boundaries is done during a *system landscape analysis*. Such an analysis for our use case of identifying third and first party tracking by apps via employing static analysis is depicted in Figure 1. It also introduces a possible extension enabling the analysis of websites. The system landscape analysis allows for the identification of various characteristics in which the employed

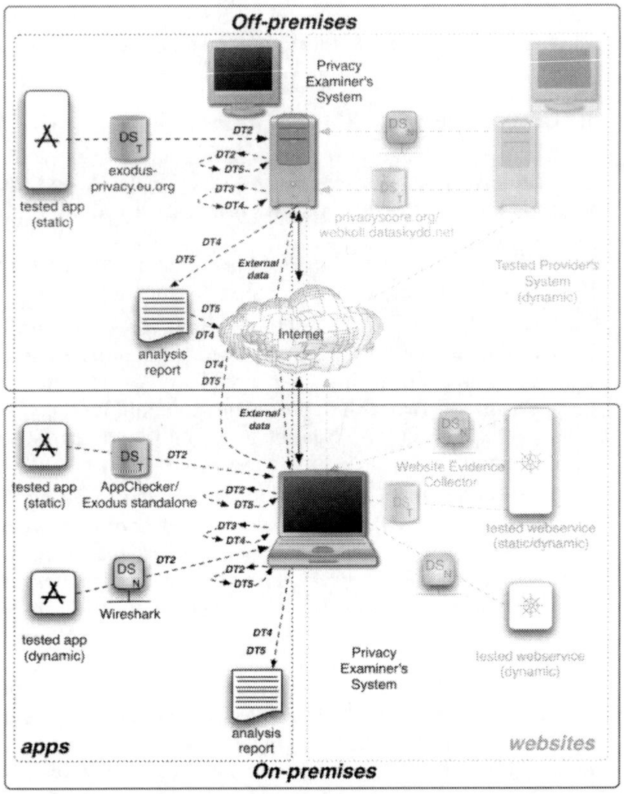

Figure 1. System landscape analysis of the examination of apps and websites regarding first and third party tracking using the categorization into *custody*, *data streams*, and *type of examination*

methods differ. These characteristics carry some implications on how these methods can be used in order to identify third and first party tracking. This affects the credibility of the results.

The first identified characteristic is *custody*. This characteristic encompasses two aspects. These aspects are *custody over the method* used for the examination and *custody over the examination item* which is an app in the context of this paper. This custody can either be *on-premises* (the examiner has custody over this component) or *off-premises* (another entity has custody over this component). If two different methods share the same characteristic in terms of custody, we refer to them as *intra-premises*. If they differ in this respect, we refer to them as *inter-premises*. Generally speaking, having custody of these two aspects implies a greater control over them and, hence, a higher credibility. Secondly, we identify the *data stream* examined by the given method as another relevant characteristic (see II-D for an introduction into the various forensic data streams). A method could analyse the binary obtained from the non-volatile memory (DS_T), the volatile memory obtained during the execution of a binary (DS_M) or the communication observed during execution (DS_N). Finally, we can categorize the *type of examination* into a *static examination* (a single snapshot of the behaviour of the website or the app) and a *dynamic examination* (a change in behaviour of an app over time).

With our stated goal of achieving comparability of tools and services for privacy examination, i.e., the sets of methods from the model from [14], this categorization provides a structure supporting the comparability between various methods. This is not affected whether these methods rely on the same internal engine (*intra-engine*) or not (*inter-engine*).

B. Comparison of methods within the forensic framework

The forensic data types shown in Section II-D are generally applicable to all data streams (see Section III-A and can be used to indicate privacy issues (primarily by their presence but also by their absence). Also they can be used to describe the methods employed to identify and examine data flows and their respective actions in a comparable manner.

One such example is shown in Table I. This table provides an overview on the three methods used for identifying trackers and permission during this paper. It includes an intra-engine comparison of two different means to employ the *Exodus Privacy Engine* and well as an inter-engine comparison to a third method.

The two means to employ the *Exodus Privacy Engine* are *Exodus Privacy* ([10], in short: *EPO*) and *Exodus Standalone* ([16], in short: *ESA*). *EPO* is a web-based service which runs remotely (*off-premises*). The user sends a request to the service which then downloads an app (in form of an .APK file) from the Google Play Store. Neither the method itself nor the examination item are in the *custody* of the examiner. *ESA* is a console application which runs on a local system and is supplied with a local .APK file to examine (*on-premises*). In this case, method and examination item in the *custody* of the examiner. Both variants examine a binary file which has to be downloaded and stored before the examination, hence the *data stream* DS_T is examined. Both employ static measures as its *type of examination*.

AppChecker ([17], in short: *APC*) provides an inter-engine comparison. This tool is a console application running on a local system (*on-premises*) with the method and examination item being in the *custody* of the examiner. Again, it employs static measures (*type of examination*) on a binary file (DS_T).

With this in mind, a closer look on the exact nature of the examination performed by these three methods is necessary with a specific focus on comparability and documentation. In both cases, access to the specific app (in form of an .APK) is required. In the case of *ESA* and *APC*, this .APK might already be available so the first action is optional. Whether the .APK has to be downloaded first (in case of *EPO*), copied from another medium or is already present on the examiners system, it represents raw data (**DT2**). This .APK is then extracted to reveal the binary (**DT2**) and the manifest which represents information about this binary (**DT3**). Following this, various pieces of information are extracted from the present data. The binary (**DT2**) is searched for hosts and ip addresses leading to a list of potential communication partners (representing **DT5**). The manifest (**DT3**) is investigated in order to compile a list of the various permissions the app is supposed to be granted by the system it runs on (representing **DT4**). In the next step, both lists are compared to *external data* which does not originate from the examined source but contributes to the examination result. This external data represents signatures which could include hosts known to be used for advertisement. In essence, these data represents a list of known trackers (in case of host names or ip addresses) or unwanted permissions. This leads to a reduced list of relevant trackers (**DT5**) or relevant permissions (**DT4**). In the final step, this data is then compiled into a report.

While the operations are identical for each three methods, the visibility to the examiner is different. In the case of *ESA* and *APC* every action was performed locally and was hence observable to the investigator. At every action, inputs and outputs could be documented in detail. In the case of *EPO* every action taking place after the process is started is not observable for the examiner. The examiner has to rely on the summary provided by *EPO* after the method is finished. However, the use of *EPO* requires far less effort from the examiner in terms of required resources.

TABLE I. FORENSIC *DATA TYPES* PROCESSED DURING THE INTERNAL ACTIONS AND THEIR VISIBILITY TO THE EXAMINER DURING STATIC ANALYSIS

Internal Action	*Data Types*	observable in ...		
		EPO - [10]	ESA - [16]	APC - [17]
Download .APK	**DT2**	✗	✓	✓
Extract .APK	**DT2**, **DT3**	✗	✓	✓
Binary: Extract Hosts	**DT2** → **DT5**	✗	✓	✓
Manifest: Extract Permission	**DT3** → **DT4**	✗	✓	✓
Host: Compare	**DT5**, *ext* → **DT5**	✗	✓	✓
Manifest: Compare	**DT4**, *ext* → **DT4**	✗	✓	✓
Generate Report	**DT4**, **DT5** → *Report*	✓	✓	✓

C. Visualization of examinations results

Since the tools and services (i.e., sets methods from [14]) typically gather a large number of results, an efficient visualization of the results of their usage is paramount. This visualization should support an easy comparison of different methods and should be easily extensible with regards to new *result categories* (horizontal view in Figure 2) and new tested apps and websites (vertical view).

We choose a DNA-graph-style representation as it allows for the additional integration of information regarding the data type (e.g., URLs of known trackers as **DT3** in the the network data stream DS_N, app permissions as configuration data **DT4**) using colouring/shading. A very important property of this visualization type is that it also depicts the *absence* using marked positions, which greatly supports the comparison of different methods to examine potentially privacy violating data flows.

IV. CASE STUDY

This section describes the creation of a test environment in order to apply various methods to examine potentially privacy violating data flows in a sample of selected apps (**ES1**) or to examine various alternative apps usable for web browsing with regards to potential privacy violations (**ES2**).

A. Building a test environment

A test environment should fulfill a number of requirements that apply to both dynamic and static tests (see Section II). To ensure the authenticity of the tested app, it should be acquired from the official distribution system. One means to access these stores and extract the app as it was downloaded is to use an Android Emulator such as the Emulator from the official *AndroidSDK* [18] or using dedicated emulators such as *Genymotion* [19]. If the option of shared access to the emulated system is used, access to the official .APK of a given app is possible. Thus, the app can be downloaded from the official distribution and yet is accessible to the tools for static evaluation by means of accessing the mass storage of the emulated system. *AppChecker* and *Exodus Standalone* as well as *Exodus Privacy* compute a SHA265 cryptographic hash, enabling also an integrity check. The maintenance of both security aspects are vital for the forensic process (see Section II-D).

Although dynamic analysis is only included in a minor role in this paper for the sake of brevity, a few short notes for a successful conduct of such a structured examination shall be provided. In this case, the creation of a "low-noise" environment is of great help for the examiner. Since in dynamic analysis the network traffic is analysed, any interference from other parts of the Android operating system should be minimized. While we consider a complete exclusion of all surplus network traffic impossible with current mobile operating systems, at least a reduced interference should be achieved by the removal of all apps and services not needed to execute a given app for testing.

B. (**ES1**): Testing eight different apps for potential privacy violations

For the tests a set of eight different apps suited for use in an educational institution was selected. The tests were conducted using the guidelines provided in Section IV-A. *Genymotion 3.1.1* [19] was used on a Lenovo T61 Laptop with 4GB RAM running *Ubuntu18.04* [20]. The Android emulator was run within a virtualized system (realized using *VirtualBox* [21] with the necessary configuration for shared access to the virtual file system. The respective apps where then downloaded from the respective Playstore on the emulated phone (emulating an Android 7.1). The downloaded binary file was then transferred using the *Terminal App* [22] to the shared folder. Here, the sha256sum for the specific binary was calculated and documented.

This binary was then examined using *Exodus Standalone* and *AppChecker*. The execution of both methods can be documented on the command line and the outputs created can be stored. Since the SHA256 checksum of the binaries are known, the results of these two methods running *on-premises* can be compared to the results provided by the *off-premises* method of *Exodus Privacy*. The three used methods are explained in detail in Section III-B including the use of forensic data types during the application of these methods.

The execution of all methods on the eight selected specimen was successful. Based on the considerations for the visualization made in Section III-C, the results are shown in Figure 2. It shows the three different methods of investigations for each of the eight different specimen as the rows while the columns show the different identified trackers (**DT5**) and the identified permissions (**DT4**). A colored box indicates that the specific tracker or permission was identified within the specific specimen using the specific method.

For the trackers, it is notable that there are very few *intra-engine* differences between *EPO* and *ESA*. The exception is *Moodle*, where *EPO* identifies the Google Firebase Analytics tracker and *ESA* does not. This might be due to a difference in the list of known tracker signatures between these versions. However, since no information on the exact version of this list used is provided by the two methods, a further examination is not possible. While *ESA* could be modified to store this list of signatures for documentation purposes (due to being open source and on-premises), this is not possible for *EPO*. Generally, both methods provide the same results, albeit the use of *ESA* provides for a better documentation on how these results are achieved. There are, however, some notable *inter-engine* differences in the results when compared to *APC*. This can be seen, for example, with DropBox, or Shazam. The reason here are different heuristics (including the signatures for the identification of trackers). An overview on these results is provided in Table II. In general, there is usually a core of trackers for any given app identified by all methods. Some trackers are only found by *EPO* and *ESA* and some only by *APC*. A review of the identified trackers show that all of them fall under DF_{tp}) since they represent connections to a third party. Based on external knowledge about the specific names of the identified trackers, these most likely all represent $DF_{tp.nrq}$.

TABLE II. NUMBER OF IDENTIFIED TRACKERS DURING **ES1** ON EIGHT SELECTED APPS AS PERFORMED IN SECTION IV-B

Application Name and Version	*ESA*	*EPO*	*APC*	common to all
Corona-Warn 1.2.1	0	0	1	0
Dropbox 194.2.6	5	5	4	2
GuitarTuna 6.4.0	10	10	11	9
Moodle 0.0.0	0	1	2	0
Pixabay 1.1.3.1	2	2	2	0
QR & Barcode Scanner 2.1.32	5	5	6	4
Shazam 10.38.0-200709	4	4	5	2
Signal 4.69.4	0	0	1	0

TABLE III. NUMBER OF IDENTIFIED PERMISSIONS DURING **ES1** ON EIGHT SELECTED APPS AS PERFORMED IN SECTION IV-B

Application Name and Version	*ESA*	*EPO*	*APC*	common to all
Corona-Warn 1.2.1	8	8	8	8
Dropbox 194.2.6	23	23	23	23
GuitarTuna 6.4.0	9	9	9	9
Moodle 0.0.0	30	30	30	30
Pixabay 1.1.3.1	9	9	9	9
QR & Barcode Scanner 2.1.32	13	13	13	13
Shazam 10.38.0-200709	14	14	14	14
Signal 4.69.4	65	65	65	65

For the permissions, the results are identical for all methods applied to all apps as can be seen in Table II. This is based on the reason that same approach for detecting permissions is used by all these methods. All the methods discussed here perform a review of the manifest to identify trackers.

C. (**ES2**): Examining various alternative apps usable for web browsing with regards to potential privacy violations

For this test, three exemplary selected apps for web browsing are examined with regards to potential privacy violations. The three mobile browsers are *Chrome*, *F-Droid Fennec* and *Mozilla Firefox*.

The tests employed the same examination setup as used in **ES1** (see Section IV-B). This includes the three methods *Exodus Standalone*, *AppChecker* and *Exodus Privacy* used for

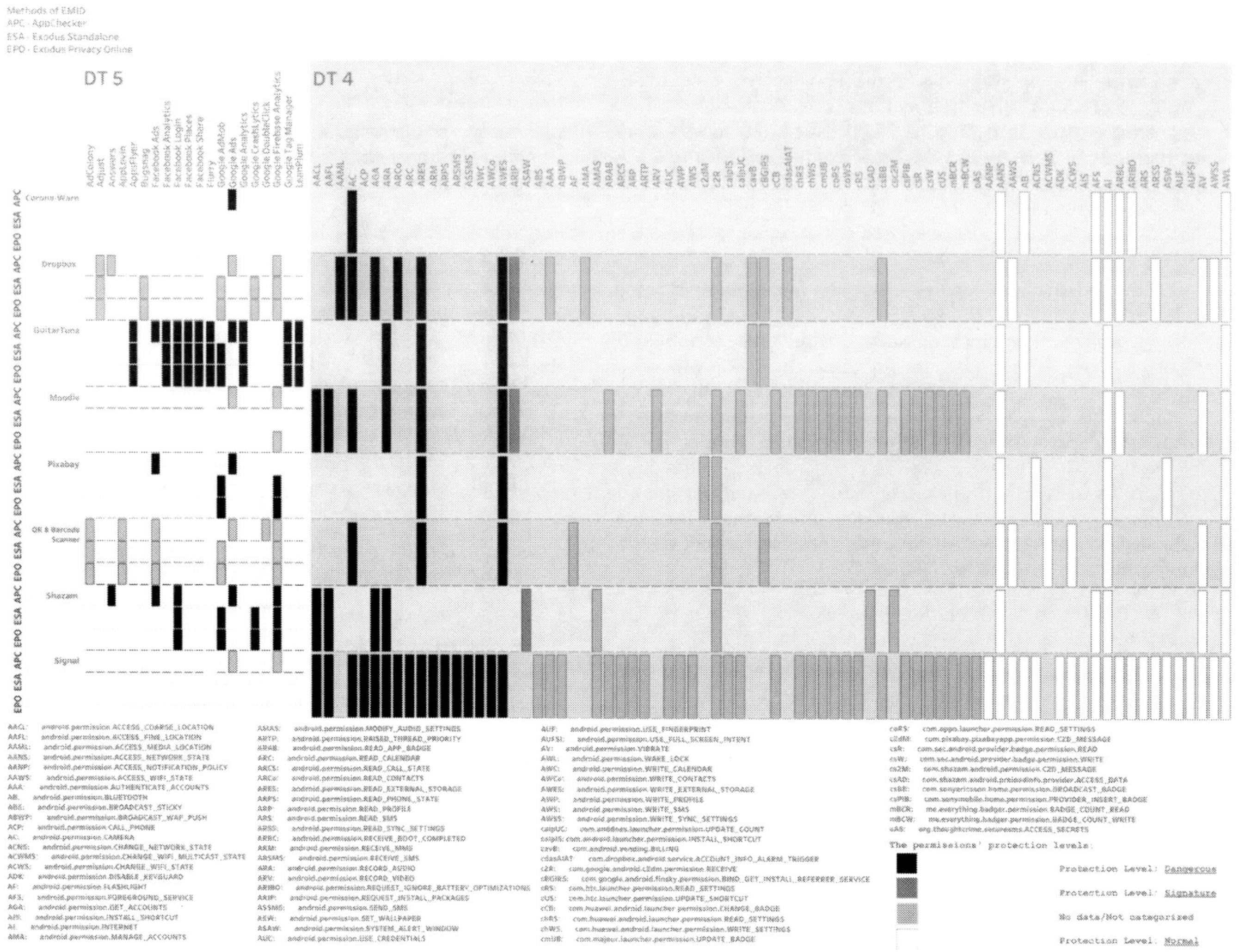

Figure 2. Trackers and permissions identified during **ES1** on eight selected apps as performed in Section IV-B

static analysis. These three methods and the forensic data types used during their application are discussed in detail in Section III-B. However, in this case dynamic analysis was employed for a more detailed insight into the results.

The execution of all methods on the three selected apps was successful. Based on the considerations for the visualization made in Section III-C, the results are shown in Figure 3. Again, the rows show the three different methods of investigation for each of the three specimen. The columns show the identified trackers (**DT4**) or permissions (**DT5**). Colored boxes indicate that a method identified the tracker or permission within the specific specimen.

In case of trackers no *intra-engine* differences between *EPO* and *ESA* are visible. There are some differences when compared to the findings of *APC*. *Chrome* contains two trackers (Google Ads and Facebook Ads) according to *APC*. *Fennec F-Droid* contains Mozilla Telemetry which *EPO* and *ESA* identify as a tracker. *Mozilla Firefox* has three trackers common to all methods. These are Facebook Ads, Google Firebase Analytics and LeanPlum. *APC* also identifies GoogleAds as a tracker. *EPO* and *ESA* identify GoogleAdMob instead. All three methods identify the same set of permissions.

Dynamic analysis can be used in order to verify these observations. The setup described in IV-A was used to execute *Fennec F-Droid* within a "low-noise" environment using *Wireshark* [11] to record the network traffic before reviewing said traffic in order to identify the data flows. In order to reduce the influence of background noise, *Fennec F-Droid* was started multiple times and the resulting communication behaviour observed. Every time the app started, a connection to firefox.settings.services.mozilla.com was attempted. Hence, we can conclude a DF_{tp}, since the host does not correspond to the provider of app. This confirms the result of the static analysis with regards to *Fennec F-Droid*.

Example **ES2** clearly shows the limitations of the approach presented here. The identification of trackers only yields DF_{tp}) and does not identify DF_{fp}). This leads to the good results of *Chrome* in this comparison without taking into account any DF_{fp}), which might cause privacy violations. Here, a thorough dynamic analysis might provide additional insight. Either

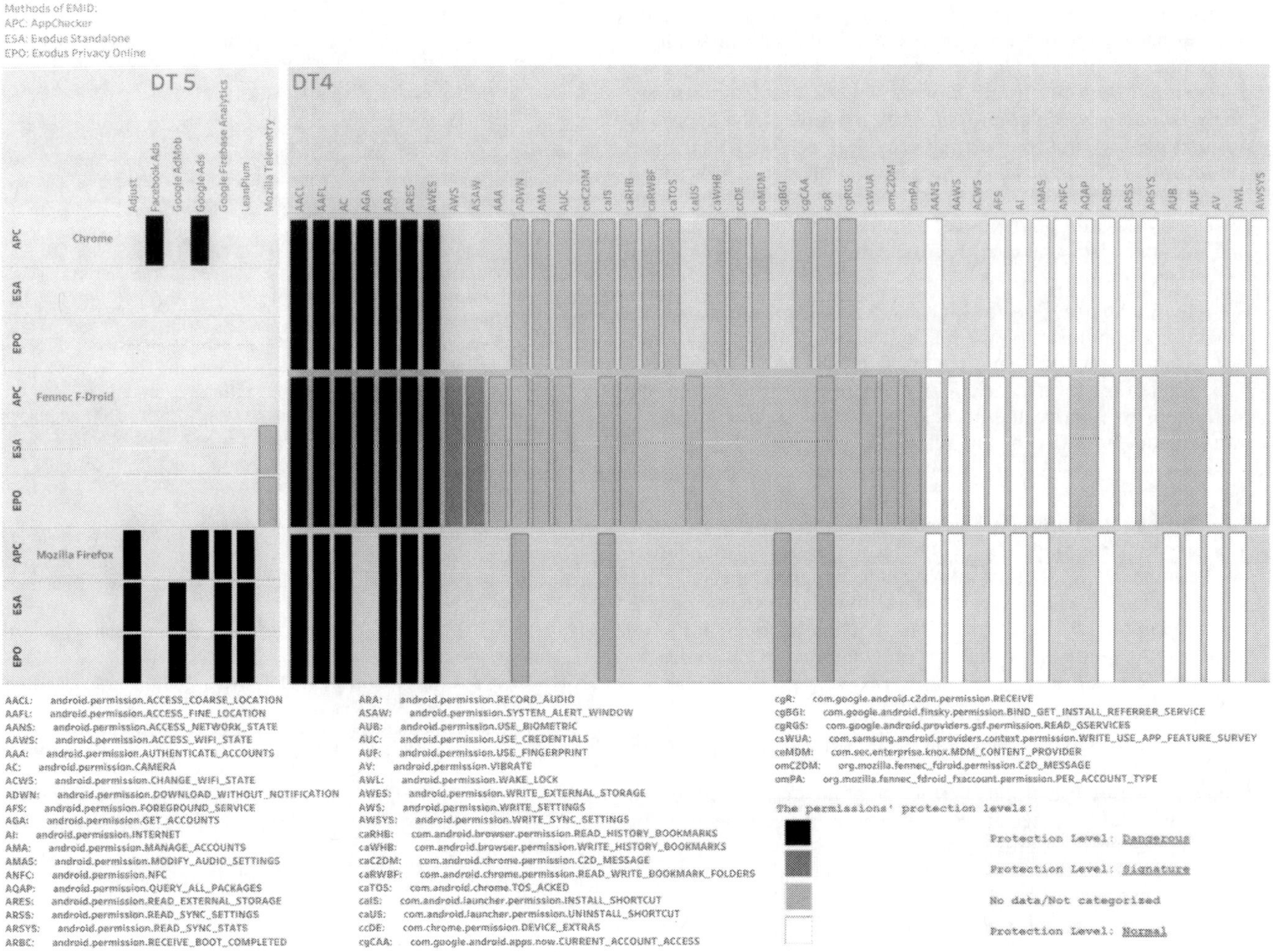

Figure 3. Trackers and permissions identified during **ES2** performed on three different web browser apps performed in Section IV-C

examining the specific data flow or blocking the specific data flow and then checking if the app still performs its function can be used to discern whether a data flows represents $DF_{fp.req}$ or $DF_{fp.nrq}$ respectively. This approach is also usable to separate $DF_{tp.req}$ from $DF_{tp.nrq}$.

V. Conclusion

This paper discusses potential privacy violations during the use of mobile apps caused by data flows to the first party and third parties. It introduces four different types of data flows with potential privacy implications and some means to detect these data flows. It discusses how the results originating from various methods can be made more reliable and more comparable. This is achieved by applying practices from computer forensics to this field and describing the examination processes from the viewpoint of a forensic investigation. This enables the identification of a set of relevant factors for selecting the methods of examination. In addition, considerations on a suitable visualization and an example for such an visualization are provided.

The approach is applied to two different Examination Scenario. In this first scenario, three different methods of static analysis to examine the potential data flows in a set of eight different apps are used. This leads to the identification of 42 trackers with 20 of them being different. In addition, 167 permissions are identified with 77 of them being different. The second scenario examines three different browser apps and identifies trackers and permissions. It shows the limits of the presented approach and gives a short example of a dynamic analysis.

The approach presented in this paper relies on static analysis and shows the limitations of this approach. The identification of trackers should use varied methods in order to achieve conclusive results since the methods presented here might provide differing results. In addition, they do not identify DF_{fp}. This would require additional methods. The advantage of the approach presented within this paper is that it provides comparability of the achieved results, which is not provided if only a single isolated method of examination is used.

The approach presented within this paper focuses on the identification of trackers from a purely technical standpoint and hence gives no guidance whether a specific tracker would violate the privacy of the user from a legal perspective. In this technological view, the approach presented within this paper supports data sovereignty. Judging the impact a specific tracker has on the privacy of the user is a difficult task. Good guidelines are provided by the *Principles relating to processing of personal data* of Article 5 of the GDPR [1]. Chief among these is *data minimisation*. A negative example is the approach of marking tracking from certain providers as less critical since these providers already have access to similar data (like done in the grading scheme seen in [8]). If certain providers obtain personal data through the use of a specific tracker, they can use the personal data obtained through different trackers in order to create a profile.

The prevention of tracking is a complex topic. Users (including administrators or teachers in care of students) can try to block trackers using technical means. Also developers who might unwittingly include trackers in their software might take steps to remove these trackers. However, these methods are beyond the scope of this paper.

A. Future Work

The approach presented here deals with the identification of trackers (representing $DF_{tp.nrq}$) but also provides a foundation to examine DF_{fp}. This would include dynamic analysis and would entail blocking specific data flows and reviewing the apps functionality following. This remains an open topic as well as the potential inclusion of code review in order to improve results.

Additional future work should include research the provision of an environment that only captures the network traffic of a given app during dynamic analysis. At present, other processes can trigger traffic, creating false positives. In addition, a future extension could include the examination of websites using the same approach.

ACKNOWLEDGMENT

This document is partly funded by the European Union Project "CyberSec LSA_OVGU-AMSL".

REFERENCES

[1] European Union, "General Data Protection Regulation (GDPR)," 2020, https://gdpr.eu/article-5-how-to-process-personal-data/ [November 05. 2020].

[2] R. Binns, U. Lyngs, M. Van Kleek, J. Zhao, T. Libert, and N. Shadbolt, "Third party tracking in the mobile ecosystem," in Proceedings of the 10th ACM Conference on Web Science, ser. WebSci '18. New York, NY, USA: Association for Computing Machinery, 2018, p. 23D31. [Online]. Available: https://doi.org/10.1145/3201064.3201089

[3] G. Maone, "NoScript," 2020, https://addons.mozilla.org/de/firefox/addon/noscript/ [November 05. 2020].

[4] pi-hole.net, "pi-hole," 2020, https://pi-hole.net/ [November 05. 2020].

[5] P. Jackson, "disconnectme - Tracker Descriptions," 2020, https://github.com/disconnectme/disconnect-tracking-protection/blob/master/descriptions.md [November 05. 2020].

[6] M. Maaß and D. Herrmann, "Privacyscore: Improving privacy and security via crowd-sourced benchmarks of websites," CoRR, vol. abs/1705.05139, 2017. [Online]. Available: http://arxiv.org/abs/1705.05139

[7] privacyscore.org, "PrivacyScore," 2020, https://privacyscore.org/ [November 05. 2020].

[8] mobilsicher.de, "So testen wir," 2020, **GERMAN** https://appcheck.mobilsicher.de/allgemein/so-testen-wir-schnelltest [November 05. 2020].

[9] android.com, "Android Operating System," 2020, https://www.android.com/ [November 05. 2020].

[10] Exodus Privacy, "Exodus Privacy," 2020, https://exodus-privacy.eu.org/en/ [November 05. 2020].

[11] wireshark.org, "Wireshark," 2020, https://www.wireshark.org/ [November 05. 2020].

[12] "A Road Map for Digital Forensic Research," DFRWS, Tech. Rep., 2001.

[13] R. Altschaffel, M. Hildebrandt, S. Kiltz, and J. Dittmann, "Digital Forensics in Industrial Control Systems," in Proceedings of 38th International Conference of Computer Safety, Reliability, and Security (Safecomp 2019). Springer Nature Switzerland, 2019, pp. 128–136.

[14] S. Kiltz, J. Dittmann, and C. Vielhauer, "Supporting Forensic Design - A Course Profile to Teach Forensics," in IMF '15: Proceedings of the 2015 Ninth International Conference on IT Security Incident Management & IT Forensics (imf 2015). IEEE, 2015.

[15] R. Altschaffel, K. Lamshöft, S. Kiltz, M. Hildebrandt, and J. Dittmann, "A Survey on Open Forensics in Embedded Systems of Systems," International Journal on Advances in Security, vol. 11, 2018, pp. 104–117.

[16] Exodus Privacy, "Exodus Standalone," 2020, https://github.com/Exodus-Privacy/exodus-standalone [November 05. 2020].

[17] J. Alemann and N.Baier and M.Streuber and T. D. Nam and L. Peters, "AppChecker," 2020, https://github.com/Tienisto/AppChecker [November 05. 2020].

[18] android.com, "Android Studio," 2020, https://developer.android.com/studio [November 05. 2020].

[19] genymotion.com, "GenyMotion," 2020, https://www.genymotion.com/ [November 05. 2020].

[20] ubuntu.com, "Ubuntu 18.04," 2020, https://releases.ubuntu.com/18.04/ [November 05. 2020].

[21] virtualbox.org, "VirtualBox," 2020, https://www.virtualbox.org/ [November 05. 2020].

[22] J. Palevich, "Android Terminal Emulator," 2020, https://play.google.com/store/apps/details?id=jackpal.androidterm& [November 05. 2020].

Towards Cybersecurity Act: A Survey on IoT Evaluation Frameworks

Maxime Puys, Jean-Pierre Krimm and Raphaël Collado

Université Grenoble Alpes, CEA, LETI, DSYS, Grenoble F-38000, France
Email: firstname.name@cea.fr

***Abstract*—On the 7th of June 2019, the Cybersecurity Act was adopted by the European Union. Its objectives are twofold: the adoption of the permanent mandate of ENISA and the definition of a European cybersecurity certification framework, which is essential for strengthening the security of Europe's digital market. Delivered certificates according to this scheme will be mutually recognized among European countries. The regulation defines three certification levels with increasing requirements. Among them, the "basic level" which typically targets non-critical, consumer objects (e.g.,smart-home or "gadget" IoT). Yet, various evaluation and certification schemes related to the IoT already exist prior to the adoption of the Cybersecurity Act. Thus, discussions are being carried on at the moment of redaction in order to either choose an existing scheme or to design a unified scheme based on existing ones. In this paper, we focus on the basic level, and assemble a survey on existing evaluation and certification schemes for consumer IoT and compare them based on various criteria. Then, we propose a unified evaluation scheme for the basic level driven by Bureau Veritas, based on existing schemes.**

Keywords–Cybersecurity Act; Internet of Things; IoT; certification; evaluation scheme; smart-home.

I. INTRODUCTION

On the 7th of June 2019, the Cybersecurity Act has officially been adopted by the European Union. Its objectives are twofold: the adoption of the permanent mandate of the European Union Agency for Cybersecurity (ENISA), the European Union Agency for Cybersecurity, and the definition of a European cybersecurity certification framework, which is essential for strengthening the security of Europe's digital market. Delivered certificates according to this scheme will be mutually recognized among European countries. Cybersecurity certification is the attestation of the conformance and robustness of a product made by a third party evaluator, according to a scheme describing the security needs of the users, and taking into account technological developments. The adoption of the Cybersecurity Act will both encourage the use of certification and recognition of certificates issued by one Member State throughout the EU, thereby contributing to the security of the single market. The regulation defines three certification levels with increasing requirements:

- The basic level which typically targets non-critical, consumer objects (e.g.,smart-home or "gadget" IoT);
- The substantial level that targets the median risk (e.g.,cloud computing or non-critical industrial IoT);
- The high level that targets critical solutions where there is a risk of attacks by actors with significant skills and resources (e.g.,vehicles, critical industry or medical devices, etc.).

Yet, various evaluation and certification schemes related to the IoT already exist prior to the adoption of the Cybersecurity Act, with companies proposing evaluation services according to these schemes. Thus, discussions are being carried on at the moment of redaction in order to either choose an existing scheme or to design a unified scheme based on existing ones.

a) Contributions:: In this paper, Bureau Veritas (BV) and CEA-Leti teamed up to focus on the "basic" level, targeting consumer IoT such as cameras, toys, or other "smart-devices". We assemble a survey on existing evaluation and certification schemes for consumer IoT and compare them based on various criteria. Then, we propose a unified evaluation scheme for the basic level driven by Bureau Veritas, based on existing schemes. The objectives of this unified scheme are twofold: (i) be a candidate for official certification scheme for the basic level; and (ii) maintain compliance with existing schemes to allow certification companies to maintain their services independently of the chosen scheme.

b) Outline:: The rest of the paper is organized as follows. Section II will present and compare existing schemes. Section III will then define our unified evaluation scheme. Finally, Section IV will introduce related works on IoT certification surveys and Section V will conclude.

II. COMPARISON OF EXISTING EVALUATION FRAMEWORKS

In this section, we propose to analyze and compare existing referential frameworks dealing with cybersecurity of consumer directed IoT devices. These evaluation schemes are candidates to become the one chosen within the Cybersecurity Act. However, it appears that theses documents have been redacted with sometimes quite different purposes and target specific audience. Moreover, their structure can vary significantly. We first propose to compare them on various criteria, such as:

a) Type of document: This describes the main purpose of the document, such as evaluation/certification or good practices. Evaluation and certification seek to ensure the compliance of the device with a predefined list of requirements. They are usually performed by a third party when the development is finished and prior to a public release. Depending on the type of evaluation, they can include compliance against functional requirements to ensure the device only does what it claims to do; but also robustness evaluation assessing the strength and the robustness of a device against cybersecurity threats. On the other hand, good practices aim at being applied during the development.

b) Targeted audience: This defines who the document is destined to. This criterion is generally linked to the type of document described above. That is, a certification scheme is usually for "conformity assessment bodies" (CAB). They are third parties conducting the evaluation of a product. However, an evaluation scheme may be applied by developers during development within continuous integration. Good practices are generally directed to developers, testers, Chief Information Security Officers (CISO), or Chief Technical Officers (CTO).

c) Structure of the document: A complete cybersecurity certification process is generally defined as presented in Figure 1. From a set of assets to protect, hypotheses (for instance on the environment), threats originating from threats origins, security objectives are obtained. Theses objectives can be seen as generic counter-measures regarding threats. For instance, if a threat is "Configuration alteration", a matching security objective could be "Secure authentication on administration interface". Then security objectives are derived on security requirements, which are more technical and related to the target of evaluation. Regarding to the objective "Secure authentication on administration interface", a requirement could be "Use two-factor authentication". Finally, security requirements are derived in technical requirements which are completely related to the programming language or framework used by the product. In parallel, security requirements are derived into tests procedures, detailing how CAB must conduct evaluation. This criterion defines which part of this structure are covered by the scheme.

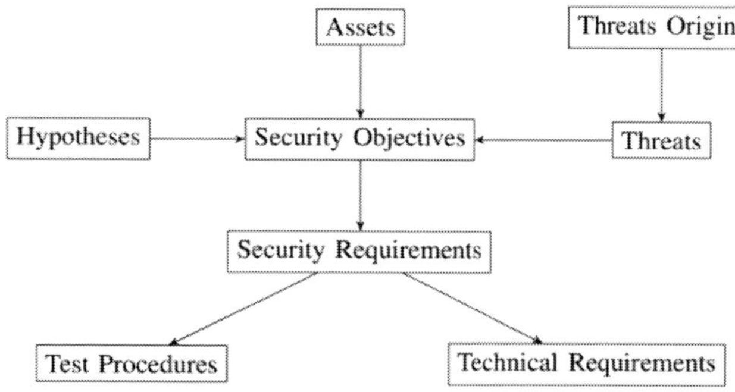

Figure 1. Structure of certification schemes

d) Split in different security levels: This criterion defines if the scheme proposes different security levels providing increasing security level and adding more security requirements to cope with. These security levels are internal to the framework and should not be mistaken with the basic, substantial and high of the Cybersecurity Act.

e) Technical perimeter: This explains how widely the scheme covers in terms of technical cybersecurity topics (network, system, cryptography, etc).

f) Level of accuracy of the requirements: This shows how precise are the requirements provided by the scheme. That is, if they stay quite generic or become quite technical.

g) Support from the community/industry: This criterion details how much the scheme is supported by either the scientific community or industry. This is a subjective criterion based on the variety of authors and members if the scheme belongs to an alliance.

We focus on five IoT evaluation schemes, known to be the best contenders for the basic level of the Cybersecurity Act, namely: ETSI, CTIA, OWASP, Eurosmart, IoT-SF. We first describe briefly every one, then we propose a summary table given the criteria we defined earlier.

h) ETSI-EN-303-645 (version 2.1.0, 2020-04): ETSI is a European standards organization based in France. In May 2018, they release the first version of TS-103-645, later officialized as EN-303-645 [1], a list of good practices in order to increase the cybersecurity of consumer IoT devices. This document is based on a "Code of Practice for Consumer IoT Security" proposed by the UK government. Destined to vendors, it is organized as a list a security objectives mixed with requirements. No separation in levels is provided. It covers a wide perimeter, going from passwords to communications, with system integrity and personal data. Requirements stay at a generic level. ETSI involves more than 850 members, drawn from 65 countries, including major universities.

i) CTIA Cybersecurity Certification Test Plan for IoT Devices (version 1.0.1, 2018-10): CTIA represents the United States wireless communications industry. In August 2018, they released the initial version of their certification plan for IoT devices [2]. Clearly destined to CAB, it is separated in three levels with increasing security features. It is not obvious if all three levels would fit in the "basic" Cybersecurity Act, given the fact that level three implies advanced security features such as two-factor authentication or secure boot. It is structured as a list of generic requirements along with test procedures, test prerequisites and test cases. The technical perimeter is wide.

j) OWASP IoT Top Ten (version 2018): The Open Web Application Security Project (OWASP) is a nonprofit foundation that works to improve the security of software. In 2018, OWASP released their Internet of Things Top 10 [3], a list of good practice. Destined to vendors, it is a list of 10 security objectives representing the 10 main kinds of vulnerabilities targeting IoT devices. It is not divided into levels but covers a wide range of topics. This list stays at a very low level of accuracy, only proposing security objectives. However, OWASP is widely known to propose a very technical set of coding rules to avoid most of the vulnerabilities. Yet, the IoT Top 10 document does not refer directly to them. OWASP has many members both from academic and industry across the world.

k) Eurosmart IoT Device Certification Scheme (version 2019-05-16): Eurosmart is a European organization based in Brussels. Their members are mainly working in hardware security (semiconductor and secure-elements) or in high-security software and include major companies and research laboratories. In April 2019, they released an initial version of their certification scheme [4] designed for CAB, however, the writing process still seems ongoing. According to published documents, they aim to cover the whole certification procedures from assets to CAB tests. Yet at the moment of redaction, they cover risk analysis (from assets to security

TABLE I. SUMMARY OF EXISTING SCHEMES

Schemes	ETSI	CTIA	OWASP	Eurosmart	IoT-SF
Type	Good practices	Certification	Good practices	Certification	Mixed
Audience	Vendors	CAB	Vendors	CAB	Vendors
Structure	Objectives Require-ments	Requirements Tests	Objectives	Complete (ongoing)	Objectives Require-ments
Levels	None	Three	None	None	Five
Perimeter	Wide	Wide	Wide	Wide	Wide
Accuracy	Generic	Generic	Low	Generic	Generic Technical
Support	World-wide	World-wide industry (mainly US)	World-wide	Sector-Specific (mainly EU)	World-wide (mainly UK)

TABLE II. MAPPING FOR FIRST BASIC LEVEL

ID	Topic	ETSI	CTIA	OWASP
1	Password management	4.1	3.2	1
2	Keeping software up to date	4.3	3.5, 3.6	4, 5
3	Securely storing sensitive data	4.4		7
4	Minimizing exposed attack surface	4.6	5.17	2, 3, 10
5	Ensuring the initial state is secure			5, 9
6	Analyzing admin. and user guides	4.2, 4.12	4.1	8
7	Third-party components management			5
(8)	Unique reference of the device			
(9)	Resistance to known vulnerabilities			10

objectives) and generic security requirements. They include a wide technical perimeter and stay a a generic level. They do not provide multiple levels of certification and according to the scheme itself, it is destined to the "substantial" level of the Cybersecurity Act.

I) IoT Security Foundation Security Compliance Framework (version 2, 2018-12): The IoT Security Foundation (IoT-SF) is composed of major companies, including almost all microchips integrators alongside major mobile network companies. Yet, smaller members and universities are mainly from UK. In 2016, they released the first version of their IoT security compliance framework [5]. Coming with a spreadsheet checklist alongside, it stands between certification and good practices as being stated as a "self-checking" framework. Destined to vendors, it is organized as a mixed list of security objectives and requirements. Five levels are introduced, based on a risk analysis to be performed on the device to assess. Depending on the importance of each security property (confidentiality, integrity, availability), the device is assigned to a minimum level. It covers a very wide perimeter, with merely all technical aspects related to security covered alongside with business, life-cycle management and governance. Interestingly, depending on the topic, requirements either stay at a generic level, or become quite technical.

Table I summarizes the criteria for all existing schemes.

III. A Unified IoT Evaluation Framework

As seen in Section II, two categories of documents are present in the current state-of-the-art. On one side, there are certification documents destined to CAB, while on the other side, there are good practice or self-assessment documents destined to vendors. It is currently (mid 2020) unclear which is preferred for the Cybersecurity Act evaluation framework, given the fact that evaluation modalities are still discussed. More precisely in the context of the basic level, it is not precised if the evaluation should be performed by CAB or vendors them-selves. According to ENISA and the European Commission during the FIC 2020 conference (Lille, 2020-01-28), such questions are likely to depend on the type of IoT device to test. In other words, there will be different evaluation schemes with different modalities for the basic level.

In this context, we propose a unified evaluation framework based on existing documents presented in Section II and driven by Bureau Veritas. Rather than providing yet another set of rules to implement, we propose a unified view detailing how existing frameworks could be mapped with each other. Thus, rather than implementing only one existing scheme, vendors and CAB can already include a global view of most of them in their process, without risking to bet on one not chosen in the end. The mapping we propose covers ETSI, CTIA, and OWASP. This choice is motivated as they seem to be the three main contenders for the final basic level of Cybersecurity Act framework, according to ongoing discussions.

A. Presentation of the Framework

The idea is to make the set-union of all topics covered in the different frameworks while pin-pointing the cross reference of related security objectives in each framework. For instance, for a common topic related to password security, we would

TABLE III. MAPPING FOR SECOND BASIC LEVEL

ID	Topic	ETSI	CTIA	OWASP
1	Password management	4.1	3.2	1
2	Keeping software up to date	4.3	**4.5, 4.6**	4, 5
3	Securely storing sensitive data	4.4		7
4	Minimizing exposed attack surface	4.6	5.17	2, 3, 10
5	Ensuring the initial state is secure			5, 9
6	Analyzing admin. and user guides	4.2, 4.12	4.1	8
7	Third-party components management			5
(8)	Unique reference of the device			
(9)	Resistance to known vulnerabilities			10
10	**Authentication and access-control**		**4.3, 4.4**	
11	**Protection of data in transit**	**4.5**	**4.8**	**7**
12	**Data input validity**	**4.13**		

note all related security objectives of each document. We divided this mapping into three levels based on – what we consider – realistic evaluation time (either performed by vendors or by CABs). The first level is intended to be completed within five business days. The second and third levels are respectively designed for nine and fifteen days. Depending on a risk analysis or marketing requirements, the device may be evaluated according to one of the three levels. The mapping for every level is provided in Tables II, III and IV.

We chose categories in Table II as they are the most simple and consensual. OWASP, designed to be as simple as possible, has almost all of his security objectives covered within the first level. Topics 1, 2 and 3 are essentially straightforward. Topic 4 refers to any software accessible from outside of the device (either from internet or from the LAN). This includes open ports, API, running servers, etc. This also includes hardware debug ports. Topic 5 refers to the guided installation of the device by the end user. The idea is to verify that default configuration and/or installation wizards put the device in a secure state. Topic 6 deals with how clear are the guides provided with the device in order to inform the end user and/or the administrator on security, privacy, and configuration. Topic 7 aims at verifying how third party components (software, libraries, stacks, etc) are manages (at least if they are clearly identified). Topics 8 and 9 (in brackets) are not directly mentioned by any of ETSI, CTIA and OWASP. Authors added these based on their experience of security. Topic 8 requires that the device can be clearly identified with a version number or equivalent while topic 9 follows topic 7 and implies that the certified version on the device is not affected by any known vulnerability (CVE). Topic 9 also applies for hardware vulnerabilities such as Meltdown [6], Zombieload [7] and more recently LVI attack [8]. No security is required for data in transit at this level which may be controversial. The idea behind is that this level should be limited to devices either that do not communicate, or do not communicate any sensitive data. Any device transferring sensitive data should be *de facto* put in level two or three.

The second basic level presented in Table III updates topic 2 to second level in CTIA and adds a few new topics (changes regarding Table II are shown in bold). Topic 10 ensures especially that no unauthenticated changes can be made and that administrator accounts must differ from user accounts. Topic 11 deals with protection of transferred data. It mainly states that messages shall be encrypted and signed and that keys must be managed securely. Finally, topic 12 requires that user inputs are checked to avoid code execution and under/overflows.

The third basic level presented in Table IV updates topic 2 to third level in CTIA and adds a few new topics (changes regarding Table III are shown in bold). Topic 13 deals with personal data and can roughly be summarized by compliance with EU's GDPR. Topic 14 requires the device to have a secure boot chain while topic 15 is related to the protection of data stored on the device. This topic differs from topic 3 "Securely storing sensitive data" in the sense that here, all the memory is protected, either by physical means such as scrambling or by file system encryption.

B. Discussions

As one can see in Tables II, III and IV regarding CTIA, our mapping can either follow CTIA levels (e.g., for topic 2. Keep software up to date); or have a fixed CTIA level in all tables (e.g., for topic 1. Password management). Depending on the topics, CTIA level following ours means we consider they are adapted to a certification at the basic level. On the other hand, a fixed CTIA level means that either lower CTIA levels are not challenging enough; or that higher CTIA levels are too demanding. Also, as the evaluation duration is currently not fixed within the Cybersecurity Act, proposing three levels has multiple benefits. First, it will help EU working groups to decide about how much requirements a device shall respect, without exceeding what will be considered as the maximal certification duration. Second, depending on specific classes of product, the Cybersecurity Act may officially require tougher evaluations. Finally, it will allow CAB to design private schemes around Cybersecurity Act, for demanding companies.

a) Coverage:: In the mapping presented above, we tried to maximize coverage, while choosing topics relatively close from one framework to others. Moreover, we tried to only select security objectives that can reasonably be asked to a device at the Cybersecurity Act basic level. Doing so, we obtain a coverage of existing framework as presented in Table V. As OWASP is simple and straightforward, it gets high coverage. ETSI is a quite balanced framework and gets a comfortable coverage at level 3. Finally, regarding CTIA, our first level already includes requirements from CTIA's level 2 and 3. Thus, we computed the coverage of all our levels against CTIA's

TABLE IV. MAPPING FOR THIRD BASIC LEVEL

ID	Topic	ETSI	CTIA	OWASP
1	Password management	4.1	3.2	1
2	Keeping software up to date	4.3	**5.5, 5.6**	4, 5
3	Securely storing sensitive data	4.4		7
4	Minimizing exposed attack surface	4.6	5.17	2, 3, 10
5	Ensuring the initial state is secure			5, 9
6	Analyzing admin. and user guides	4.2, 4.12	4.1	8
7	Third-party components management			5
(8)	Unique reference of the device			
(9)	Resistance to known vulnerabilities			10
10	Authentication and access-control		4.3, 4.4	
11	Protection of data in transit	4.5	4.8	7
12	Data input validity	4.13		
13	**Personal data management**	**4.8, 4.11**		**6**
14	**Secure boot**	**4.7**	**5.11**	
15	**Protection of data at rest**	**4.4**	**5.15**	**6**

level 3. It appears that this level is actually quite challenging for devices targeting a Cybersecurity Act basic level. For instance, topics such as "5.12 – Threat monitoring" or "5.16 – Tamper evidence" seem more destined to a Cybersecurity Act substantial or even high level of certification. This explains that we purposely exclude such topics and got a low coverage of CTIA.

TABLE V. COVERAGE OF EXISTING FRAMEWORKS

Level	ETSI	CTIA	OWASP
1	46%	29%	90%
2	62%	47%	90%
3	85%	59%	100%

IV. Related Works

There are some works on consumer IoT security certification. In may 2018, Cihon et al. [9] wrote a report on how to increase adoption of the proposed European cybersecurity certification framework. This document was written prior to the adoption of the Cybersecurity Act but studies the political, societal and economic aspects resulting from a common policy. In June 2018, Brass et al. [10] published a survey on cybersecurity standards for IoT. This work is really complete and provides a very precise overview of all IoT certification schemes existing at the time. Their survey is not directly related to the Cybersecurity Act and thus does not focus on the main candidates (including US regulations). Moreover, it lists existing standards rather than comparing them. Yet it sheds a light on most crucial aspects and challenges of certification of IoT devices and show the trade offs between maximizing the security of product and have legislations actually applicable. It is worth noting that given the rapid pace of the domain, frameworks such as Eurosmart and CTIA were not published at that time and thus are not included in the comparison.

In July 2019, the US NIST institute released the first version of NISTIR 8259 [11]. This internal report aims at giving manufacturers voluntary recommendations regarding cybersecurity of their devices. No mention seem to be made about regulation in this document. However in September 2019, the US Chamber of Commerce released a public letter [12] to the authors of NISTIR 8259. They state that they support the NIST report and mention that they believe policymakers in the U.S. and internationally need to align their IoT security with NISTIR 8259. Still in September 2019, the ENISA Advisory Group proposed an opinion paper [13] related to the security of consumer IoT. As an important note, this group is made of stakeholders including industry and academia and does not necessarily convey the view of ENISA. They recall the key elements of cybersecurity for such market and what ENISA can bring as a cybersecurity agency. While this article does not explicitly compares existing evaluation frameworks, it lays the foundations of which requirements could actually be selected for the basic level. In particular, authors emphasize the importance of certification schemes at European level but in contrast state that it should not impede the pace of innovation. In November 2019, Softic [14] proposed an analysis of the impact European certification of IoT on devices, consumers and business. Sadly, this thesis seem now inaccessible following the demand of the author.

V. Conclusion

In this paper, we discussed about the upcoming common cybersecurity certification framework for Europe in the context of the Cybersecurity Act. We proposed a survey of existing evaluation and certification schemes for consumer IoT and compared them based on various criteria. This allowed to (i) place them in the context of a global certification process, (ii) see how they are designed to and, (iii) what are the technical content they tackle and at which level of precision. We then proposed a unified evaluation scheme for the basic level of the Cybersecurity Act, based on existing schemes. This unified scheme lead by Bureau Veritas has two main objectives: (i) be a candidate for official certification scheme for the basic level; and (ii) maintain compliance with existing schemes to allow certification companies to maintain their services independently of the chosen scheme. Future works include speaking in depth with both ENISA, association and groups authoring existing framework in order to have their opinion on the unified mapping and to allow interested stakeholders to discuss with Bureau Veritas. Some use cases on various products with different purpose and security level could help seeing if the mapping brings enough security to components and does not miss critical properties.

REFERENCES

[1] ETSI, "Etsi en-303-645," Tech. Rep., May 2018.

[2] CTIA, "Cybersecurity certification test plan for iot devices," Tech. Rep., Aug. 2018.

[3] OWASP IoT Security Team, "Internet of things: Top 10," OWASP, Tech. Rep., 2018.

[4] Eurosmart, "Iot device certification scheme," Tech. Rep., Apr. 2019.

[5] R. Atoui, J. Bennett, S. Cook, P. Galwas, P. Gupta, J. Haine, H. Trevor, C. Hills, R. Marshall, M. John et al., "Iot security compliance framework," IoT Security Foundation, 2016.

[6] M. Lipp, M. Schwarz, D. Gruss, T. Prescher, W. Haas, A. Fogh, J. Horn, S. Mangard, P. Kocher, D. Genkin, Y. Yarom, and M. Hamburg, "Meltdown: Reading kernel memory from user space," in 27th USENIX Security Symposium (USENIX Security 18), 2018.

[7] M. Schwarz, M. Lipp, D. Moghimi, J. Van Bulck, J. Stecklina, T. Prescher, and D. Gruss, "ZombieLoad: Cross-privilege-boundary data sampling," in CCS, 2019.

[8] J. Van Bulck, D. Moghimi, M. Schwarz, M. Lipp, M. Minkin, D. Genkin, Y. Yuval, B. Sunar, D. Gruss, and F. Piessens, "LVI: Hijacking Transient Execution through Microarchitectural Load Value Injection," in 41th IEEE Symposium on Security and Privacy (S&P'20), 2020.

[9] P. Cihon, G. M. Guitierrez, S. Kee, M. Kleinaltenkamp, and T. Voigt, "Why certify? increasing adoption of the proposed eu cybersecurity certification framework," Master's thesis, Cambridge Judge Business School, May 2018.

[10] I. Brass, L. Tanczer, M. Carr, M. Elsden, and J. Blackstock, "Standardising a moving target: The development and evolution of iot security standards," June 2018.

[11] M. Fagan, K. Megas, K. Scarfone, and M. Smith, "Core cybersecurity feature baseline for securable iot devices: A starting point for iot device manufacturers," National Institute of Standards and Technology, Tech. Rep., July 2019.

[12] K. Megas and M. Fagan, "Subject: Draft NISTIR 8259, core cybersecurity feature baseline for securable iot devices: A starting point for iot device manufacturers," Sept. 2019.

[13] E. A. Group, "Opinion: Consumers and iot security," Tech. Rep., Sept. 2019.

[14] D. Softic, "Cybersecurity and certification: The impact of the european cybersecurity certification framework on the security and safety of iot devices, consumers and businesses," Master's thesis, University of Oslo, Nov. 2019.

Towards Reducing the Impact of Data Breaches

George O. M. Yee
Computer Research Lab, Aptusinnova Inc., Ottawa, Canada
Dept. of Systems and Computer Engineering, Carleton University, Ottawa, Canada
e-mail: george@aptusinnova.com, gmyee@sce.carleton.ca

Abstract— **Organizations are increasingly being victimized by breaches of private data, resulting in heavy losses to both the organizations and the owners of the data, i.e., the people described by the data. For organizations, these losses include large expenses to resume normal operation and damages to its reputation. For data owners, the losses may include financial loss and identity theft. To defend themselves from such data breaches, organizations install security controls (e.g., encryption) to secure their vulnerabilities. While such controls help, they are far from being fool proof. This paper examines the behaviour of Business-to-Consumer (B2C) e-commerce companies, in terms of why they collect and store personal data. It then proposes an approach that reduces the impact of a data breach by limiting the amount of private data that the company stores in its computer system, while preserving the company's ability to accomplish its purposes for collecting the private data. The paper illustrates the approach by applying it to different types of B2C e-commerce companies.**

Keywords-reducing impact; data breach; private data loss; B2C e-commerce.

I. Introduction

Data breaches of personal data or personal information are appearing more and more often in the news, devastating the victim organizations. The losses have serious negative consequences both to the consumer (e.g., financial loss, identity theft) and to the organization (e.g., loss of reputation, loss of trust). Recently in the news is a report that MGM Resorts has suffered a data breach in which the personal details of over 10.6 million guests who stayed at its hotels have appeared on a hacking forum [1]. MGM Resorts is being sued for this breach [2]. In the first half of 2019, there were 3,800 publicly disclosed breaches worldwide, exposing 4.1 billion records. This represents an increase of 54% in the number of reported breaches compared to the first half of 2018 [3].

In response to attacks that result in data breaches, organizations attempt to identify the vulnerabilities in their computer systems and secure these vulnerabilities using security controls. Example security controls are firewalls, intrusion detection systems, encryption, two-factor authentication, and social engineering awareness training for employees. Unfortunately, securing vulnerabilities with security controls is far from being foolproof. One major weakness is that it is impossible to find all the vulnerabilities in a computer system. This means that it is highly likely that a determined attacker will find an attack path into the organization's system that has been overlooked and cause a data breach, even though the organization believes that it has done due diligence and secured all its vulnerabilities. Nevertheless, security controls do help to prevent breaches, and we are not advocating that they be eliminated. Rather, the approach in this work can be considered as an addition to the existing arsenal of security controls.

In this work, we propose an approach in which most of the private data collected is stored on the user's device. Thus, a smaller quantity of private data remains on the company's computer system, reducing the impact or the loss of private data should the company stored data ever be breached. The approach also ensures that the needs of the company to carry out its purposes for collecting the private data are satisfied. The user's device could be a desktop computer, a laptop, or a smart phone. The approach is intended for Business-to-Consumer (B2C) e-commerce companies, since B2C companies appear to collect large quantities of personal data and are often victimized by data breaches. Note that in this work when we write about data storage on or in the "company's computer system", we mean that the data is stored on company premises or in the cloud.

This paper is organized as follows. Section II examines the behaviour of B2C companies in terms of why they collect and store personal information. It also looks at the nature of the collected information. Section III presents the approach. Section IV contains examples of how the approach can fit with different types of e-commerce companies. Section V describes related work. Section VI gives conclusions and future work.

II. The Collection and Storage of Personal Information by B2C Companies

In this section we examine why B2C companies collect personal information and discuss the nature of this information.

A. Private Data

Private information consists of data about a person that can identify or be linked to that person and is owned by that person. Thus, private information is also "personal information", and consists of "personal data". For example, a person's height, weight, or credit card number can all be used to identify the person and are considered as personal information. There are other types of personal information, such as buying patterns and navigation habits (e.g., websites visited) [4]. In many countries, personal information is protected by legislation in which the concept of "purpose" for collecting the personal information (how the collected information will be used) is important. Companies must disclose the purpose for collecting the personal information and cannot use the information for any other purpose.

B. *Purposes for Collecting Personal Information*

Companies engaged in B2C e-commerce, collect personal information for the following purposes (the first two purposes are self-evident):

- Transaction Requirements: Personal information is needed and used in carrying out the transaction. For example, making an online purchase requires your name and address for goods delivery.
- Communication: Personal contact information is needed to communicate with customers for resolving order issues or to answer product questions.
- To Secure Other Data: A personal biometric is needed for further authentication, e.g., a voice print, prior to allowing the customer to access more secure areas of his or her account [5]. The biometric may also be required for use in multi-factor authentication.
- Establishing Loyalty: A personal history of past transactions may be required to establish a customer's loyalty in order to reward the customer with certain benefits such as free shipping or product discounts [6].
- Targeted Advertising: A personal history of past transactions is needed to understand the type of products a particular customer has purchased in the past, and thereby create more appealing and effective ads directed at the customer [7].
- Market Research: The personal histories of past transactions for all customers are studied in order to understand what products appeal to customers in order to make decisions for stock purchases, or to provide a better customer experience in terms of app or website design [5].
- Sharing or Selling: Personal information collected is shared or sold to other organizations for a profit [5].

C. *E-Commerce Data*

In B2C e-commerce, online companies sell items and services to consumers. Example types of such companies include sellers of goods and services (e.g., Amazon.com), hotels (e.g., Mariott.com), travel agencies (e.g., Expedia.ca), financial services (e.g., CIBC.com), and the list goes on. All these companies share common data types. Each company offers products that customers purchase. Table 1 identifies the products for the e-commerce company types mentioned above.

Each customer has a set of personal identifying information, such as name, postal address, and phone number that identify the customer, and depending on the service provided by the company, include personal information such as credit card details, date of birth, amount of mortgage on house, and so on. We group all such personal identifying information under the heading Customer Personal Data (CPD). Each customer makes one or more product selections and effects payment for the product(s) selected. In addition, there is ancillary data, such as type of payment, date ordered, date shipped, date delivered (from delivery agent, e.g., courier), and so on. Table 2 shows these data types and whether they originate from the company or the customer.

TABLE 1. PRODUCTS ASSOCIATED WITH EACH COMPANY TYPE.

Company type	Products
Sellers of goods and services (e.g., Amazon.com)	Physical items such as pots, clothing, and electronics; services such as selling your items for you
Hotels (e.g., Mariott.com)	Rooms
Travel Agencies (e.g., Expedia.ca)	Travel bookings
Financial services (e.g., CIBC.com)	Fee-based banking accounts

TABLE 2. DATA TYPES AND WHERE THEY ORIGINATE.

Data type	Origin
Products	Company
CPD	Customer
Product selection	Customer
Amount paid	Company
Ancillary data	Company

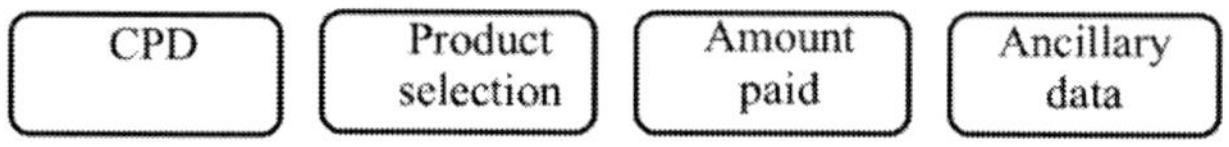

Figure 1. Data collection for a customer order.

We can see that each online customer order involves the data types shown in the left column of Table 2. Depending on the company, the instantiation of these data types will be different, with the possible exception of Amount paid. For example, the "Products" of Amazon.com would be different from the "Products" of eBay.com and the CPD for CIBC.com may be different from that for TD.com (another Canadian bank). Thus, each customer order may be represented by a data collection as shown in Figure 1. We wish to emphasize that there is no implied ordering of the data types in Figure 1, i.e., Figure 1 does not state that the data types should be stored in any particular order one after the other. These data collections would be stored by the company in its own databases, which may be on company premises or on a cloud server. If the company were to suffer a data breach, this data (including CPD) would be exposed.

III. Approach

This section details our approach for reducing the impact of data breaches.

A. Strategy for Storing a Customer's Personal Data

The goal of this strategy is to reduce the storage of personal data on the company's computer system by storing the bulk of the personal data on customers' own devices, while allowing for all the purposes described in Section II-B to be carried out. The strategy consists of five parts, as follows:

1. Identification of data (Figure 1) to be stored on the customer's device: CPD.
2. Design for linking the data on the customer's device to the rest of the data stored on the company's computer system: Use a Unique Customer Identifier (UCI) that the company assigns to each customer. The UCI is the hash (e.g., SHA-3) of the customer's User ID and password for accessing the company. It will form part of the records shown in Figure 2 (shown as relational records without loss of generality since we could have shown them as other types of data structures, e.g., linked lists).

UCI	CPD

a) Record of personal data stored on customer's device.

UCI	Product selection	Amount paid	Ancillary data

b) Record of order data stored on company's system.

Figure 2. Data records corresponding to a customer order. Encrypted data types are shaded.

3. Design for enabling the company to carry out its communication purpose: Use the "Contact information" data record in Figure 3 to contact the customer, where "Contact information" consists of email address and telephone number. Figure 4 shows how the UCI links the three types of data records together.

UCI	Contact information

Figure 3. Data record for a customer's contact information. Encrypted data types are shaded.

4. Design to keep the CPD record should the customer a) use a new device with the company after using other devices, or b) loses a device used with the company. For a), the customer can register a new device with the company on its website after logging in. The company would then transfer the CPD record from a previously used device (on which the customer is also logged in) to the new device. For b), the customer may have used other devices with the company and wishes to replace the lost device, in which case the resolution for a) applies. If the lost device is the only device used with the company, the customer would need to re-enter his/her CPD. See also the third paragraph of Section III-C.
5. Enabling security: Use authenticated symmetric encryption (e.g., AES-GCM [8]) to encrypt the UCI and CPD in Figure 2(a), as well as the Contact information in Figure 3 (encrypted data types are shaded). The UCI in Figure 3 is not encrypted. The UCI and remaining data types in Figure 2 (b) are not encrypted, as it would be difficult for the attacker to use them alone to identify the customer, should the data be breached.

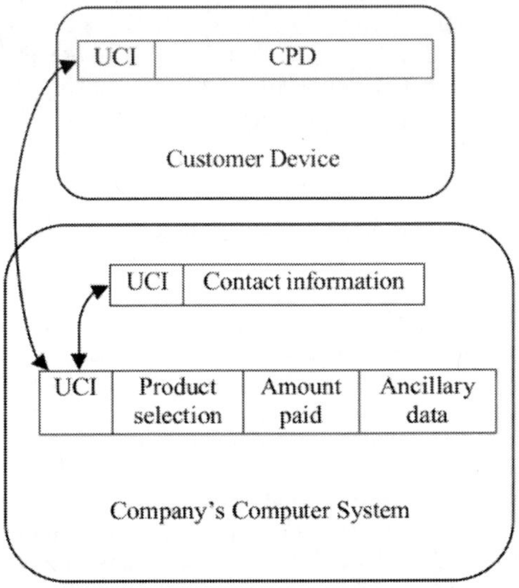

Figure 4. How the UCI links data records together.

B. Customer Walk-Through of the Strategy

1. The customer accesses the company using its website, running either on a desktop computer or on a mobile device such as a smart phone or tablet. In the following, all data transfers between the user's device and the company's system is done though a secure channel (e.g., TLS).

2. If it's the customers first use of the website on this device (detected by the absence of the CPD record), he/she will be asked if he/she has a different device that was used with the website. If not, he/she will be prompted to enter his/her CPD. The company then generates the UCI, forms the record in Figure 2(a), encrypts it, and stores this encrypted record on the customer's device. The company then uses the unencrypted CPD entered by the customer for processing the current order. In addition, the company checks if the customer's Contact information is already in the system (possible if the customer's device was lost or stolen) and if not, creates and stores the record in Figure 3, after encrypting the Contact information (obtained from the CPD). If the customer has used the website before on a different device, he/she will be asked to also login using the other device, at which point the company stores the CPD

record from the old device on the new device, decrypts the CPD record, and uses it for the current transaction.

If the customer has used the website before on this device (detected by the presence of the encrypted CPD record), the company automatically retrieves the encrypted CPD record (Figure 2(a)) from the customer's device and decrypts it for use in the current transaction.

Note that the only time the company retrieves the CPD record from a customer device is when the customer logs in to do a new transaction.

3. The customer proceeds with his/her shopping. Once the customer completes the shopping, the company creates and stores the customer's order data record as shown in Figure 2(b). Note that this record may have to be updated for some ancillary data (e.g., date delivered) once the data is available. This update process as out of scope for this work.

C. *Security Analysis*

We first consider outside attacks against the company. Such attacks would result in breaching the company's data stores leading to the loss of the Contact information and the order data (Figure 4). This loss could be in the form of a copy taken of the data, deletion of the data from the company's data stores, modification of the data in the company's data stores, or certain combinations of these, namely copy followed by deletion, and copy followed by modification. However, the attacker fails to read the Contact information since it is encrypted. The attacker would be able to read the UCI from both the Contact information and the order data records but the UCI would appear as meaningless (hash). The attacker could also read the order data but would have a hard time identifying the customer using only this data. Further, deleting or modifying the data will also fail to damage the company provided that the company is aware of the attack and is able to re-populate the data stores using data back-ups. We assume that the company has implemented other security measures, including making data backups and having ways to detect attacks (e.g., intrusion detection system). Any modification of the encrypted Contact information would also be detected by a failure to decrypt the modified version, i.e., the modified encrypted data fails authentication. Note that for the rest of this paper, whenever we refer to failing to decrypt attacker-modified encrypted data, we mean that the modified encrypted data has failed authentication. In any case, the probability of being attacked after applying the approach is low, since the only attraction for attackers is encrypted Contact information, consisting only of email address and telephone number. Attacks on the company side could also involve malware, that for example, exfiltrates the customer's CPD while in the clear. However, these attacks are not peculiar to the approach and can occur for any website that collects information from users. We assume that the company already has security measures for such attacks.

As for insider attacks against the company, we admit that our security scheme is vulnerable to such attacks. For example, an insider could simply access the CPD in its unencrypted form. Insider attacks are always among the harder ones to defend against and given their seriousness, we expect the company to have implemented other security measures (e.g., [9]) specifically against insider attacks. An exploration of these measures is outside the scope of this paper.

Attacks on the customer side with the device in the customer's possession or not (device lost or stolen) could also result in a copy taken of the customer's CPD record, deleting it, modifying it, or combinations thereof. Since the data is encrypted, the attacker would not be able to read the data if a copy is taken. Deletion or modification of the encrypted CPD record would be detected by the company's system when it fails to find it or fails to decrypt it, in which case the company's system would inform the customer that he/she needs to re-enter his/her CPD or have it transferred from another device (see Section III-A, part 4).

The secure communication channel between the company's system and the customer device may also be attacked, but this is again not peculiar to the approach. Such attacks would be handled the same way as is done for the many other applications of secure communication channels.

D. *Implementation Notes*

The following are suggestions on how the above strategy should be implemented.

- On the company side, the implementation should include functionality to warn that its data stores have been compromised when it is unable to decrypt attacker-modified encrypted data, or when it finds its data stores empty. The implementation should also warn the customer that his/her device has been attacked when the encrypted CPD record was expected but is missing, or when it is unable to decrypt the attacker-modified record.
- If the customer changes or forgets his/her password for accessing the service (if forgotten, a conventional password reset procedure would be used), the company's computer system will need to generate a new UCI corresponding to the new user-ID/password combination. The company will have to create a new CPD record with the new UCI, and upload this new record to all customer devices via the website. The company will also have to update the UCI in the records of Figure 2(b) and Figure 3.
- The company's system needs to allow the customer to update his/her CPD and/or Contact information, and update the relevant records with the new information. For CPD, the system would need to upload an updated CPD record to all customer devices.

E. *Verification of Purposes*

We verify that the approach allows the company to carry out its purposes (Section II-B) for collecting personal data.

- Transaction Requirements: The customer's CPD record is obtained from the customer's device for every transaction (either pre-existing or currently entered) and is available for carrying out the transaction.

- Communication: For contacting the customer, the customer's Contact information (Figure 3) can be obtained using the UCI link from the order data records since contacting is done for an order issue. The customer can contact the company by logging into the company's website. The company can determine the customer's UCI from the customer's User ID and password, and use it to access the contact information for the reply.
- To Secure Other Data: The personal biometric, once captured, can be stored as part of the customer's CPD record on the customer's device. Once the customer logs in for a new transaction, the CPD record is retrieved from the customer's device, at which point the personal biometric is available for use.
- Establishing Loyalty: The company has access to a customer's order history in the form of the order data records. These records (Figure 2(b)) are identified as belonging to a particular customer through the UCI link to the Contact information records. The company can thus establish the loyalty of a particular customer.
- Targeted Advertising: Understanding the type of products a customer has purchased in the past may be done by accessing the customer's order data records, as explained above for establishing loyalty.
- Market Research: The histories of past transactions for all customers can be studied by accessing the order data records, ignoring the UCI in each order record, since there is no need to identify the customers. We assume that market research is carried out without the CPD records, since the company probably does not have the customer's consent for such use of his/her CPD. If the company does require the CPD records, the company can always capture and store them, but would have to accept the risks of those records being breached and being sued for illegally using the CPD for market research.
- Sharing or Selling: There is nothing stopping the company from copying each customer's CPD record and sharing or selling the data. The company would have to accept the risks of the CPD records being breached and being sued for illegally sharing or selling the customer's CPD.

F. Strengths and Weaknesses of the Approach

The approach has the following strengths: a) it is straightforward, which may make it easier to "sell" to upper management for approval, b) it is efficient in that attackers would have to breach the devices of all the company's customers, in order to breach the same quantity of personal data that are traditionally all stored in the company's system, c) it makes the company less attractive to attackers who intend to cause a data breach due to its efficiency as stated above and the fact that the only private data left on the company's system to be breached is the encrypted customer Contact information, and d) it should please customers who want more control over their private data, since most of it is stored only on their own devices.

The approach seems to have three weaknesses: a) the storage/retrieval of the CPD record may attract attacks on the secure transmission channel, b) there is additional overhead cost due to encryption / decryption operations, and c) it is vulnerable to insider attack. Weakness a) does not represent significant extra risk over conventional transactions since personal data is transmitted in conventional transactions as well. For weakness b), the extra overhead should not be significant. Finally, weakness c) is not exclusive to this approach, since it can arise wherever there are insiders. Potential remedies include the installation of specific security measures to defend against insider attacks [9].

IV. Application Examples

We instantiate the data types in Figure 1 for two types of B2C companies, demonstrating that the approach can fit with different B2C companies.

Example 1: Seller of goods (e.g., Amazon.com). Table 3 shows the instantiation of the data types for this example.

TABLE 3. INSTANTIATION OF DATA TYPES FOR EXAMPLE 1.

CPD	Product selection	Amount paid	Ancillary data
Name	Camera	$159.00	Date ordered
Billing address	Hair clipper	$49.00	Date shipped
Default shipping address	Laser printer toner	$68.00	Date delivered
Alternate shipping address			Payment method
Email address			Product returned
Phone number			Reason for return
Credit card data			Refund status

Example 2: Hotel (e.g., Mariott.com). Table 4 shows the instantiation of the data types for this example.

TABLE 4. INSTANTIATION OF DATA TYPES FOR EXAMPLE 2.

CPD	Product selection	Amount paid	Ancillary data
Name	Room - double	$200 / night	Date of reservation
Billing address			Arrival date
Home address			Departure date
Email address			Payment method
Phone number			Airport shuttle y/n
Credit card data			Daily laundry y/n
Loyalty ID number			Daily cleaning y/n
Country of origin			Wake-up call y/n
Passport country			Stay extended y/n
Passport number			
Room preferences			
Floor preference			

We could have included other examples here, but the above examples suffice for our purposes.

V. RELATED WORK

Work that is most closely related to this work are as follows: Aggarwal et al. [10] propose that an organization outsource its data management to two untrusted servers to break associations of sensitive information. They show how the use of two servers, together with the use of encryption where needed, enables efficient data partitioning and guarantees that the contents of any one server does not violate data privacy. However, it is unclear if attackers can re-construct the sensitivity associations by breaching both servers. Ciriani et al. [11] present what they claim to be a solution that improves over Aggarwal et al. [10] by first splitting the information to be protected into different fragments so that sensitive associations represented by confidentiality constraints are broken, and minimizing the use of encryption. The resulting fragments may be stored at the same server or at different servers. Our work differs from Aggarwal et al. [10] and Ciriani et al. [11] as follows: a) the above two papers are solutions for securing databases, whereas our work is focused on reducing the loss of data in the event of a data breach by simply not storing some of the data in the company's computer system, b) we do not use data partitioning or fragmentation; rather, our data is distributed between the company and its customers from the point of data creation, c) we do not need to rely on breaking any sensitivity associations, d) our approach has been designed to satisfy the business needs of the organization, and e) our approach is more straightforward, and is therefore easier to apply.

Other work in the literature mostly deal with the prevention or risks of data breaches, the discovery of a data breach, and the aftermath of a data breach. Within these categories, the most closely related works have to do with preventing or evaluating the risks of data breaches. We describe some of these papers below, to give the reader a sense of this research. Note that these works all differ from this paper in that this paper aims to reduce the impact or data lost if a breach were to happen, whereas the works described in the following are largely focused on preventing breaches from happening. Panou et al. [12] describe a framework for monitoring and describing insider behaviour anomalies that can potentially impact the risks of a data breach. The framework also enhances a company's understanding of cybersecurity and increases awareness of the threats and consequences related to breaches, and eventually enable faster recovery from a breach. Guha and Kandula [13] propose a data breach insurance mechanism together with risk assessment methodology to cover the risk from accidental data breaches and encourage best practices to prevent the breaches. They also present data supporting the feasibility of their approach. Zou and Schaub [14] interviewed consumers after the Equifax data breach and discovered that consumers' understanding of credit bureaus' data collection practices was incomplete. As such, consumers did not take sufficient protective actions to deal with the risks to their data. The authors describe the implications of their findings for the design of future security tools with the aim of empowering consumers to better manage their data and protect themselves from future breaches. Nicho and Fakhry [15] look at the application of system dynamics to cybersecurity, specifically to the Advanced Persistent Threat (APT) that can employ technical, as well as organizational factors to cause a data breach. They applied system dynamics to the APT that led to the Equinox breach and identified key independent variables contributing to the breach. Their work provides insights into the dynamics of the threat and suggests "what if" scenarios to minimize APT risks that could lead to a breach. Luh et al. [16] present an ontology for planning a defence against APTs that can lead to a data breach. The ontology is mapped to abstracted events and anomalies that can be detected by monitoring and helps with the understanding of how, why, and by whom certain resources are targeted. There are other references in this category which have not been included here due to lack of space.

VI. CONCLUSIONS AND FUTURE WORK

We have presented an approach, applicable to B2C e-commerce companies, that reduces the impact of a data breach by storing most of a customer's private data in his/her own device rather than in the company's computer system. The word "most" is key, since we still allow some necessary personal data (customer contact information) to be stored on the company's system. We also verified that the approach allows the company to carry out its purposes for collecting private data. Some readers may consider the approach overly simple, but if a simple solution gets the job done, it should be preferred over a complex solution. As well, we do not claim that the approach as presented is complete, as there may be details that we have overlooked. We look forward to receiving feedback and correcting this in a future paper.

In terms of future work, we would like to explore the application of the approach to other types of businesses and organizations, and adapt it where necessary. We would also like to have implementations of the approach in order to fine tune it, measure implementation effort, and check performance.

ACKNOWLEDGMENT

The author is grateful to Aptusinnova Inc. for financially supporting this work. He expresses his thanks to the conference reviewers of this paper for their detailed and useful comments.

REFERENCES

[1] ZD Net, "Exclusive: Details of 10.6 million MGM hotel guests posted on a hacking forum," [retrieved: October, 2020] https://www.zdnet.com/article/exclusive-details-of-10-6-million-of-mgm-hotel-guests-posted-on-a-hacking-forum/

[2] Reuters, "MGM Resorts sued over data breach that possibly involved 10.6 million guests," [retrieved: October, 2020] https://www.reuters.com/article/us-mgm-resorts-intl-cyber-lawsuit/mgm-resorts-sued-over-data-breach-that-possibly-involved-10-6-million-guests-idUSKCN20G062

[3] Norton, "2019 Data breaches: 4 billion records breached so far," [retrieved: October, 2020]

https://us.norton.com/internetsecurity-emerging-threats-2019-data-breaches.html

[4] E. Aïmeur and M. Lafond, "The scourge of Internet personal data collection," Proc. 2013 International Conference on Availability, Reliability and Security (AReS 2013), Sept. 2013, pp. 821-828.

[5] Business News Daily, "How businesses are collecting data (and what they're doing with it)," [retrieved: October, 2020] https://www.businessnewsdaily.com/10625-businesses-collecting-data.html

[6] R. Sarcar, "How to set up an ecommerce loyalty program to improve retention, build community and drive 5X in sales," [retrieved: October, 2020] https://www.bigcommerce.com/blog/online-customer-loyalty-programs/#how-to-create-and-implement-a-customer-loyalty-program

[7] PC, "How companies turn your data into money," [retrieved: October, 2020] https://www.pcmag.com/news/how-companies-turn-your-data-into-money

[8] M. Dworkin, "Recommendation for block cipher modes of operation: Galois/Counter Mode (GCM) and GMAC," NIST Special Publication 800-38D, November 2007.

[9] CERT National Insider Threat Center, "Common Sense Guide to Mitigating Insider Threats, Sixth Edition," Technical Report CMU/SEI-2018-TR-010, Software Engineering Insititute, Carnegie Mellon University, December 2018.

[10] G. Aggarwal et al., "Two can keep a secret: a distributed architecture for secure database services," Proc. Second Biennial Conference on Innovative Data Systems Research (CIDR 2005), Jan. 2005, pp. 1-14.

[11] V. Ciriani et al., "Combining fragmentation and encryption to protect privacy in data storage," ACM Transactions on Information and System Security (TISSEC), Vol. 13, Issue 3, article 22, pp. 1-33, July 2010.

[12] A. Panou, C. Ntantogian, and C. Xenakis, "RiSKi: A framework for modeling cyber threats to estimate risk for data breach insurance," Proc. 21st Pan-Hellenic Conference on Informatics (PCI 2017), article no. 32, Sept. 2017, pp. 1-6.

[13] S. Guha and S. Kandula, "Act for affordable data care," Proc. 11th ACM Workshop on Hot Topics in Networks (HotNets-XI), Oct. 2012, pp. 103-108.

[14] Y. Zou and F. Schaub, "Concern but no action: consumers' reactions to the Equifax data breach," Extended Abstracts, 2018 CHI Conference on Human Factors in Computing Systems (CHI EA '18), paper no. LBW506, Apr. 2018, pp. 1-6.

[15] M. Nicho and H. Fakhry, "Applying system dynamics to model advanced persistent threats," Proc. 2019 International Communication Engineering and Cloud Computing Conference (CECCC 2019), Oct. 2019, pp 29-33.

[16] R. Luh, S. Schrittwieser, and S. Marschalek, "TAON: an ontology-based approach to mitigating targeted attacks," Proc. 18th International Conference on Information Integration and Web-based Applications and Services (iiWAS '16), Nov. 2016, pp. 303-312.

Forensic Behavior Analysis in Video Conferencing Based on the Metadata of Encrypted Audio and Video Streams - Considerations and Possibilities

Robert Altschaffel, Jonas Hielscher, Christian Kraetzer, Kevin Lamshöft and Jana Dittmann

Otto von Guericke University Magdeburg
Magdeburg, Germany
Email: robert.altschaffel@iti.cs.uni-magdeburg.de

Abstract—**This paper discusses the possibility to perform a forensic behavior analysis on the network recordings of video conferences in order to identify different activities taking part during such conferencing. This behavior analysis is based on the audio- and video streams of such software. While the connections are usually encrypted, the possibility of using and deriving heuristic metadata from the encrypted stream in order to identify various activities (use cases) is explored. This paper shows first results of such an approach to identify various activities, which could then be used to construct a biometric pattern. Furthermore, a model for communication flows during video conferences is introduced, formalizing which specific data can be gathered at various points by an observer. A first case study employs a set of four different test cases applied to two different solutions for video conferencing.**

Keywords*—*Security, Video conferencing, Zoom, Big Blue Button, User and traffic profiling, Network forensics.

I. Introduction

Video Conferencing (VC) systems are used to communicate using video, audio and text streams. They are used in business contexts, as well as in the private life of many people, receiving additional relevance during the trend of social distancing associated with the COVID-19 epidemic.

This paper evaluates the possibility to perform a forensic behavior analysis on network data captures of VC. This forensic behavior analysis aims at identifying certain activities during VC sessions. The analysis is based on the audio-, video- and text streams common in this kind of software. While the network traffic is usually encrypted, the possibility of using metadata still available, as well as heuristic metadata derived from the encrypted stream has been explored in different application scenarios (see Section II-B). This paper discusses first results of this approach tested with two different VC solutions and the impact these results have for forensic use and also the potential impact on the privacy of the users during such conferencing sessions is discussed.

The paper is structured as follows: Section II of this paper gives an overview on the VC systems used for the first tests discussed in this paper, the impact of biometrics on privacy, approaches used to perform activity identification in encrypted traffic and general considerations on using such an approach during a forensic investigation. Section III introduces the overall approach used during these tests. Section IV describes the tools required to conduct such forensic activity identification. An exemplary case study based on the two selected VC systems is provided in Section V. A discussion of the potential impacts of the results presented in this work as well as a discussion on potential future topics conclude this paper in Section VI.

II. State of the Art

This section gives some general background to establish the foundations of the work done during this paper.

A. Video conferencing

This paper discusses systems used to enable the communication between users utilizing text, audio and video. These systems are referred to as *VC solutions* during the course of this paper (based on the definition of this term in [1]). They are used for business discussions as well as for private conversations. These two use cases establish a clear need of confidentiality of the communication and in some cases also of the resulting metadata of the communication (this includes the identity of the participants or the date and time of the communication). If the contents of the communication are disclosed, private information and business secrets might be revealed. In this paper, we focus on conferencing systems which rely on a central (conferencing) server which handles the communication (in contrast to peer-to-peer systems).

B. Activity and Content Identification in Encrypted Traffic

This section provides an overview on the various approaches designed to identify activities within encrypted traffic.

An early approach was published in 2001 by Song et al. [2]. The study found that the reconstruction of single user inputs in an SSH session is possible based on the packet size and keystroke dynamics. Statistical models to successfully extract biometric features from the encrypted traffic of the TeamViewer application were researched in Altschaffel et al. [3]. White et al. [4] separated encrypted VoIP-traffic into single phonemes and were able to show that at least parts of the encrypted spoken conversations can be reconstructed.

Dupasquier et al. [5] used a dynamic time warping algorithm based on the size of encrypted packets, as well as the timing information as input in order to predict between 60%-83% of spoken sentences correctly. Korczynski et al. [6] applied statistical protocol identification on encrypted Skype traffic in order to distinguish different types of communication (audio, video, chat, file sharing, etc.). With their approach they were able to predict the type of communication with accuracy between 60.3% and 100%, depending on the type. Zhu et al. [7] used packet inter-arrival-times and packet size as parameters to identify speakers in a Skype session. They also proposed countermeasures to restore privacy, e.g. the harmonization of packet sizes between different speakers. Zhang et al. [8] were able to track Skype users mobility (determine their ever-changing public IP-Addresses), by creating unique fingerprints of their Skype-network-traffic.

Besides the potential risks originating from such transcription attacks and user tracking analyses, Whiskerd et al. [9] demonstrated that biometric user information can also be easily derived from such encrypted communication sessions. In their work they achieved an EER of roughly 5% while doing keystroke dynamics (KD) analyses in the encrypted domain, a performance which, for their setup, is not significantly worse than biometric KD verification on the ground truth (i.e. unencrypted) input.

C. Digital forensics

Digital forensics is defined by [10] as *"[...] the science of identifying and analyzing entities, states, and state transitions of events that have occurred or are occurring"*. In essence, forensics is used to reconstruct events. Digital forensics performs this reconstruction in the digital domain. This event reconstruction might be useful in various contexts, including judicial proceedings.

Forensic proceedings follow a distinct pattern. Forensic process models describe this pattern. In this paper, the forensic process model as described in [11] is used. This model has two primary advantages useful for the approach used within this model. At first, the forensic process described in this model contains a *Strategic Preparation* (**SP**) which consists of activities taken before a specific forensic investigation in order to support or even enable the possibility of said investigation. The other advantage is the use of various *Data Types* which represent groups of data handled in a specific way during a forensic investigation.

During this paper, the enhanced definitions presented in [12] are used. Hence, the following definitions for the *Investigation Steps* are used to describe the forensic behavior identification:

- **Strategic preparation (SP)** represents measures taken by the operator of an IT-system, prior to an incident, which might support a forensic investigation
- **Operational preparation (OP)** represents the preparation for a forensic investigation after a suspected incident
- **Data gathering (DG)** represents measures to acquire and secure digital evidence
- **Data investigation (DI)** represents measures to evaluate and extract data for further investigation
- **Data analysis (DA)** represents the detailed analysis and correlation between digital evidence from various sources
- **Documentation (DO)** represents the detailed documentation of the investigation

This identification is based on data which belongs to a range of different *Data Types*. The *Data Types* relevant for this approach are defined as follows by [13]:

- **Raw data (DT2)**: *A sequence of bits within the Data Streams of a computing systems not (yet) interpreted.*
- **Details about data (DT3)**: *Data added to other data, stored within the annotated chunk of data or externally*
- **Functional data (DT9)**: *Data content created, edited, consumed or processed as the key functionality of the system*

These *Data Types* are related to each other. **DT2** is the pure not interpreted data flow between the systems. This contains some **DT3** in order to facilitate the communications between the systems (in this case network addresses or ports). If the **DT2** could be completely interpreted (incl. decryption and decoding), the **DT9** would be obtained. This would include the video, audio and text streams. This data might also contain annotations (**DT3**). The approach presented in this paper relies on *Strategic Preparation* (providing among others the evaluation setup) and has to address the fact that different *Data Types* are available at different locations of the use case scenarios common with VC systems.

III. Usability of Audio and Video Streams in Video Conferencing for Activity Analysis

Section II-B has shown that different activities might lead to a notable change in communication behavior. This change in network behavior might enable the identification of various activities in a communication flow without the ability to interpret the communication flow directly (e.g. by using the audio codec to reconstruct the transmitted audio). Such an approach might be useful in cases in which the used codec is unknown or not available or where such reconstruction is not possible since the communication channel itself is encrypted.

In order to implement such an approach several steps are necessary. At first, the various activities in VC which might lead to discernible difference in communication behavior have to identified. This is performed in Section III-A. After this, the discernible difference in the communication behavior has to be identified. These differences can be used to establish the properties usable for an identification of the various activities. This process is described in Section III-B. Section III-C describes where in the communication structure these properties are available during the use of a VC solution. Section III-D then explores the technical process used in order to identify different activities within communication flows. This approach is based on pattern recognition which evaluates said properties. During the use of the system, these properties are compared to a model created during a training phase. This process is akin to the pattern recognition pipeline.

A. Activities in video conferencing

First considerations on the various activities usually performed in VC are listed here. This list describes some basic behaviors which we suspect to have a notable impact on the observable communication behavior. For example, these activities each require a different amount of data to be transmitted to the other participants during the video conference. This list contains eleven elements at this point of time but is expandable. However, a distinction between more similar activities might require additional insight into the communication behavior and the resulting properties.

Activities in Text

TE_1 inactive / not typing
TE_2 typing
TE_3 sending text

Activities in Audio

A_1 deactivated / muted
A_2 unmute and silent
A_3 unmute and speaking fluently
A_4 unmute and speaking chopped off

Activities in Video

V_1 deactivated
V_2 black screen
V_3 one person in front
V_4 multiple persons in front

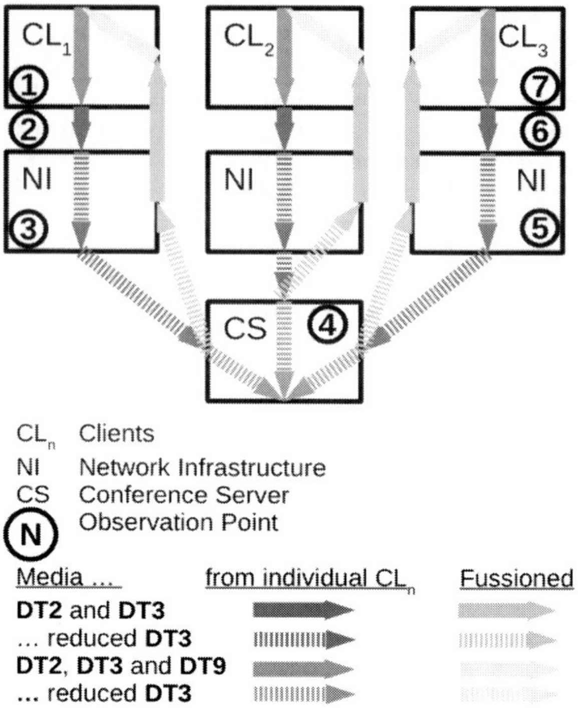

Fig. 1. Communication infrastructure in VC solutions and potential available *Data Types* at various observation points

B. Features

Various features usable to distinguish activities within encrypted communication sessions have been proposed by the literature examined in Section II-B. A common theme here is the size of the transmitted packets in correlation to the timing information. Our approach uses these two sets of inputs as the foundation for the resulting features. The specific features used in this approach are based on the hierarchy of features proposed in [3]. Here, *Window-based features using fixed time windows* are selected as best representing the results found in other research work presented in Section II-B. These features are based on *Packet features* and aggregated over a specific amount of packets. Hence, the used features consist of information about the specific *packet size*. This is then aggregated to the *minimum*, *maximum*, *mean* and *standard deviation* of *packet size* over a specific window of packets.

However, obtaining these features relies on the possibility to separate the various communication streams as understood by the feature hierarchy. In order to do so, the presence of additional information might be necessary. This information includes identifiable network addresses.

C. Availability of features in the communication infrastructure

Some of the information discussed in III-B is only available at certain points within the communication infrastructure. This is due to the fact that the media streams are encrypted on their path between the various clients and the conference server. In addition, the conference server fuses the various media streams of the clients together and delivers them back to the attached clients. This is illustrated in Figure 1.

It is of relevance to understand where which exact *Data Types* (and hence features) are available within this communication infrastructure. Hence, assuming Client CL_1 is the target of the activity identification, the available *Data Types* at the specific Observation Points (**OP**) are:

- $\mathbf{OP}_1$ provides access to the entire unencrypted media streams front Client CL_1 (**DT9**) as well as its representation on the network (**DT2**) and the metadata necessary for the network communication (**DT3**).
- $\mathbf{OP}_2$ provides access to the raw representation of the encrypted media streams on the network (**DT2**) as well as the metadata necessary for the network communication (**DT3**).
- $\mathbf{OP}_3$ provides the same access as $\mathbf{OP}_2$ but might alter some of the metadata necessary for the network communication (**DT3**).
- $\mathbf{OP}_4$ can decrypt the encrypted media streams and has access to all unencrypted media streams from all clients (**DT9**). In addition, access to the individual encrypted streams (**DT2**) and the individual metadata from the network communication (**DT3**) is available, although potentially in a form altered by the network infrastructure.
- $\mathbf{OP}_5$ has access to the encrypted and combined media

streams (**DT2**) as well as to some metadata necessary for the communication from the Conference Server to Client CL_3 which might be altered due to intervening Network Infrastructure (**DT3**).

- **OP_6** has the same access to **DT2** as **OP_5** but has access to the original metadata for the communication between Conference Server and Client CL_3 (**DT3**).
- **OP_7** can decrypt the combined **DT2** in order to achieve the combined media streams from all Clients CL_n (**DT9**). In addition, the metadata from the communication between Conference Server and Client CL_3 is available (**DT3**).

D. Using pattern recognition to identify activities in VC to support a forensic investigation

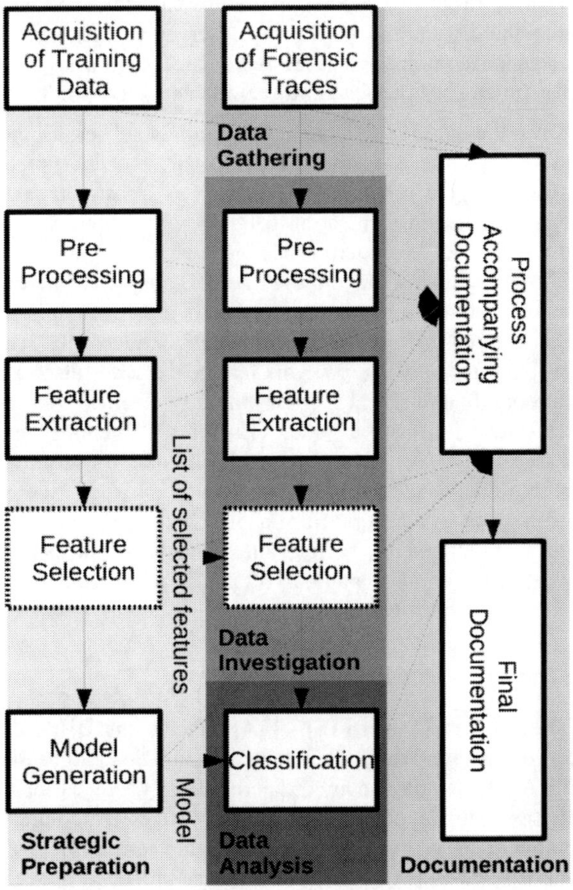

Fig. 2. Mapping of the pattern recognition approach to the forensic *Investigation Steps*, based on [12].

In order to use pattern recognition to identify activities within an encrypted VC session, various activities during the forensic process are necessary.

At first, the pattern recognition relies on a classification model. This model has to be created before a specific forensic investigation takes place. This has to occur during the **SP**. In addition to the steps already described in the pattern recognition pipeline, the acquisition of training data is a complicated topic and requires special attention. Section III-C discussed the availability of features at various spots within the communication infrastructure. The training data should be as close as possible to the data acquired during the forensic investigation in order to achieve an usable classification model. Hence, the training data should be captured at the spot most likely used by the forensic investigator during a forensic investigation. The rest of the **SP** covers the creation of the model which involves the Pre-Processing, Feature Extraction, Feature Selection and the Model generation itself.

Once a specific forensic investigation is started the potential forensic data sources are identified during the **OP**. This leads to the exact locations where forensic data is acquired during **DG** and will aim at acquiring the greatest extent of possible data while maintaining integrity and authenticity of the captures. Hence, a capture location which is entirely under the control of the investigator might enable a greater degree of integrity and authenticity. In this step, **DT2** is acquired.

Once these forensic traces are acquired, the data is interpreted. **DT3** is extracted from **DT2**. If no encryption is used (or the encryption keys are known to the investigator), **DT9** could also be reconstructed. This data is then used for the Feature Extraction.

Finally, the model generated during the **SP** is used to classify the forensic traces yielding information about the activities performed during the VC session investigated here. During the entire process the performed actions and steps are documented in order to create a final documentation usable to judge the potential evidentiary value of the classification results.

IV. EXEMPLARY IMPLEMENTATION AND PRELIMINARY RESULTS

In order to test our hypothesis that the features presented in III-B are sufficient to identify the various possible activities in VC (see III-A) even within encrypted communication a test setup using two different VC solutions was created. First preliminary tests have been conducted in order to show the validity of this approach.

The two video conference solutions Zoom [14] and Big Blue Button (BBB) [15] are chosen for a first practical case study. Zoom is selected for its high market share among commercial VC solutions (as can be seen in [16]). BBB is an Open Source VC solution. The prevalence of self-hosted instances of BBB hinders extensive use statistics for this solution. However, it is broadly used in various educational institutes. Both follow the communication structure as laid out in Section III-C and are hence representative for the technologies used in VC.

In case of Zoom we use the educational accounts of our university and in case of BBB a self-hosted instance (denoted as **BBB**). Zoom offers a desktop-client and a web-client which are both used (denoted as **Zoom-Web** and **Zoom-App** respectively). BBB offers only a web-client.

A. Setup

Three clients (CL_1, CL_2, CL_3) are used during these tests. While CL_1 is used in every test-run and actively using functionalities like the microphone or webcam to generate corresponding data, CL_2 is only used in those occasions in which multiple active clients are required for the tests. CL_3 is a passive observer (participating in the conferences but not actively using any functionality). The Observation Point for forensic data is located outside the decryption performed by the client located on this system. Hence, the observation takes place at **OP**$_6$. All incoming traffic is captured using Wireshark. Different hardware is used for the clients (and therefore the possible quality of audio and video data differs): An *iPad (2017)* is used for CL_1, an *iPhone 11* for CL_2 and a *Lenovo Thinkpad Carbon X1 3th Gen* for CL_3. The following tests are performed in this setup:

[T1] - Audio: CL_1 is using the microphone to send audio data. Different levels of audio usage are compared: 1. The microphone is muted in the conference client and on the hardware (A_1). 2. The microphone is activated in the conference client but deactivated on the hardware (A_2). 3. The microphone is fully activated and a monotone voice is recorded (A_3). 4. The microphone is fully activated and a voice which varies in vocal pitch and volume is recorded (A_4). **[T2] - Video**: CL_1 is using the built-in webcam to send video data. Different levels of video usage are compared: 1. The webcam is deactivated in the client (V_1). 2. The webcam is activated and a black image is recorded (V_2). 3. The webcam is activated and a static video (without visible movement) is recorded (V_3). 4. The webcam is activated and and a moving video (movement of a person) is recorded (V_4). The aim is to test whether an observer can identify user behavior, e.g. whether a person is visible in the camera or not. **[T3] - Video2x**: CL_1 and CL_2 are using the built-in camera and both perform tests like in [T2] (V_5). The aim is to test whether an observer can identify the number of active participants or not. **[T4] - Video-Audio**: CL_1 is using different audio- and video features like described in [T1] and [T2]. The aim is to test whether the stream of audio and video data can be distinguished on network level in order to evaluate them separately. This adds up to twelve test cases from **OP**$_6$ (four tests with three different clients). Additional tests cases are performed to test the validity of our approach in regards to keystroke dynamics. **[T5] - Keystroke** CL_1 is using the chat functionality of the client and in case of BBB also the *Shared Notes*. Simple text strings are typed and sent. In this test the outgoing traffic is captured at CL_1 (observation point 2) as well as the incoming traffic at CL_3 (observation point 6). In addition traffic without any user interaction is captured at both points. Each of the tests presented here is repeated twice in order to reduce the risk of data corruption.

B. Training

For each of these tests, an initial run during the preparation (as discussed in III-D) is performed in order to obtain training data. Pre-processing is done using the filter options of Wireshark in order to clean up the captures from easily identifiable noise and in order to separate the specific streams. The necessary steps are different according to the specific conferencing software used. These pre-processing steps are provided here in order to present an overview on potentially necessary actions:

BBB: The audio and video streams are transferred using WebRTC[17] which is based on UDP. Other data, like information about the session itself and the text chat is transferred using Websockets based on TCP. Hence, TCP packets are removed. **Zoom-Web**: The video streams are transferred exclusively via UDP. The audio streams are transferred using Websockets (TCP) and WebRTC (UDP). Depending on the test scenario, UDP or TCP packets are filtered out. **Zoom-App**: The audio and video streams are transferred over UDP exclusively. Additional data is transferred partly via TCP. Therefore all TCP packets are filtered out. In all cases, only the incoming traffic is observed, filtered by the source IP address. While the IP address of the BBB server is unique over all conference sessions, the addresses of the Zoom server change every time. The filters need to be adapted accordingly.

Since the data is collected at **OP**$_6$, only a subset of potential data is available. As discussed in III-C, the encrypted and combined media streams (**DT2**) as well as some metadata necessary for the communication between the Conference Server and Client CL_3 is available which prevents the separation of (**DT2**) into streams specific to either CL_1 or CL_2. This data is then used as training data in order to create models. Here, a self-created feature extractor which extracts the features mentioned in III-B is used. This feature extractor also extracts additional features which were initially deemed not useful for the decision task at hand. The WEKA machine learning workbench[18] is used to create the model. In addition, the captures are visualized using the I/O-Graph tool inherent in Wireshark in order to perform a first visual inspection of the features predicted to be relevant. Wireshark allows for the visualization of *(F1)* number of packets per time *(pck/sec)* and *(F2)* the throughput *(byte/sec)*.

C. Tests and Results

The test cases cover **[T1]** - **[T4]** either using **BBB**, **Zoom-App** or **Zoom-Web**. The J48 classification algorithm in WEKA was employed in order to identify the various user activities. This algorithm uses decisions trees which are interpretable in order to identify the relevant feature (as has been demonstrated in [3]). However, this was preceded by a purely visual inspection of the respective data.

a) Visual Inspection: A first visual inspection was performed using the Wireshark I/O Graph for every test case as shown in Figure 3. The identifiable activities for each test case (see Section IV-A) are shown in the following way: "/" means a distinction is possible between the activities on the left and the right side. "∧" indicates that the activities on the left and right side can not be distinguished from each other, but together form a combined class. An X denotes that no separation was possible.

This approach allows for the extraction of user behavior in ten out of twelve test cases. An overview of the results is provided in Table I.

During the inspection, only $F2$ shows significant differences between the different user behavior features and thus only this feature is used for the visualization. **[T4]** in **Zoom-Web** does not show any difference between the activation of one or two cameras. This is due to the fact that **Zoom-Web** can only show one incoming stream per time and the Zoom server decides which is chosen. **[T3]** in **BBB** cannot be used to differentiate between audio and video streams, since both are sent over the same protocol and port. In **[T3]** in **Zoom-Web** the audio and video streams can easily be distinguished based on the protocol (video: UDP only, audio: UDP and TCP). In the **Zoom-App**, the distinction is possible based on different port numbers per stream. In **[T4]** in both **Zoom-Web** and **Zoom-App**, $F1$ differs heavily, based on the quality of the used camera which potentially allows to extract additional information about the used hardware. The same is not possible in case of **BBB**.

Fig. 3. In the case of Zoom, the amount of incoming UDP data at $\mathbf{OP_6}$ varies, depending on the audio-channel usage of CL_1. An activated microphone (A_2) can be distinguished from a deactivated (A_1) and a continuous voice (A_3) from a choppy voice (A_4).

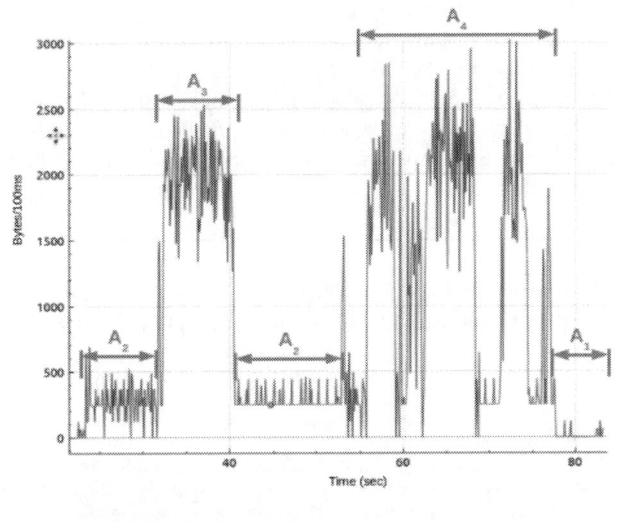

TABLE I. RESULTS OF THE VISUAL INSPECTION EMPLOYING THE WIRESHARK I/O GRAPH FOR ACTIVITY IDENTIFICATION

Test	Zoom-Web	Zoom-App	BBB
[T1]	A_1 / A_2 / A_3 / A_4	A_1 / A_2 / A_3 / A_4	$(A_1 \wedge A_2)$ / $(A_3 \wedge A_4)$
[T2]	V_1 / V_2 / V_3	V_1 / V_2 / V_3	V_1 / $(V_2 \wedge V_3)$
[T3]	V_1 / V_2 / V_3 / A_1 / A_2 / A_3 / A_4	V_1 / V_2 / V_3 / A_1 / A_2 / A_3 / A_4	X
[T4]	X	V_1 / V_2 / V_3 / V_4	$(V_1 \wedge V_2 \wedge V_3)$ / V_4

[T5] shows that no keystroke biometrics is possible in either **Zoom-App** or **Zoom-Web** at all. Single keystrokes are not transferred over the network and other clients have no indication about, whether a client is currently typing or not. In **BBB** keystroke biometrics is possible on different levels: At OP_2 every keystroke in the text chat is visible on the network as an TCP request to the server, which is directly answered. The size of the transferred packets does not differ, since the concrete keystroke (character) is not transferred but only the information about the occurence of a keystroke event. At OP_6 packets are received whenever the status of another user changes between *writing* and *not writing*. The first event is triggered after the first keystroke is received by the server, the second approximately 1.5 sec after the last keystroke was received. Even stronger keystroke biometrics are possible with the shared notes: Here every keystroke is also visible at OP_6 and the network packets differs in size, based on the transferred content (e.g. the packet is larger if one chunk of text was inserted by just one keystroke like using the insert shortcut).

b) Classification Results: The promising first results from the visual inspection are confirmed using pattern recognition in the form of the J48 algorithm. In this case, the derivation of user behavior is possible in nine out of the twelve test cases as can be seen in Table II. Here, Kappa Statistics are used. They range between 0 and 1 with 1 indicating optimal classification.

The identification is possible to a greater degree than those based on visual inspection. Indeed, the missing three entries are the result of non-sufficient training data and are not indicative of the impossibility to discern the user behavior in these cases.

The first results lead to the surprising observation that the most distinct features are those based on the transfer dynamic during the communication (especially a feature referred to as *syn_transfer_drop_freq* which denotes the rate with which windows of a certain amount of packets each have a lower throughput than the previous window). The extraction of this feature is present in the feature extractor used here. However, when filtering out the STUN protocol, these features lose their usefulness in the case of BBB. STUN - or Session Traversal Utilities for NAT - is commonly used protocol which enables clients to access servers which are based behind a NAT-firewall.

Therefore, we suspect that these features are highly susceptible to changes in the network infrastructure. However, this question remains open for additional work and for this paper we removed these features from further considerations.

TABLE II. KAPPA STATISTICS FOR DIFFERENT TEST CASES IN THE CONTEXT OF ACTIVITY IDENTIFICATION

Test	Zoom-Web	Zoom-App	BBB
[T1]	0.9989	0.9947	1
[T2]	0.9993	0.9953	1
[T3]	NA	NA	1
[T4]	0.9993	0.9947	NA

A detailed example of this can be seen in Table III where the confusion matrix for **[T2]** using **Zoom-Web** is provided.

The confusion matrix shows a clear distinctness between the various classes of activities.

TABLE III. CONFUSION MATRIX FOR **[T2]** USING **ZOOM-WEB** IN THE CONTEXT OF ACTIVITY IDENTIFICATION

Classified as	V_1 **deactivated**	V_2 **black screen**	V_3 **one person in front**
V_1 **deactivated**	44	0	0
V_2 **black screen**	1	1221	0
V_3 **one person in front**	1	0	2898

The J48 decision tree allows for an interpretation of the features this distinction is based on:

```
winn_totlen_stddev1 <= 124
|   str_totlen_stddev1 <= 6: NoCamera
|   str_totlen_stddev1 > 6: Black
winn_totlen_stddev1 > 124: MovingImage
```

The feature *winn_totlen_stddev* denotes the standard variation of the total length of the payload of various packets during windows of 500 packets. Even when these features are removed, other features would be used without degrading the classification quality.

Beyond the possibilities of visual inspection is for example the identification of all specific activities in the case of **[T2]** using **BBB**:

```
str_entropy_mean1 <= 6.38381: NoCamera
str_entropy_mean1 > 6.38381
|   winn_kbps1 <= 0.069221: Black
|   winn_kbps1 > 0.069221
|   |   winn_ia_pl_mean1 <= 0.01912: MovingImage
|   |   winn_ia_pl_mean1 > 0.01912
|   |   |   str_totlen_mean1 <= 796: MovingImage
|   |   |   str_totlen_mean1 > 796: Black
```

Here, *str_entropy_mean1* (the entropy) is used to distinguish between NoCamera and a Black image. This seems to be the case since there is less variance in the video stream. Hence, additional features might be useful.

V. Discussion

The results presented in this paper can be seen as a preliminary trend indicating the potential benefits of a forensic behavior analysis in encrypted VC sessions (the resulting capture files can be found online [19]). While it is freely and openly admitted by us authors that the amount of training and test data used within this first evaluation is not sufficient for any generalization, the used features (mainly those covering the transfer rate of data) seem promising. The use of $\mathbf{OP}_6$ for the **DG** impacts the attribution of a given behavior to a specific client since a separation of the specific streams is often impossible after they have been aggregated by the conference server. On one hand this might make the approach presented in this paper impractical for a larger amount of communication participants, on the other hand is this segmentation problem not that hard: For example in the case of audio streams in VC, only one participant is likely to speak at any given point of time. For larger analyses, the separation of different types of media streams on the network layer, like it is possible in both Zoom clients, is nevertheless very important.

VI. Conclusion

In this paper we have demonstrated an approach for forensic behavior analysis on encrypted VC communications. First results indicate that an activity identification is possible. This approach relies on the creation of knowledge (in the form of decision models) before a specific investigation takes place. Then, these models are applied to the captured data. The first tests conducted in this paper have to be repeated on a greater amount of data for training and test in order to increase the generalization of the potential this approach offers in terms of forensic activity identification.

In addition, the first tests identified potentially useful features beyond the use of those based on network throughput. The multitude of different communication scenarios and the specific data available at the various points of the network has been discussed in Section III-C providing a clear definition of the specific Observation Points. It has to be investigated how accurate a model created with training data from one specific Observation Point is when applied to test data obtained from another observation point. Also, the network connection characteristics might have an influence on the specific models since such a connection could limit bandwidth. This might influence the investigation into the use of specific features (like for example *syn_transfer_drop_freq*).

While the presented approach might prove useful in reconstructing potential security events in a given network, it could also lead to certain privacy related risks. Although the use of biometrics to identify persons within these streams is not explored in this paper, this seems like a potential field for additional research.

Acknowledgment

The research shown in this paper is partly funded by the European Union Project "CyberSec LSA_OVGU-AMSL".

References

[1] "Merriam-Webster.com Dictionary - Videoconferencing," Merriam-Webster, Tech. Rep., 2020.

[2] D. X. Song, D. Wagner, and X. Tian, "Timing analysis of keystrokes and timing attacks on ssh," in *Proceedings of the 10th Conference on USENIX Security Symposium - Volume 10*, ser. SSYM'01. USA: USENIX Association, 2001.

[3] R. Altschaffel, R. Clausing, C. Kraetzer, T. Hoppe, S. Kiltz, and J. Dittmann, "Statistical pattern recognition based content analysis on encrypted network: Traffic for the teamviewer application," 03 2013, pp. 113–121.

[4] A. M. White, A. R. Matthews, K. Z. Snow, and F. Monrose, "Phonotactic Reconstruction of Encrypted VoIP Conversations : Hookt on fon-iks," in *2011 IEEE Symposium on Security and Privacy*, 2011.

[5] B. Dupasquier, S. Burschka, K. Mclaughlin, and S. Sezer, "Analysis of information leakage from encrypted skype conversations," *Int. J. Inf. Sec.*, vol. 9, pp. 313–325, 10 2010.

[6] M. Korczynski and A. Duda, "Classifying service flows in the encrypted skype traffic," 06 2012, pp. 1064–1068.

[7] Y. Zhu and H. Fu, "Traffic analysis attacks on skype voip calls," *Computer Communications*, vol. 34, pp. 1202–1212, 07 2011.

[8] S. Le Blond, C. Zhang, A. Legout, K. Ross, and W. Dabbous, "I know where you are and what you are sharing: Exploiting p2p communications to invade users' privacy," in *Proc. 2011 ACM SIGCOMM Conference on Internet Measurement Conference*. New York, NY, USA: ACM, 2011, p. 45–60.
[9] N. Whiskerd, N. Körtge, K. Jürgens, K. Lamsöft, S. Ezennaya-Gomez, C. Vielhauer, J. Dittmann, and M. Hildebrandt, "Keystroke biometrics in the encrypted domain - a first study on search suggestion functions of web search engines," in *EURASIP J. on information security*, 2020.
[10] M. Bishop, *Computer Security - Art and Science*, 2nd ed. Addison-Wesley, 2018.
[11] S. Kiltz, J. Dittmann, and C. Vielhauer, "Supporting Forensic Design - A Course Profile to Teach Forensics," in *Proc. 9th Int. Conf. on IT Security Incident Management & IT Forensics (IMF 2015)*. IEEE, 2015.
[12] R. Altschaffel, K. Lamshöft, S. Kiltz, M. Hildebrandt, and J. Dittmann, "A Survey on Open Forensics in Embedded Systems of Systems," *Int. Journ. on Advances in Security*, vol. 11, pp. 104–117, 2018.
[13] R. Altschaffel, M. Hildebrandt, S. Kiltz, and J. Dittmann, "Digital Forensics in Industrial Control Systems," in *Proceedings of 38th International Conference of Computer Safety, Reliability, and Security (Safecomp 2019)*. Springer Nature Switzerland, 2019, pp. 128–136.
[14] Zoom Video Communications, Inc., "Zoom - Video Conferencing, Web Conferencing, Webinars," 2020, https://zoom.us [September 20. 2020].
[15] BigBlueButton, "BigBlueButton - Open Source Web Conferencing," 2020, https://bigbluebutton.org/ [September 20. 2020].
[16] datanyze, "Web Conferencing Market Share," 2020, https://www.datanyze.com/market-share/web-conferencing--52 [November 05. 2020].
[17] C. Jennings, H. Boström, and J.-I. Bruaroey, "WebRTC 1.0: Real-Time Communication Between Browsers," 2020, https://www.w3.org/TR/webrtc/ [September 20. 2020].
[18] University of Waikato, "WEKA - The workbench for machine learning," 2020, https://www.cs.waikato.ac.nz/ml/weka/ [September 20. 2020].
[19] Jonas Hielscher, "Forensic in Video Conferencing Results," 2020, https://gitti.cs.uni-magdeburg.de/jhielscher/forensicinvideoconferencingresources [November 06. 2020].

Towards Situation-based IT Management During Natural Disaster Crisis

Abdelmalek Benzekri
Institut de Recherche en Informatique de Toulouse
Université de Toulouse 3 Paul Sabatier
Toulouse, France
Abdelmalek.Benzekri@irit.fr

Romain Laborde
Institut de Recherche en Informatique de Toulouse
Université de Toulouse 3 Paul Sabatier
Toulouse, France
Romain.Laborde@irit.fr

Arnaud Oglaza
Institut de Recherche en Informatique de Toulouse
Université de Toulouse 3 Paul Sabatier
Toulouse, France
Arnaud.Oglaza@irit.fr

Maleerat Sodanil
Faculty of Information Technology and Digital Innovation
King Mongkut's University of Technology North Bangkok
Bangkok, Thailand
Maleerat.m@itd.kmutnb.ac.th

Hatahairat Ketneechairat
Department of Information and Production Technology Management
College of Industrial Technology
King Mongkut's University of Technology North Bangkok
Bangkok, Thailand
hathairat.k@cit.kmutnb.ac.th

***Abstract*—To face disaster relief challenges, crisis management requires operational commitment and efficient coordination of all stakeholders. Deployment of new communication channels at the level of the infrastructure but also at the level of social media streams needs strengthened emergency response processes. We discuss open questions in building an effective decision support system to help crisis decision cells identifying early warnings and situation-specific awareness and figure out the right actions/partnerships to coordinate.**

Keywords*— *crisis management ; policy-based management ; situation awareness ; network infrastructure ; social media ; machine learning ; natural language processing.

I. Introduction

Resilience against natural disasters is a field of growing importance, especially given the current changes in climate and environment. A crisis, whose cause can be accidental or intentionally induced, is a sudden situation, unexpected with severe adverse consequences for humans and organizations.
According to Asia-Pacific Economic Cooperation (APEC) Business Advisory Council, the Asia-Pacific region experiences over 70% of the world's natural disasters [1]. With the heavy floods, earthquakes and storm damaging parts of Asia-Pacific over the past years, it has become clear that disaster preparedness is an absolute must for this area. Nevertheless, this issue is not specific to Asia-Pacific countries only and European Environment Agency reported in 2017 [2] that "efforts to reduce disaster risk and at the same time adapt to a changing climate have become a global and European priority". As a consequence, research in this field is of joint interest being a challenge for both, European and Asian partners. As IT infrastructures are playing an increasing role in our economy, their resilience against natural disasters is of utmost importance. Promoting disaster resilient Information and Communication Technology (ICT) frameworks was one of the main recommendations of APEC Business Advisory Council to APEC Leaders in its 2014 report [3]. Network service providers also share this objective in the 2015 reports of the NGMN Alliance [4] that requires resilience of 5G networks during natural disasters.
Crisis management requires efficient collaboration between a certain number of public, as well as private actors, acting in a coordinated way in order to solve the crisis and reduce its impacts. Mobilizing institutional stakeholders, launching assessed processes, deploying emergency communications for disaster relief are among the response facilities.

The increasing adoption of wireless communication technologies – LTE/4G/5G, wifi, satellite – and the commercial infrastructures widely available or deployed on demand in case of a disaster, are at the heart of the information systems to consider [5]. Because of their nature, and the services they render, these information systems allow for incredible and amazing new usages and/or new sources of information. Actors may exchange and share all types of multimedia information (voice, photos, live videos, georeferenced information, etc) and content-rich services (social media) providing a better appreciation and awareness of the current situation allowing a more efficient and reliable coordination for decision making and strengthening emergency response.

These new communication channels allow crisis cells to involve citizens in a participative approach to extend and leverage both the information dissemination and collection perimeters [6]. They can be seen as a "place for harvesting" information during a crisis event to determine what is happening on the ground and providing relevant direct real-time feedbacks.

Given the huge amount of raw data from a large diversity of sources mostly unstructured, it becomes impossible for a human to process the whole and take the right decisions related to the identified crisis situations. Information sources analytics should help not only in defining and identifying situations, but also in building a decision support system. Such cross-fertilization analysis should be gathered within a dedicated environment integrating support functions such as storage, filter, aggregation, inference and fusion of data and their associated meta-data.

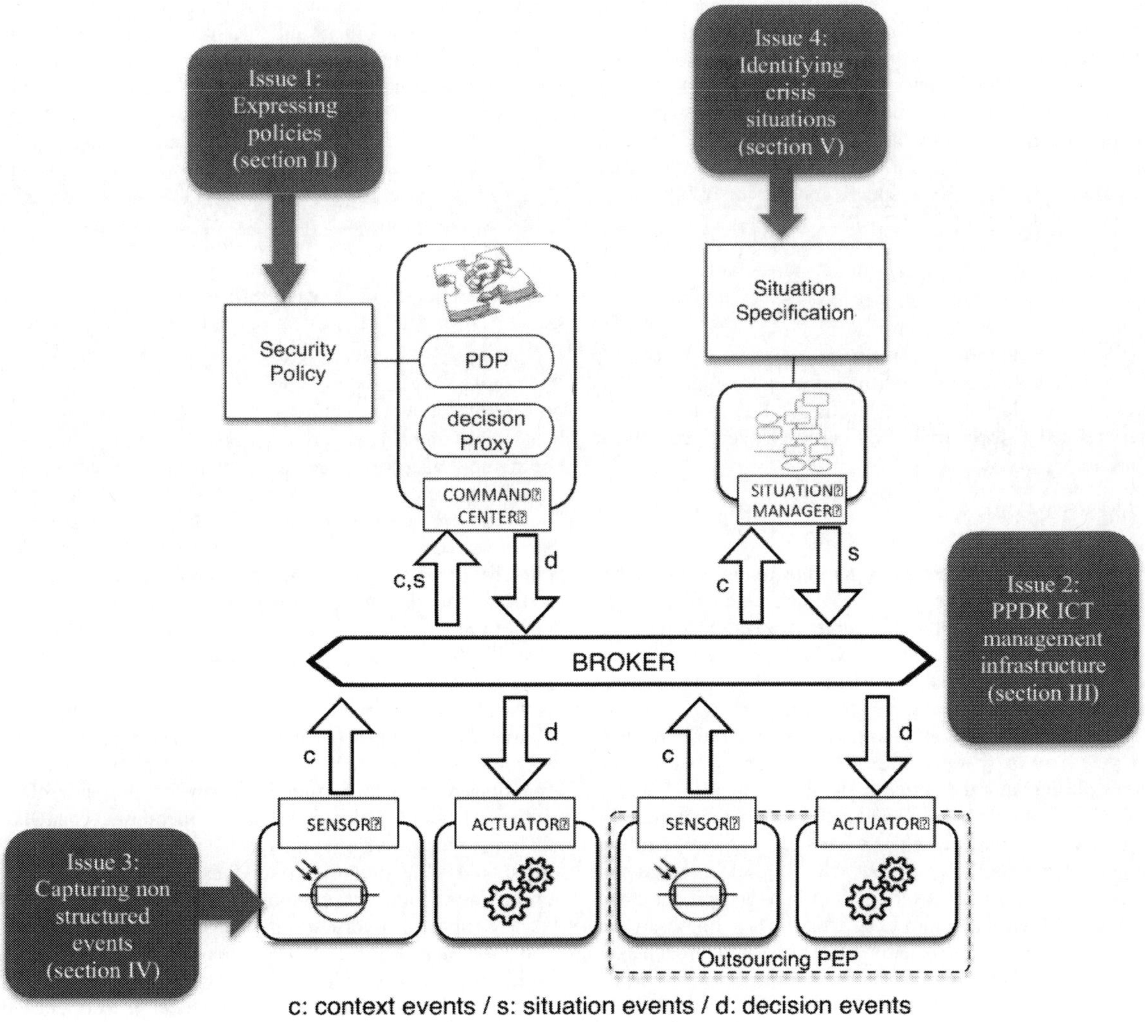

Figure 1. Open research questions

Crisis management processes involve complex management decisions to automatically adapt the deployed IT systems. As a consequence, crisis IT management systems require a better understanding of the dynamics of the environment which raises important research challenges on:

- Eliciting/expressing/validating adaptive systems requirements.
- Expressing/managing/validating adaptive security and/or management policies.
- Dynamically enforcing adaptive security and/or management policies.

Situational Awareness (SA), describes the idealized state of understanding what is happening in an event involving many actors and other moving entities, especially with respect to the needs of command and control operations. SA theory provides an interesting construct to structure the dynamics of the environment in a consistent way [7]. Endsley and Garland [8] define SA as "the perception of the elements in the environment within a volume of time and space (level 1), the comprehension of their meaning (level 2), and the projection of their status in the near future (level 3)". Since "knowing what's going on so you can figure what to do" [9] is a good principle, situation awareness can facilitate the decision making process. Although this construct was initially developed in the military domain, researchers are now trying to apply it to other areas such IT risk management [10] or incidence management in 5G networks [11].

In this article, we intend to consider open issues related to a holistic approach to improve crisis management efficiency during disaster by applying situation awareness principles to dynamic IT crisis management.

A situational awareness perspective is sound for anticipating how individuals, groups and communities can use information contributed by others especially in a social media context. We will discuss what social media may contribute to situational awareness. We expect to launch situation characteristics extraction as well as situational updates labeling from, for instance tweets in the Thai language. Natural Language Processing techniques will be assessed contributing in detecting and extracting emergency knowledge from the social media streams. These situational information will be hence transformed into structured information relevant for the definition of operational policies.

Besides, we have developed dynSMAUG, a dynamic security management framework driven by situations [12] that combines a dynamic policy based management system with situation awareness. On the basis of our dynSMAUG system (Figure 1), we investigate how to integrate unstructured information coming from social media to dynamic IT management and adapt our management system to crisis management. This analysis highlights broader open research questions related to governing the operational IT infrastructure resilience as well as aligning crisis information system during natural disaster crises.

The rest of the article is structured as follows. Sections 2 to 5 describe the open research questions and related works. Section 6 complements this analysis by listing recent and current related research projects. Finally, Section 7 concludes the article.

II. EXPRESSING EMERGENCY/CRISIS PROCEDURES INTO THE MANAGEMENT SYSTEM

Our dynamic management system has to operate within a global crisis management plan. The security and management decisions taken by our command centre must comply with the existing emergency procedures. The main goal should be to investigate the expression of emergency procedures using a situation driven policy language. The idea consists in finding official crisis procedures and express them into our language. However, how to write policies to dynamically manage IT systems during natural disaster crisis?

McHugh and Sheth [13] describe how to construct an emergency procedure flowchart where "The objective of the emergency procedures is to be able to protect lives and minimize damage to assets and to try to 'nip the incident in the bud' before it escalates into a disaster." They highlight the process to develop flow charts for emergency procedures, which in themselves are only able to summarize what needs to be done and should be used during top-level designs, trainings and awareness campaigns.

Hanachi et al. [14] advocate to go further "transforming a plan into a process providing an accurate and machine-readable specification of actions to be done in the field, a better common understanding between stakeholders responsible for these actions and a means to analyse, simulate and evaluate the crisis response before launching it…"

The ideal crisis policy language should address the expression of the policies governing crisis resolution at the business level. This language should also allow decision crisis cells to base their policies on relevant facts observed by the sensors in the impacted field and on the available business knowledge extracted from the plans, the stakeholders and their capacities.

We think that our situational awareness policy language is a good candidate to meet the crisis resolution processes requirements. In dynSMAUG, security policiesare expressed in a generic way: "when situation and conditions then authorization decision and/or obligation(s)".

On the one hand, situations allow capturing the dynamic constraints (time, location, etc.) and organize them into a stable and logical concept. Situation oriented policies are simpler and more readable. Also, managing high level policies, close to the decision crisis cell needs, reduces the gap between policies requirements and the effective policy enforced by stakeholders, and then limits the policy translation errors. On the other hand, making policies more independent from technical constraints minimizes the impact of changing mechanisms and simplifies the policy life cycle management.

This approach has proven to be generic being applied to different use cases such as dynamic security management [12], service-oriented architectures [15], virtual organizations [16], healthcare urgency management by enforcing break-the-glass [17] or permissions-based workflow management [18].

III. HOW TO ADAPT THE DYNSMAUG ARCHITECTURE TO NATURAL DISASTER CRISIS ENVIRONMENT?

Resilience of networks is also under active consideration by network service providers being one of the main goals of future 5G networks. The NGMN Alliance [4] requires that "5G should be able to provide robust communications in case of natural disasters such as earthquakes, tsunamis, floods, hurricanes, etc." From a more technical point of view, 5G networks are expected, by the 5GPP (https://5g-ppp.eu/), to be a multi-access network in order to deserve 7 trillion wireless devices serving over 7 billion people creating a secure, reliable and dependable Internet with a "zero perceived" downtime for services provision. To reach such one-network-fits-all concept, 5G adopts a new paradigm for computing and infrastructure including Software Defined Networks (SDN), Network Function Virtualization (NFV) and Cloud Computing [4], [19]. The objective is enabling the automation of network service provisioning and management as software functions running on commodity hardware to support efficient network resource utilization, quicker operational changes, and faster service provisioning cycles. The benefits expected are the shared infrastructure, the services deployment cost and the promising disruptive technologies [13], [20], [21].

We envision building a self-organized Public Protection and Disaster Relief (PPDR) network using a two-tier architecture that introduces two classes of spectrum users: a) primary users -- the users owning a license to operate on a particular frequency, and b) secondary users – unlicensed users who access a particular frequency only if the respective primary users do not need it. The PPDR will act as primary user in the frequencies allocated to it (698 – 703/753 – 758 MHz and 733 – 736/788 – 791 MHz) and use it for mission-critical application such as voice. On the other hand, to enable new application, such as the exchange of high-definition videos and images, PPDR will access other spectrum in the role of secondary user.

This architecture can significantly improve the performance of the PPDR network, however, it requires the PPDR radios, especially when acting as secondary user, to be cognitive. This means radios capable of intelligently adapting parameters, such as transmission frequency, power, etc.

The vision we would like to share can get materialized thanks to the 3 following actions:

- Technologies such as mmwave, drones, MIMO and C-RAN can be combined and utilized in the design of the new network architecture. The idea is to adapt the network to priorities and users/network conditions so as to deliver ultra-high bit rates over targeted geographical areas. In case of emergency, mobile access network elements (mainly BS elements carried by drones and ground mobile BSs) can be utilized for better spectrum management and throughput delivery. In this context, we plan to conceive algorithms able to dynamically and quickly make decisions on optimal number and locations of resources to be allocated.

- The design of a mechanism that, depending on the traffic's quality of service requirements and possibly on external events (e.g. an emergency situation), can decide dynamically whether to transmit the traffic over the PPDR dedicated frequencies, thus setting the radio to act as primary user, or over spectrum accessed opportunistically, thus setting the radio to act as secondary user. This mechanism can also participate in the dynamic reconfiguration of network components (such as edge gateways) and can be implemented as part of a Network Functions Virtualization (NFV) architecture deployed at the PPDR level [20], [22].
- The current design of dynSMAUG includes single points of failure (the command center and the situation manager) which does not meet crisis IT requirements. We intend to distribute this entity to dynamically adapt dynSMAUG to 5G network requirements during natural disaster crisis.

IV. How to capture non structured context events? For instance, tweets in Thai

This section targets situation characteristics extraction as well as situational updates labelling from social media in general and for instance tweets in the Thai language. Natural Language Processing (NLP) techniques are contributing in detecting and extracting emergency knowledge from the social media streams. These situational information are hence transformed into structured information relevant for the characterization of the situations under operational deployment.

NLP is a kind of machine learning and artificial intelligence that can be used to interact with human and computers in natural languages. The objective of NLP is to achieve human-like comprehension of texts/languages. Named Entity Recognition (NER) is a part of NLP information extraction that seeks to locate and classify named entities in text into pre-defined categories such as the names of persons, organizations, locations, expressions of times etc. NER solutions can be divided into rule-based, machine learning based and hybrid methods [23].

Many related works have analysed twitter streams for crisis detection. Thusly in [24], the authors analysed the contribution of twitter to situational awareness during two natural hazards events. Corvey et al. [25] pointed out that using twitter in mass emergency requires NLP techniques. Neubig et al. [26] quickly created a NLP system to aid the relief efforts during the 2011 East Japan Earthquake and were able to effectively deliver new information about the safety of over 100 people in the disaster stricken area to a central repository for safety information. Ifrim et al. [27] proved that aggressive lettering of tweets based on length and structure, combined with hierarchical clustering of tweets and ranking of the resulting clusters, achieves encouraging results in detecting events from twitter. Klein et al. [28] proposed a combined structural and content based analysis approach to detect and extract emergency knowledge from twitter streams. Finally, Imran et al. [29] presented human-annotated Twitter corpora collected during 19 different crises that took place between 2013 and 2015. They used these corpora to train machine-learning classifiers to demonstrate the utility of the annotations.

However, these related works do not deal with Thai language that has specific features such as not marking word boundaries. As a consequence, an NLP model dedicated to twitter messages in Thai is required. We can reuse some existing tools like LexTo [30] or pyThaiNLP [31]. They will let us focus on how to turning text-based social media stream into structured events augmenting the knowledge on the disaster relief and the crisis resolution.

All these cited related works show how to turn social media streams into structured events augmenting the knowledge one may have in the disaster relief and in the crisis resolution. However, social media being not trusted information may convey fake news. This issue is still an open question but more and more researchers are focussing on it [32].

V. How to calculate a natural disaster crisis situation?

As pointed out by Castillo [33], "Social media is an invaluable source of time-critical information during a crisis. However, emergency response and humanitarian relief organizations that would like to use this information struggle with an avalanche of social media messages that exceeds human capacity to process." Situation awareness theory provides a relevant support to deal with such issues.

A situation is a particular time frame of interest that has a beginning, a life span and an end [34]. The beginning and the end of a situation are determined by combining multiple events coming from multiple sensors and occurring at different moments. Indeed, a situation involves multiple entities and multiple conditions. The beginning and the end of a situation cannot be simple events captured by a unique sensor. In addition, events being instantaneous, combining multiple events requires complex temporal operators (event ordering, event existence/absence, time windows, etc.) to specify the beginning and end of situations.

Currently, situations in dynSMAUG are described using Complex Event Processing techniques [35]. CEP solutions allow to specify complex events through complex event patterns that match incoming event notifications on the basis of their content as well as some ordering relationships on them. We choose the open source event processing implementation called Esper, which is maintained by Espertech. For specifying complex event patterns, Esper offers a stream-oriented language called Event Processing Language (EPL) that is an extension of SQL for processing events (e.g., windows definition and interaction, timed-data arithmetic definition, etc.). We previously showed it is possible to combine real time events with log events to calculate situations [36].

This specification-based identification approach does not scale because situations identification rules become too hard for a human in such a Big data context that includes plenty of sensors and very complex situations [14].Therefore, we have to investigate Machine Learning for crisis situations identification. We can benefit from initiatives like The Humanitarian Data Exchange that provides open crisis data related to previous disasters such as Typhoon Yolanda [37].

VI. RELATED RESEARCH PROJECTS

Many research projects have investigated these issues and we can list the following ones.

The H2020 TransCrisis project [38] - Enhancing the EU's transboundary crisis management capacity (2015 - 2018) has studied the crisis management capacities the EU and how political leaders have made use of these crisis management capacities. This framework deals with transboundary crisis management at the EU level.

The H2020 DARWIN project [39] - Expecting the unexpected and know how to respond (2015 - 2018) has focused on improving responses to expected and unexpected crises affecting critical societal structures during natural disasters (e.g. flooding, earthquakes) and man-made disasters (e.g cyber-attacks). To achieve this, DARWIN developed European resilience management guidelines aimed at critical infrastructure managers, crisis and emergency response managers, service providers, first responders and policy makers.

The H2020 5G-MoNArch project [40] - 5G Mobile Network Architecture for diverse services, use cases, and applications in 5G and beyond (2017-2020) proposes a flexible, adaptable, and programmable 5G architecture by combining virtualisation, slicing and orchestration of access with inter-slice control and cross-domain management, experiment-driven optimization, cloud-enabled protocol stack.

The H2020 MATILDA [41] - A Holistic, Innovative Framework For The Design, Development And Orchestration Of 5g-Ready Applications And Network Services Over Sliced Programmable Infrastructure (2017-2020) designed and implemented a holistic 5G end-to-end services operational framework tackling the lifecycle of design, development and orchestration of 5G-ready applications and 5G network services over programmable infrastructure, following a unified programmability model and a set of control abstractions.

The H2020 SLICENET [42] - End-to-End Cognitive Network Slicing and Slice Management Framework in Virtualised Multi-Domain, Multi-Tenant 5G Networks (2017-2020) aimed at creating and demonstrating the tools and mechanisms to achieve "networks as a service" where logical network slices are created and allocated to flexibly and efficiently in a multi-operator environment.

The H2020 5G ENSURE [43] – 5G Enablers for Network and System Security and Resilience (2015 – 2018) proposed the design of an overall security architecture including authentication, authorization and accounting, privacy, trust, security monitoring, and network management and virtualization isolation.

The H2020 SELFNET [44] – A Framework for Self-Organized Network Management in Virtualized and Software Defined Networks (2015 – 2018) designed an autonomic network management framework targeting the integration of SDN, NFV, Self-Optimizing Network, Cloud Computing, Artificial Intelligence and Quality-of-Experience, to address self-protection (to prevent distributed cyber-attacks), self-healing (to deal with network failures) and self-optimization (to enhance the QoE and network performance), and virtual infrastructure management.

The H2020 COHERENT [45] – Coordinated control and spectrum management for 5G heterogeneous radio access networks (2015 – 2018) defined a programmable unified management framework for heterogeneous 5G Radio Access Networks (flexible spectrum management, radio resources coordination and modelling, and RAN sharing).

The H2020 5G NORMA [46] – 5G Novel Radio Multiservice Adaptive Network Architecture (2015 – 2018) developed an adaptive networking architecture with flexible and context-aware network functions deployment in a multi-tenant scenario involving software defined network control, joint optimization of access and core network functions, and adaptive decomposition and allocation of network functions.

The ANR GéNéPi project (2014-2017) proposed a Mediation Information System dedicated to support the collaborative management of crisis situation. Especially, it aimed at exploiting very large quantities of and flows of data generated from crisis sites.

None of the previous works integrate social media crisis information and the crisis IT architecture deployment. The originality of our approach is thus twofold. First, we consider natural disaster crisis management as a big data issue and we would like to exploit social media especially in Thai language using machine learning techniques. Secondly, we advocate for a crisis IT management framework that integrates information coming from social media to dynamically adapt the network architecture and support the crisis management services.

VII. CONCLUSION

Crisis management is definitely a big data issue given the incredible diversity, heterogeneity and number of channels that can contribute to a crisis resolution. To allow more efficient and reliable coordination for decision making and strengthening emergency response, crisis cells have to govern the operational IT infrastructure resilience as well as align its information system for a better appreciation and awareness of the situation being managed.

As it becomes impossible for a human to "harvest" and process the whole information, machine-learning techniques can help in identifying the right situations in which the right decision might be taken. Situation awareness theory provides the tools for expressing and deploying the right policies.

Using the dynSMAUG system as a concrete example, we highlighted open questions in building an effective decision support system to help crisis cells identifying early warnings and situation-specific awareness figuring out the right actions/partnerships to coordinate. Our future work will tackle these open questions to propose a situation-based IT management system during natural disaster crisis.

REFERENCES

[1] H. KAMEZAKI, "ICT Infrastructure resilience against natural disasters in the Asia-Pacific region," Mar. 2015. [Online]. Available: http://www.adrc.asia/acdr/2015/documents/PF520_05_ABAC.pdf.

[2] European Environment Agency, "Climate change adaptation and disaster risk reduction in Europe," 15/2017, 2017. [Online]. Available: https://www.eea.europa.eu/publications/climate-change-adaptation-and-disaster/.

[3] APEC Business Advisory Council, "Building Asia-Pacific Community Mapping Long-Term Prosperity," 2014.

[4] 5G Initiative team, "NGMN 5G White paper," Next

Generation Mobile Networks Alliance, 2015. [Online]. Available: https://www.ngmn.org/fileadmin/ngmn/content/downloads/Technical/2015/NGMN_5G_White_Paper_V1_0.pdf.
[5] E. Villebrun, "Le Réseau Radio du Futur (RRF)," Jun. 14, 2018.
[6] "Risques : Prévention des risques majeurs." [Online]. Available: https://www.gouvernement.fr/risques.
[7] M. R. Endsley, "Situation awareness misconceptions and misunderstandings," *Journal of Cognitive Engineering and Decision Making*, vol. 9, no. 1, pp. 4–32, 2015.
[8] M. R. Endsley and D. J. Garland, "Theoretical underpinnings of situation awareness: A critical review," *Situation awareness analysis and measurement*, vol. 1, p. 24, 2000.
[9] E. C. Adam, "Fighter cockpits of the future," in *Digital Avionics Systems Conference, 1993. 12th DASC., AIAA/IEEE*, 1993, pp. 318–323.
[10] J. Webb, A. Ahmad, S. B. Maynard, and G. Shanks, "A situation awareness model for information security risk management," *Computers & Security*, vol. 44, pp. 1–15, Jul. 2014, doi: 10.1016/j.cose.2014.04.005.
[11] L. I. Barona López, Á. L. Valdivieso Caraguay, J. Maestre Vidal, M. A. Sotelo Monge, and L. J. García Villalba, "Towards Incidence Management in 5G Based on Situational Awareness," *Future Internet*, vol. 9, no. 1, p. 3, Jan. 2017, doi: 10.3390/fi9010003.
[12] R. Laborde, A. Oglaza, A. S. Wazan, F. Barrère, and A. Benzekri, "A situation-driven framework for dynamic security management," *Annals of Telecommunications*, vol. 74, no. 3–4, pp. 185–196, 2019.
[13] C. M. Machuca *et al.*, "Technology-related disasters: A survey towards disaster-resilient Software Defined Networks," in *2016 8th International Workshop on Resilient Networks Design and Modeling (RNDM)*, Sep. 2016, pp. 35–42, doi: 10.1109/RNDM.2016.7608265.
[14] J. Ye, S. Dobson, and S. McKeever, "Situation identification techniques in pervasive computing: A review," *Pervasive and Mobile Computing*, vol. 8, no. 1, pp. 36–66, Feb. 2012, doi: 10.1016/j.pmcj.2011.01.004.
[15] R. Laborde, F. Barrère, and A. Benzekri, "Toward authorization as a service: a study of the XACML standard," in *Proc of the 16th Communications & Networking Symposium*, 2013, p. 9.
[16] B. Nasser, R. Laborde, A. Benzekri, F. Barrere, and M. Kamel, "Dynamic creation of inter-organizational grid virtual organizations," *First International Conference on e-Science and Grid Computing*, pp. 405–412, 2005.
[17] B. Kabbani, R. Laborde, F. Barrère, and A. Benzekri, "Managing Break-The-Glass using Situation-oriented authorizations," in *9ème Conférence sur la Sécurité des Architectures Réseaux et Systèmes d'Information-SAR-SSI 2014*, 2014, p. 0, Accessed: Aug. 28, 2015. [Online]. Available: https://hal.archives-ouvertes.fr/hal-01120112/.
[18] B. Kabbani, R. Laborde, F. Barrere, and A. Benzekri, "Specification and enforcement of dynamic authorization policies oriented by situations," in *New Technologies, Mobility and Security (NTMS), 2014 6th International Conference on*, 2014, pp. 1–6, Accessed: Aug. 28, 2015.
[19] G. Arfaoui, J. M. S. Vilchez, and J.-P. Wary, "Security and Resilience in 5G: Current Challenges and Future Directions.," 2017, pp. 1010–1015.
[20] A. S. da Silva, P. Smith, A. Mauthe, and A. Schaeffer-Filho, "Resilience support in software-defined networking: A survey," *Computer Networks*, vol. 92, pp. 189–207, Dec. 2015, doi: 10.1016/j.comnet.2015.09.012.
[21] P. N. Tran and H. Saito, "Disaster Avoidance Control against Tsunami," in *2016 28th International Teletraffic Congress (ITC 28)*, Sep. 2016, vol. 01, pp. 26–34
[22] K. Nguyen, Q. T. Minh, and S. Yamada, "A Software-Defined Networking Approach for Disaster-Resilient WANs," in *2013 22nd International Conference on Computer Communication and Networks (ICCCN)*, Jul. 2013, pp. 1–5, doi: 10.1109/ICCCN.2013.6614094.
[23] X. Dong, H. Lin, R. Tan, R. K. Iyer, and Z. Kalbarczyk, "Software-defined networking for smart grid resilience: Opportunities and challenges," in *Proceedings of the 1st ACM Workshop on Cyber-Physical System Security*, 2015, pp. 61–68.
[24] S. Vieweg, A. L. Hughes, K. Starbird, and L. Palen, "Microblogging during two natural hazards events: what twitter may contribute to situational awareness," in *Proc of the SIGCHI conference on human factors in computing systems*, 2010, pp. 1079–1088.
[25] W. J. Corvey, S. Vieweg, T. Rood, and M. Palmer, "Twitter in mass emergency: what NLP techniques can contribute," in *Proc of the NAACL HLT 2010 Workshop on Computational Linguistics in a World of Social Media*, 2010, pp. 23–24.
[26] G. Neubig, Y. Matsubayashi, M. Hagiwara, and K. Murakami, "Safety Information Mining—What can NLP do in a disaster—," in *Proceedings of 5th International Joint Conference on Natural Language Processing*, 2011, pp. 965–973.
[27] G. Ifrim, B. Shi, and I. Brigadir, "Event detection in twitter using aggressive filtering and hierarchical tweet clustering," 2014.
[28] B. Klein, X. Laiseca, D. Casado-Mansilla, D. López-de-Ipiña, and A. P. Nespral, "Detection and extracting of emergency knowledge from twitter streams," in *International Conference on Ubiquitous Computing and Ambient Intelligence*, 2012, pp. 462–469.
[29] M. Imran, P. Mitra, and C. Castillo, "Twitter as a lifeline: Human-annotated twitter corpora for NLP of crisis-related messages," *arXiv preprint arXiv:1605.05894*, 2016.
[30] "LexTo : เล็กซ์โต (โปรแกรม ตัดคำภาษาไทย แบ่งคำภาษาไทย)." http://www.sansarn.com/lexto/ (accessed Nov. 02, 2020).
[31] *PyThaiNLP/pythainlp*. PyThaiNLP, 2020.
[32] A. Bondielli and F. Marcelloni, "A survey on fake news and rumour detection techniques," *Information Sciences*, vol. 497, pp. 38–55, 2019.
[33] C. Castillo, *Big crisis data: social media in disasters and time-critical situations*. Cambridge University Press, 2016.
[34] A. Adi and O. Etzion, "Amit-the situation manager," *The VLDB Journal—The International Journal on Very Large Data Bases*, vol. 13, no. 2, pp. 177–203, 2004.
[35] D. Luckham, "An Introduction to Complex Event Processing in Distributed Enterprise Systems," in *The Power of Events*, Springer, 2002.
[36] A. Benzekri, R. Laborde, A. Oglaza, D. Rammal, and F. Barrère, "Dynamic security management driven by situations: An exploratory analysis of logs for the identification of security situations," in *2019 3rd Cyber Security in Networking Conference (CSNet)*, 2019, pp. 66–72.
[37] "Open Crisis - Humanitarian Data Exchange." https://data.humdata.org/organization/open-crisis (accessed Nov. 02, 2020).
[38] "Home," *TransCrisis*. https://www.transcrisis.eu/ (accessed Nov. 02, 2020).
[39] "DARWIN," *DARWIN*. https://h2020darwin.eu/ (accessed Nov. 02, 2020).
[40] "5G Mobile Network Architecture – for diverse services, use cases, and applications in 5G and beyond." https://5g-monarch.eu/ (accessed Nov. 02, 2020).
[41] "The Matilda Project." https://www.matilda-5g.eu/ (accessed Nov. 02, 2020).
[42] "SLICENET – SLICENET." https://slicenet.eu/ (accessed Nov. 02, 2020).
[43] "5G ENSURE," *5G ENSURE*. http://www.5gensure.eu/ (accessed Nov. 02, 2020).
[44] "SELFNET-5G – SELFNET-5G." https://selfnet-5g.eu/ (accessed Nov. 02, 2020).
[45] "EU H2020 COHERENT | EU H2020 COHERENT." http://www.ict-coherent.eu/coherent/ (accessed Nov. 02, 2020).
[46] "5G NORMA - 5G Novel Radio Multiservice adaptive network Architecture." http://www.it.uc3m.es/wnl/5gnorma/ (accessed Nov. 02, 2020).

A Concept of an Attack Model for a Model-Based Security Testing Framework

Introducing a holistic perspective of cyberattacks in software engineering

Tina Volkersdorfer, Hans-Joachim Hof
Security in Mobility
CARISSMA Institute of Electric, Connected, and Secure Mobility (C-ECOS)
Technische Hochschule Ingolstadt, Germany
Email: tina.volkersdorfer@carissma.eu, hans-joachim.hof@thi.de

Abstract — **In this paper, we present a framework for model-based security testing. The primary advantage of our framework will be the automation of manual security reviews as well as automation of security tests like penetration testing. The framework can be used to decide on single steps for the test procedure. This paper focuses on the concept of the framework, describing the necessary components and their use. Our framework can simulate the behaviour of an adversary that executes multiple attacks to reach his primary goal. Using our approach, it is possible to continuously and consistently address security in software development, even in the early phases of software engineering when no running code is available. Due to the consistency, some of the necessary tests can be executed with less effort. This makes security tests more efficient. Our preliminary evaluation shows that it is possible to use our attack model in a wide range of domains and that there is potential reuse of modelled elements.**

Keywords-attack model; adversary model; model-based testing; security testing; penetration test.

I. INTRODUCTION

The research project MASSiF (Modellbasierte Absicherung von Security und Safety für umfeldbasierte Fahrzeugfunktionen) addresses model-based safety and security testing in the automotive software domain. In the automotive domain, software engineers thoroughly use model-based safety engineering and model-based safety testing. However, to our best knowledge, there are currently no approaches for holistic attack-model-based security testing. This argument is also supported by [1]. Depending on what the use case requires, a suitable attack model of the existing multitude of isolated solutions is used. If the use case changes or new questions arise, the applied model may have to be updated, or further models may have to be used, e.g., the MITRE ATT&CK Framework [2] (used for details of a specific adversary profile) in contrast to attack trees [3] (focusing the system security on identifying security improvements). Using different models or the constant development of new models is time-consuming and causes security to be inconsistent and untraceable, which in turn may have a negative impact on the quality of security testing. This paper and the associated master thesis [4] introduce a holistic modelling framework for attacks that provides an adversary-based and target-based foundation for a guided model-based security testing to close this gap. As model-based security testing is likely of benefit for other domains than automotive software, our framework is domain-agnostic. For example, penetration testing is usually applied towards the end of software engineering to evaluate implemented security controls

Penetration is a common means to evaluate implemented security controls [5]. However, penetration testing usually takes place in the late phases of software development, when it is expensive to fix security problems. Also, the effectiveness and efficiency of penetration test depend on the skills of the tester[5]. Vulnerabilities could go unnoticed. In contrast, a holistic attack model that provides automated mechanisms for generating security test cases could be applied in the early design phase. Hence, it mitigates some of the shortcomings of penetration testing. Our approach is a complement for penetration tests. The automatable test execution is more cost-effective, and early weaknesses can already be detected. The primary focus of this paper is on the attack model and its use in the framework.

The rest of this paper is structured as follows: Section II discusses related work on attack modelling. Section III states the requirements for the holistic modelling framework for security testing. Section IV presents our approach to attack modelling. Section V shows the preliminary evaluation of the part of the modelling framework presented in this paper. Section VI concludes the paper.

II. RELATED WORK

Several adversary and attack models exist. Dependent on the perspective of the attack, there are various modelling concepts.

The process modelling approach focuses on representing the attack based on phases. For example, the Lockheed Martin Cyber Kill Chain [6] defines an attack with seven phases that have to be passed through by the adversary. The kill chain model intends to model Advanced Persistent Threats (APTs) and malware behaviour. Hence, an attack is seen as a linear process, and it does not represent information about the attack surface that is provided for an adversary. Testing requires exploring multiple attack techniques, so bare process modelling approaches are typically not sufficient for testing.

Another standard method is graph-based modelling that uses attack graphs to represent various attack opportunities. Kaynar [7] presents examples of this class of adversary and attack models in the domain network security.

A specific graph representation of attacks is the attack tree by [3]. An attack tree focuses on the primary goal of an adversary. This primary target represents the root of the attack tree, the elementary attack steps to are the leaves, and the various associated subgoals link these nodes. Existing attack trees can easily be reused or combined to form more comprehensive attack trees for threat and risk analysis. Attack trees incorporate multiple paths adversaries may take, but they do not include any characteristics of an adversary or about an adversary's decision on next steps in an attack. Efficient testing requires an approach that also takes into consideration realistic assumptions about attack paths. Our work uses tree structures in combination with adversary modelling and target modelling to overcome the shortcomings of attack trees.

Classification modelling approaches model attacks on different abstraction levels. For example, MITRE proposes the ATT&CK framework [2] to model attacks based on the adversary's perspective. Tactics, techniques, and procedures define adversary behaviour. MITRE ATT&CK can be used both to derive behaviour-based adversary scenarios and to establish attack profiles of an implemented system. It is suitable for testing and verifying the security of a software product. However, the MITRE ATT&CK framework is not designed for use in the early design phase to support a model-based security testing based on a specific adversary strategy. Our work closes this gap.

There are also combined approaches to attack aspects shown above. Adepu and Mathur [1] present unified adversary and attack models with a focus on both security and safety aspects in the context of Cyber Physical Systems in [8]. The relevant system information is part of an attack domain model. However, Adepu and Mathur limit the proposed framework by not considering the characterization of an adversary, e.g., the adversary's current knowledge about the target. However, realistic assumptions about an adversary are necessary for comprehensible modelling the strategic and tactical attack actions of this adversary.

ADVISE [8] is the work most similar to our approach. It addresses the structured and goal-oriented procedure of an adversary. ADVISE is based on an executable security model on system-level to generate security metrics. Our work can be applied earlier in the design process of a system. The application of ADVISE is neither limited to a specific domain nor a certain level of detail. In contrast to our work, the adversary's decision function of ADVISE for the simulated attack procedure does not include the different aspects of designing and launching an attack, e.g., reconnaissance actions. ADVISE is proposed for a repeatable usage in the security engineering to support the evaluation of system security. However, this security analysis method is not designed to support security testing by providing a guideline for performing security tests based on a specific adversary.

III. Requirements

In this paper, we propose a concept for a holistic attack modelling to support the model-based security testing by simulating the strategic actions of an adversary in terms of traceability. The general basis for the requirements engineering is [9] by interpreting security tests as business processes. Concerning the modelling of dynamic behaviour, there are analogies between model-based testing and models for business processes [9] [10]. Using models, complex scenarios can be simulated. The suggested model is intended to be used to decide on the next steps during testing activities, e.g., the structured use of existing penetration testing tools. Hence, relevant requirements for the design of our approach can be derived from [9]:

a) Model-based: The expectation is that applying a model-based perspective to an attack presents a suitable basis for formalization similar to the formalization of the software development process in IT that came with the introduction of model-based software engineering [11]. This formalization is a basis for automation of security testing of system models.

b) Expressive: The purpose is to model as many attacks as possible by the proposed general attack model. A generic attack model should express all necessary information regarding attack, adversary, and target. As already shown in Section II, most attack models only incorporate certain aspects of an adversary and the target. Area of application is a relevant factor for the choice of an attack model. Using a holistic attack model for multiple use cases can involve less effort than the application of several different attack modelling techniques, and it offers a widespread usage.

c) Reusable: The holistic attack model should consist of reusable components to reduce the time-consuming modelling of new attacks [9]. For example, already modelled elements of the attack model should be reusable for as many different use cases as possible (e.g., change of target, change of adversary, change of attack). The requirements a) "model-based" and b) "expressive" support this requirement "reusable".

d) Systematic: The proposed model should ensure a systematic and continuous (re-)use of attack information in all phases of the software engineering process. Today's software development often lacks such a systematic and continuous reuse of information about attacks.

e) Consistent: The proposed attack model should be consistent. A consistent model can be verified and validated. Formalization and automated tool support require a consistent model.

f) Visualizable: The model should use visual means to model attacks. An appropriate visual graphic representation of attacks facilitates the readability and understandability, especially of complex attacks. Visual illustrations are more intuitive for humans than prose text [9] [10]. The use of visual elements supports the formalization as it is missing the ambiguity and inaccuracy of prose. The aim is to achieve a concise expressiveness of the model. The connection of individual attack model components should be easily identifiable, such that security can be consistently verified and software quality increases.

g) Understandable: Software engineers that are no security experts should be able to use our models throughout the software development process. Hence, our models should be understandable, easy to learn and uncomplicated to use. Complex models tend to be difficult to understand [11]. This disadvantage should be avoided.

IV. Design Of An Attack Model for a Model-Based Security Testig Framework

This paper introduces a holistic modelling framework for attacks that provides an adversary-based and target-based foundation for a guided model-based security testing. We postulate the following scope for our approach. Future work will probably leverage some of these restrictions:

- The proposed attack model is limited to one or more cyber-enabled capabilities [12] as a target. The term "cyber-enabled capability" describes any software enabled technology that can be influenced by an adversary in various ways [12]. Attacks targeting on humans (e.g., Social Engineering) are out of scope.
- Our model is limited to adversaries that follow a rational goal. Random attacks are out of scope of this work. The method is limited to goal-oriented adversaries.
- The focus of this paper is to identify the necessary conceptional elements for a suitable, holistic attack modelling framework. Completeness, detailed specification and implementation of these elements are out of the scope of this paper.

A. Overview

In our attack model, we associate each attack with an adversary and the system under attack (target). An adversary plans, develops, and executes attacks against the target by using specific resources. The target may provide one or more access points for an attack. Both for the construction of the proposed model and its execution, it requires this basis of the content in the context of attacks.

Figure 1 shows the essential elements of our framework: the attack model, adversary model and the target model. The adversary model characterizes a specific adversary. Each adversary is defined by descriptive attributes, the goal of his attack, and his current knowledge about the target (called adversary perspective model in Figure 1). The target model represents the system under attack and all necessary associated components of the environment that can be exploited by an attack attempt. The attack model connects all components of the framework. Each attack is simulated within an iteration of defined steps. For this purpose, all necessary information from the attack base is used.

Figure 2 illustrates the pictorial representation of the context of two elementary attack iterations. In each step of the attack simulation, one elementary attack iteration is executed. The adversary's primary goal sets the direction for each attack iteration. Depending on the current adversary's knowledge, he attempts to exploit the target by an available access point. The attack base provides all actions that an adversary could possibly execute in an elementary attack iteration. For example, it stores knowledge about possible weaknesses, available attack techniques, and exploits for the vulnerabilities. The simulation of the target model provides the effect of the attack on the target. The use of a target model allows executing attacks on systems that do not yet exist. Each simulation step ends with an update of the adversary and the target model. When the adversary reached his primary goal, the simulation terminates. Otherwise, the next iteration starts.

Our executable attack model simulates the strategical approach of a specific adversary to attack a particular target. It takes into consideration the properties of this adversary as well as the knowledge the adversary has about a target system at a given time. Security testers can use each iteration to derive security tests. Thus, this holistic method for attack modelling provides a holistic basis for model-based security tests.

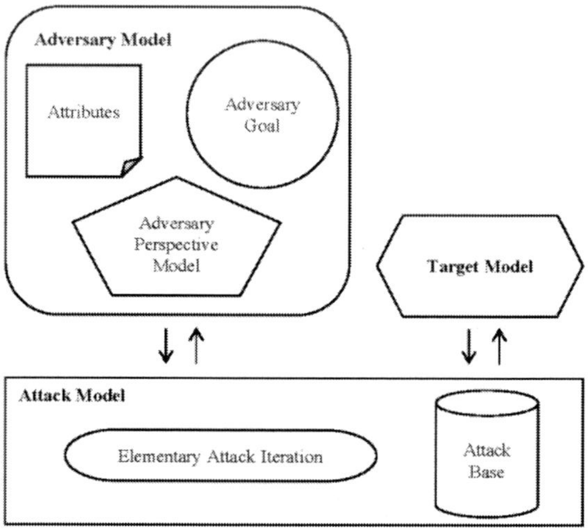

Figure 1. Components of the framework.

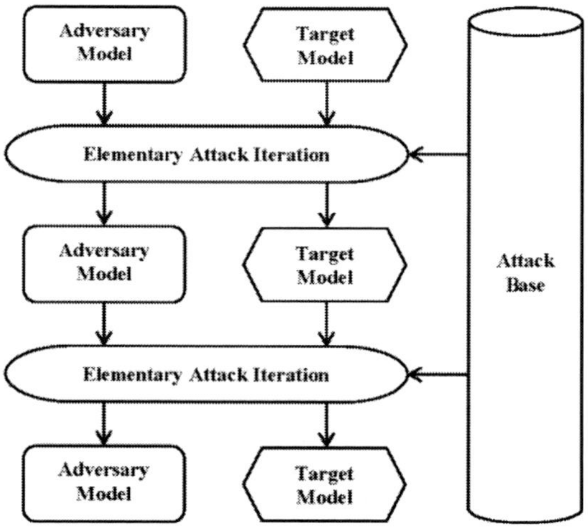

Figure 2. Interaction of the components shown for two elementary attack iterations.

B. Adversary Model

The adversary model consists of three main components: Adversary primary goal, characteristic attributes, and the adversary perspective model, as shown in Figure 1.

The adversary primary goal indicates the direction of the attack. For example, the primary goal of an adversary may be the extraction of financial data from a financial data transfer system. During modelling, the adversary's goal does not change. The adversary's goal is used to derive the behaviour of an adversary during an attack simulation. In the example above, the goal derives attractive data stores in the target system. The adversary tries to navigate from any access points available to the adversary to these data stores.

Attributes characterize each adversary. Attributes include, e.g., the location of an adversary (remote adversary, local adversary) and his skills.

The adversary perspective model represents the adversary's knowledge about the target at a given time. During the attack simulation, each elementary attack iteration increases this knowledge, thus changes the adversary perspective model. For example, the adversary may get access to further access points after the first attack iteration, that he can use for an attack attempt in the next attack iteration. As long as the adversary's current knowledge is not sufficient to achieve his primary goal, the adversary tries to expand his knowledge in the appropriate direction through further attack attempts.

The difference between the target model and the adversary perspective model is that the target model holds only correct information. Still, the adversary perspective model may keep incomplete or blurry details on the target. It represents the current, preliminary view an adversary usually has on the target.

C. Target Model

The target model represents one or more cyber-enabled capabilities that an adversary wants to attack. For example, the target model holds information about available access points of the target. An access point, based on [13], provides adversaries unintended access or unintended information disclosure. The access point is either part of or related to a cyber-enabled capability. During an attack iteration, an adversary analyzes or uses access points to gain knowledge or to control or manipulate the target.

When an adversary chooses to execute an exploit as part of an elementary iteration, this exploit is applied to the target model. The outcome of the exploitation updates both the target model and the adversary model. Thus, the target model is a necessary element for holistic attack modelling.

D. Attack Characterization and Simulation

The attack model shows various perspectives of an attack. The process perspective focuses on the execution of an attack. The attack model simulates each attack within one iteration that incorporates four steps. We call such an iteration an elementary attack iteration, as shown in Figure 1, as it constitutes the smallest attack unit possible from a process perspective. Each elementary attack iteration includes the four steps: (1) Identify available access points, (2) Select one access point, (3) Probe the target, and (4) Update adversary's knowledge. To achieve the adversary's primary goal, usually, several elementary iterations are necessary.

The technical perspective focuses on the selection of available exploits in a proper order to achieve the adversary's goal. An exploit is an umbrella term for various means of actions to execute attacks [14]. It represents one specific step of an attack and is the elementary element of the technical perspective. An attack technique summarizes the necessary exploits to achieve an adversary's primary goal. Selection and execution of an exploit in our simulation can be subject to preconditions [2]. For example, the adversary first has to ensure that the provided access point is vulnerable before he can take further actions in this regard.

The strategic perspective brings together both the process perspective and the technical perspective. It simulates the strategical behaviour of the adversary in the attack simulation, as exemplarily shown in Figure 2. To do so, it selects the next iteration in the attack simulation as well as decides, when the adversary reached his primary goal.

V. Preliminary Evaluation

In this section, we evaluate if our attack model framework meets the requirements of Section III. We evaluated the attack model framework under the following restrictions (future work will leverage some of these restrictions):

- The application of the modelling is limited in each case to one attack iteration.
- The attack scenarios under consideration focus the first activities of an attack, comparable to Reconnaissance of the Lockheed Martin Cyber Kill Chain [6].
- The proposed attack model is applied to two significant attack scenarios by way of example. The first example incorporates vulnerabilities of the OWASP Top Ten 2017 [15], hence is highly relevant in the domain of web application. In contrast, the second example stems from the automotive domain. We use the idea of UML activity diagrams [16] and attack tree [3] for our examples. We choose UML as it is common in many relevant application domains.

A. Evaluation Criteria

The following criteria were identified for the evaluation:

a) Model-based: The criterion refers to the extent to which the attack modelling method is based on a model.
b) Relevant attacks: The criterion refers to the extent to which relevant attacks can be modeled using the proposed attack model.
c) Application domain independence: The criterion refers to the ability to model different attacks independently of the application domain.
d) Reusable elements: The criterion refers to the extent to which the modelled contents and elements of the attack model can be easily reused in conjunction with other attack scenarios.

e) Systematic structures: The criterion refers to the extent to which there is a systematic approach to the structure and procedure of the proposed attack modelling concept so that an attack can be modelled in a comprehensible and repeatable way.
f) Visual elements: The criterion refers to the extent to which the proposed attack model has graphic elements or can be illustrated visually at a glance.

A consistent model is a requirement for the use of automatism [9] and thus, a suitable basis for supporting security tests. Therefore, proper syntax and semantic for the necessary elements have to be defined. The specification of the individual elements of the proposed concept is out of the scope of this paper. Therefore, we omit the evaluation of the model consistency. The understandability of a model helps to evaluate its usefulness. Also, we omit the evaluation of the requirement understandability. We will survey relevant stakeholders to assess the understandability of the model at the end of the still running research project MASSiF.

B. Findings

We iterated through the proposed attack model based on two exemplary attack scenarios. For the sake of briefness, we only present an extract of exciting findings in Figure 3 and Figure 4 concerning the elementary attack step (3).

In the first scenario, we model an identity theft attack on a social media platform. This scenario incorporates attacks from the OWASP Top Ten 2017 [15]. Figure 3 shows a technical perspective of an attack on the user input field of a web application. Visualized using tree structures, the adversary selected Credential Stuffing as an attack technique and utilizes an associated exploit.

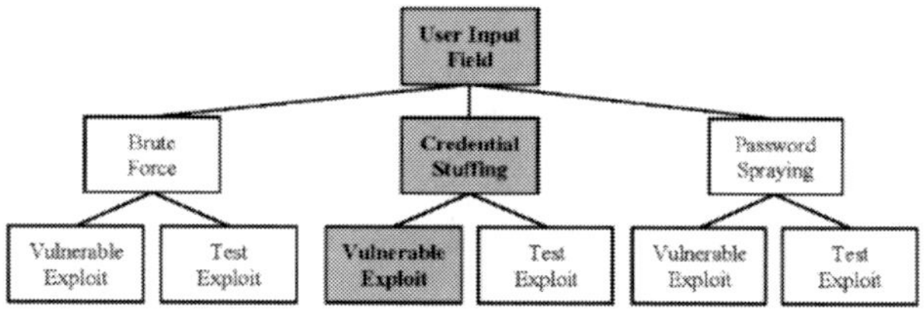

Figure 3. Selected exploit based on the access point "User Input Field".

In the second scenario, based on the research project MASSiF, an adversary tries to manipulate data on an Electronic Control Unit (ECU) in a vehicle. Figure 4 shows a technical perspective of an attack on the standardized interface OBD-2 (On-board-diagnose) Connector in a vehicle. The adversary selected Extraction Technique to extract data from the vehicle.

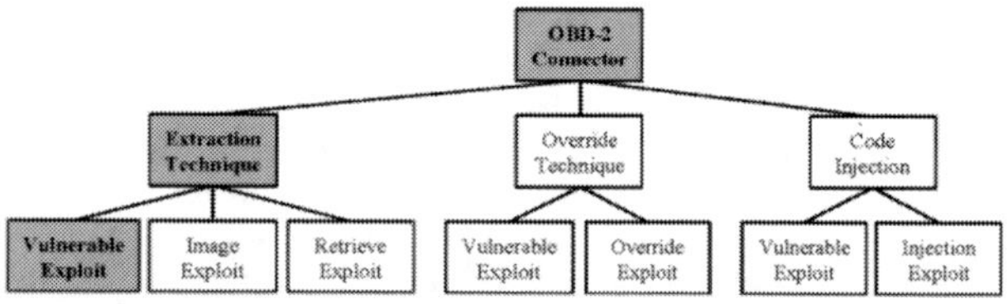

Figure 4. Selected exploit based on the access point "OBD-2 Connector".

The respective application of the exploits on the corresponding target model for the scenario leads to new information for the adversary, e.g., the specific access point is vulnerable. During the next iteration, the adversary can select the next exploit based on the new information the adversary gained from the previous attack iteration.

C. Interpretation

Using the example of tree structures and UML activity diagrams, model-based elements could be used systematically for attack modelling. The criterion model-based can be confirmed insofar as the developed attack model provides a suitable foundation for different modelling approaches.

The criterion relevant attacks can be confirmed to the extent that we were able to model two representative examples from very different application domains. In our opinion, the proposed concept provides a suitable basis for modelling attacks, independent of the domain. Consequently, the proposed concept accomplishes the criterion application domain independence. However, it is still an open question to what extent the specific characteristics of individual domains must or can be captured.

The content of the attack basis, e.g., defined exploits, attack techniques, or access points, as well as the elementary attack iteration process itself are exemplary representatives of reusable elements. Likewise, and regarding the criterion reusable elements, the adversary model can be applied repeatedly, e.g., with different starting positions of the adversary's knowledge for the attack modelling.

The elementary attack iteration represents the basic, systematic guideline for the execution of the attack model. Likewise, the adversary model, target model and the attack basis represent a suitable foundation for a systematic deployment, representation and reuse of attack information. In this respect, the criterion systematic structures is accomplished.

The exemplary use of tree structures and UML activity diagrams shows that the attack modelling concept provides a suitable basis for the integration of graphical model elements. In this respect, the criterion of visual elements is accomplished.

We evaluated five out of seven requirements. In the context of the criteria, our attack model meets the requirements model-based, expressive, reusable, systematic, and visualizable. Requirements III.e) "consistent" and III.g) "understandable" can only be meaningfully evaluated in a later stage of the research project MASSiF. Hence, we did not evaluate these criteria.

VI. Conclusion and Future work

In this paper, we present the concept of a framework for model-based security testing. The framework addresses security throughout the software engineering process. The main goal of the framework is the automation of security tests, especially of security tests in early phases of software engineering (e.g., manual security review).

The central part of our framework is the attack model. The attack model offers several perspectives on security. It can simulate an attack against a target system model. Using a target system model allows simulating attacks on software systems that are not yet implemented. The primary goal that the adversary wants to achieve drives the simulation and offers multiple paths of attacks. Our approach can be used to drive security testing to increase its quality. The preliminary evaluation of the attack model shows that the model is expressive, reusable, systematic, and visualizable.

Future work will focus on detailed specification, implementation of the proposed elements, particularly the attack base and the testing part of the proposed framework.

ACKNOWLEDGMENT

This work is part of the project MASSiF (Modellbasierte Absicherung von Security und Safety für umfeldbasierte Fahrzeugfunktionen). It is supported by the German Federal Ministry of Education and Research (BMBF) under the KMU-innovative program.

Federal Ministry of Education and Research

REFERENCES

[1] S. Adepu and A. Mathur, "Generalized Attacker and Attack Models for Cyber Physical Systems," in *2016 IEEE 40th Annual Computer Software and Applications Conference*, Piscataway, NJ, IEEE, 2016, pp. 283-292.

[2] B. E. Strom *et al.*, "MITRE ATT&CK: Design and Philosophy," July 2018. [Online]. Available: https://www.mitre.org/sites/default/files/publications/pr-18-0944-11-mitre-attack-design-and-philosophy.pdf. [retrieved: 2020.09.25].

[3] B. Schneier, "Attack Trees," *Dr. Dobb's Journal,* vol. 24, no. 12, pp. 21-29, 1999.

[4] T. Volkersdorfer, *Methodik zur Angriffsmodellierung für Security-Tests [Attack Modelling Methodology for Security Tests],* Technische Hochschule Ingolstadt, Germany: Master thesis at Department for Computer Science, 2020.

[5] K. Scarfone, M. Souppaya, A. Cody, and A. Orebaugh, *Technical Guide to Information Security Testing and Assessment,* 800-115 ed., Gaithersburg, MD 20899-8930: National Institue of Standards and Technology, 2008.

[6] E. Hutchins, M. Cloppert, and R. Amin, "Intelligence-Driven Computer Network Defense Informed by Analysis," *Leading Issues in Information Warfare & Security Research,* vol. 1, pp. 80-106, January 2011.

[7] K. Kaynar, "A taxonomy for attack graph generation and usage in network security," *Journal of Information Security and Applications,* vol. 29, pp. 27-56, August 2016.

[8] E. LeMay *et al.*, "Adversary-Driven State-Based System Security Evaluation," in *Proceedings of the 6th International Workshop on Security Measurements and Metrics*, New York, NY, USA, Association for Computing Machinery, 2010, pp. 1-9.

[9] A. Drescher, A. Koschmider, and A. Oberweis, Modellierung und Analyse von Geschäftsprozessen [Modelling and Analysis of Business Processes], Berlin, Boston: De Gruyter Oldenbourg, 2017.

[10] M. Winter, T. Roßner, C. Brandes, and H. Götz, Basiswissen modellbasierter Test [Basic Knowledge Model-Based Test], Heidelberg: dpunkt.verlag, 2016.

[11] J. M. Borky and T. H. Bradley, Effective Model-Based Systems Engineering, Cham, Switzerland: Springer, 2019.

[12] The MITRE Corporation, "CAPEC Glossary," 4 April 2019. [Online]. Available: https://capec.mitre.org/about/glossary.html. [retrieved: 2020.08.07].

[13] J. Bryans *et al.*, "A Template-Based Method for the Generation of Attack Trees," in *Information Security Theory and Practice*, Cham, Springer International Publishing, 2020, pp. 155-165.

[14] H. Siller, "Exploit," Springer Gabler, 19 February 2018. [Online]. Available: https://wirtschaftslexikon.gabler.de/definition/exploit-53419/version-276511. [retrieved: 2020.09.15].

[15] The OWASP Foundation, "OWASP Top 10 - 2017: The ten most critical web application security risks," 2017. [Online]. Available: https://owasp.org/www-project-top-ten/. [retrieved: 2020.08.13].

[16] Object Management Group, "Unified Modeling Language," 5 December 2017. [Online]. Available: https://www.omg.org/spec/UML/2.5.1/PDF. [retrieved: 2020.09.10].